Lecture Notes in Computer Science 12404

More information about this series at http://www.springer.com/series/7410

Zhixiong Chen · Laizhong Cui ·
Balaji Palanisamy · Liang-Jie Zhang (Eds.)

Blockchain – ICBC 2020

Third International Conference
Held as Part of the Services Conference Federation, SCF 2020
Honolulu, HI, USA, September 18–20, 2020
Proceedings

 Springer

Editors
Zhixiong Chen
Mercy College
Dobbs Ferry, NY, USA

Balaji Palanisamy
University of Pittsburgh
Pittsburgh, PA, USA

Laizhong Cui
Shenzhen University
Shenzhen, China

Liang-Jie Zhang 🆔
Kingdee International Software Group
Co, Ltd.
Shenzhen, China

ISSN 0302-9743   ISSN 1611-3349   (electronic)
Lecture Notes in Computer Science
ISBN 978-3-030-59637-8   ISBN 978-3-030-59638-5   (eBook)
https://doi.org/10.1007/978-3-030-59638-5

LNCS Sublibrary: SL4 – Security and Cryptology

This Springer imprint is published by the registered company Springer Nature Switzerland AG
The registered company address is: Gewerbestrasse 11, 6330 Cham, Switzerland

Preface

The International Conference on Blockchain (ICBC) aims to provide an international forum for both researchers and industry practitioners to exchange the latest fundamental advances in the state-of-the-art technologies and best practices of blockchain, as well as emerging standards and research topics which would define the future of blockchain.

This volume presents the accepted papers for the International Conference on Blockchain (ICBC 2020), held as a fully virtual conference during September 18–20, 2020. All topics regarding blockchain technologies, platforms, solutions, and business models align with the theme of ICBC. Topics of interest included, but were are not limited to, new blockchain architecture, platform constructions, blockchain development, and blockchain services technologies as well as standards and blockchain services innovation lifecycle, including enterprise modeling, business consulting, solution creation, services orchestration, services optimization, services management, services marketing, and business process integration and management.

We accepted 15 papers, including 14 full papers and 1 short paper. Each was reviewed and selected by at least three independent members of the ICBC 2020 International Program Committee. We are pleased to thank the authors whose submissions and participation made this conference possible. We also want to express our thanks to the Program Committee members for their dedication in helping to organize the conference and reviewing the submissions. We owe special thanks to the keynote speakers for their impressive speeches.

July 2020

Zhixiong Chen
Laizhong Cui
Balaji Palanisamy
Liang-Jie Zhang

Organization

General Chairs

J. Leon Zhao   City University of Hong Kong, China
Richard Brooks   Clemson University, USA

Program Chairs

Zhixiong Chen   Mercy College, USA
Laizhong Cui (Vice-chair)   Shenzhen University, China
Balaji Palanisamy   University of Pittsburgh, USA
  (Vice-chair)

Services Conference Federation (SCF 2020)

General Chairs

Yi Pan   Georgia State University, USA
Samee U. Khan   North Dakota State University, USA
Wu Chou   Vice President of Artificial Intelligence & Software
                 at Essenlix Corporation, USA
Ali Arsanjani   Amazon Web Services (AWS), USA

Program Chair

Liang-Jie Zhang   Kingdee International Software Group Co., Ltd, China

Industry Track Chair

Siva Kantamneni   Principal/Partner at Deloitte Consulting, USA

CFO

Min Luo   Georgia Tech, USA

Industry Exhibit and International Affairs Chair

Zhixiong Chen   Mercy College, USA

Operation Committee

Jing Zeng   Yundee Intelligence Co., Ltd, China
Yishuang Ning   Tsinghua University, China
Sheng He   Tsinghua University, China
Yang Liu   Tsinghua University, China

Steering Committee

Calton Pu (Co-chair)	Georgia Tech, USA
Liang-Jie Zhang (Co-chair)	Kingdee International Software Group CO., Ltd, China

ICBC 2020 Program Committee

Artem Barger	IBM Research, Israel
Salman Baset	Independent
Luca Cagliero	Politecnico di Torino, Italy
Shiping Chen	CSIRO, Australia
Roberto Di Pietro	Hamad Bin Khalifa University, Qatar
Praveen Jayachandran	IBM Research, India
Nagarajan Kandasamy	Drexel University, USA
Qinghua Lu	CSIRO, Australia
Reza M. Parizi	Kennesaw State University, USA
Catalin Meirosu	Ericsson, Sweden
Vallipuram Muthukkumarasamy	Griffith University, Australia
Roberto Natella	Federico II University of Naples, Italy
Gowri Ramachandran	University of Southern California, USA
Rudrapatna Shyamasundar	Indian Institute of Technology Bombay, India
Andreas Veneris	University of Toronto, Canada
Jiuyun Xu	China University of Petroleum, China
Xiwei Xu	CSIRO's Data61 and The University of New South Wales, Australia
Rui Zhang	Institute of Information Engineering, Chinese Academy of Sciences, China

Conference Sponsor – Services Society

Services Society (S2) is a nonprofit professional organization that has been created to promote worldwide research and technical collaboration in services innovation among academia and industrial professionals. Its members are volunteers from industry and academia with common interests. S2 is registered in the USA as a "501(c) organization," which means that it is an American tax-exempt nonprofit organization. S2 collaborates with other professional organizations to sponsor or co-sponsor conferences and to promote an effective services curriculum in colleges and universities. The S2 initiates and promotes a "Services University" program worldwide to bridge the gap between industrial needs and university instruction.

The services sector accounted for 79.5% of USA's GDP in 2016. The world's most service-oriented economy, with services sectors accounting for more than 90% of GDP. S2 has formed 10 Special Interest Groups (SIGs) to support technology and domain specific professional activities:

- Special Interest Group on Web Services (SIG-WS)
- Special Interest Group on Services Computing (SIG-SC)
- Special Interest Group on Services Industry (SIG-SI)
- Special Interest Group on Big Data (SIG-BD)
- Special Interest Group on Cloud Computing (SIG-CLOUD)
- Special Interest Group on Artificial Intelligence (SIG-AI)
- Special Interest Group on Edge Computing (SIG-EC)
- Special Interest Group on Cognitive Computing (SIG-CC)
- Special Interest Group on Blockchain (SIG-BC)
- Special Interest Group on Internet of Things (SIG-IOT)

About the Services Conference Federation (SCF)

As the founding member of the Services Conference Federation (SCF), the First International Conference on Web Services (ICWS 2003) was held in June 2003 in Las Vegas, USA. Meanwhile, the First International Conference on Web Services - Europe 2003 (ICWS-Europe 2003) was held in Germany in October 2003. ICWS-Europe 2003 was an extended event of ICWS 2003, and held in Europe. In 2004, ICWS-Europe was changed to the European Conference on Web Services (ECOWS), which was held in Erfurt, Germany. SCF 2019 was held successfully in San Diego, USA. To celebrate its 18th birthday, SCF 2020 was held virtually during September 18–20, 2020.

In the past 17 years, the ICWS community has been expanded from Web engineering innovations to scientific research for the whole services industry. The service delivery platforms have been expanded to mobile platforms, Internet of Things (IoT), cloud computing, and edge computing. The services ecosystem is gradually enabled, value added, and intelligence embedded through enabling technologies such as big data, artificial intelligence (AI), and cognitive computing. In the coming years, all the transactions with multiple parties involved will be transformed to blockchain.

Based on the technology trends and best practices in the field, SCF will continue serving as the conference umbrella's code name for all service-related conferences. SCF 2020 defines the future of New ABCDE (AI, Blockchain, Cloud, big Data, Everything is connected), which enable IOT and enter the 5G for Services Era. SCF 2020's 10 collocated theme topic conferences all center around "services," while each focusing on exploring different themes (web-based services, cloud-based services, big data-based services, services innovation lifecycle, AI-driven ubiquitous services, blockchain driven trust service-ecosystems, industry-specific services and applications, and emerging service-oriented technologies). SCF includes 10 service-oriented conferences: ICWS, CLOUD, SCC, BigData Congress, AIMS, SERVICES, ICIOT, EDGE, ICCC, and ICBC. The SCF 2020 members are listed as follows:

[1] The International Conference on Web Services (ICWS 2020, http://icws.org/) is the flagship theme-topic conference for Web-based services, featuring Web services modeling, development, publishing, discovery, composition, testing, adaptation, delivery, as well as the latest API standards.

[2] The International Conference on Cloud Computing (CLOUD 2020, http://thecloudcomputing.org/) is the flagship theme-topic conference for modeling, developing, publishing, monitoring, managing, delivering XaaS (Everything as a Service) in the context of various types of cloud environments.

[3] The International Conference on Big Data (BigData 2020, http://bigdatacongress. org/) is the emerging theme-topic conference for the scientific and engineering innovations of big data.

[4] The International Conference on Services Computing (SCC 2020, http://thescc.org/) is the flagship theme-topic conference for services innovation lifecycle that includes enterprise modeling, business consulting, solution creation, services orchestration,

services optimization, services management, services marketing, and business process integration and management.

[5] The International Conference on AI & Mobile Services (AIMS 2020, http://ai1000. org/) is the emerging theme-topic conference for the science and technology of AI, and the development, publication, discovery, orchestration, invocation, testing, delivery, and certification of AI-enabled services and mobile applications.

[6] The World Congress on Services (SERVICES 2020, http://servicescongress.org/) focuses on emerging service-oriented technologies and the industry-specific services and solutions.

[7] The International Conference on Cognitive Computing (ICCC 2020, http:// thecognitivecomputing.org/) focuses on the Sensing Intelligence (SI) as a Service (SIaaS) which makes systems listen, speak, see, smell, taste, understand, interact, and walk in the context of scientific research and engineering solutions.

[8] The International Conference on Internet of Things (ICIOT 2020, http://iciot.org/) focuses on the creation of IoT technologies and development of IoT services.

[9] The International Conference on Edge Computing (EDGE 2020, http:// theedgecomputing.org/) focuses on the state of the art and practice of edge computing including but not limited to localized resource sharing, connections with the cloud, and 5G devices and applications.

[10] The International Conference on Blockchain (ICBC 2020, http://blockchain1000. org/) concentrates on blockchain-based services and enabling technologies.

Some highlights of SCF 2020 are shown below:

- **Bigger Platform:** The 10 collocated conferences (SCF 2020) are sponsored by the Services Society (S2) which is the world-leading nonprofit organization (501 c(3)) dedicated to serving more than 30,000 worldwide services computing researchers and practitioners. Bigger platform means bigger opportunities to all volunteers, authors, and participants. Meanwhile, Springer sponsors the Best Paper Awards and other professional activities. All the 10 conference proceedings of SCF 2020 have been published by Springer and indexed in ISI Conference Proceedings Citation Index (included in Web of Science), Engineering Index EI (Compendex and Inspec databases), DBLP, Google Scholar, IO-Port, MathSciNet, Scopus, and ZBlMath.

- **Brighter Future:** While celebrating the 2020 version of ICWS, SCF 2020 highlights the Third International Conference on Blockchain (ICBC 2020) to build the fundamental infrastructure for enabling secure and trusted service ecosystems. It will also lead our community members to create their own brighter future.

- **Better Model:** SCF 2020 continues to leverage the invented Conference Blockchain Model (CBM) to innovate the organizing practices for all the 10 theme conferences.

Contents

Research Track

Blockchain Based Full Privacy Preserving Public Procurement

Prem Ratan Baranwal$^{(\boxtimes)}$ ⬤

Research and Development, Talentica Software (India) Pvt Ltd, Pune, India
`premb@talentica.com`

Abstract. Public procurement is one of the government activities most prone to corruption, and e-procurement systems have been recommended to increase transparency, outreach, and competition. Other benefits include ease of access to public tenders and easier detection of irregularities. One of the main challenges with the existing e-procurement/auction systems is ensuring bid privacy of the losing bidders and collusion between bidders and auctioneer. Most of the auction systems, proposed, depend either upon auctioneer(s) or on the trusted third party, which, according to us, is the biggest problem for addressing corruption. We propose a blockchain based solution for Public Procurement, which eliminates auctioneers/third-parties using secure multi-party computation (MPC). Our solution fully preserves bid privacy and is secure against malicious bidders.

Keywords: Public Procurement · Sealed-bid auction · Multi-party computation · Homomorphic encryption · Blockchain · Privacy

1 Introduction

1.1 Background and Motivation

Public Procurement refers to the goods, services, and construction work purchased by the government and state-owned enterprises. As per the OECD report [9], it accounts for 12% of the GDP of OECD countries, which makes it most prone to corruption. Up to 20–25% of the contract value may be lost to corruption in public procurement in these countries. This results in a non-competent working environment, higher cost of goods and services, and ultimately a lack of transparency and trust in the government. Besides the sound procurement rules, adequate administrative infrastructure is required to build an auction system trusted by both government and companies, especially small and medium enterprises (SMEs).

Around the world, governments have started using E-procurement (electronic procurement) systems to increase transparency, to provide easy access to public tenders, to reduce direct interaction between officials and companies, and to allow for easier detection of irregularities. U.S. government has used the e-procurement system for tracking and managing a vendor's past performance [9].

© Springer Nature Switzerland AG 2020
Z. Chen et al. (Eds.): ICBC 2020, LNCS 12404, pp. 3–17, 2020.
https://doi.org/10.1007/978-3-030-59638-5_1

A suitable auction mechanism is an essential part of these systems. For our paper, we will be using *First Price Sealed-Bid Auction* as the auction mechanism in our protocol. The private data, in this case, is each bidder's bid and auction result is the highest bid price (or lowest bid price in case of a reverse auction). Some significant challenges faced by these auction systems are as follows:

- **Public Auditability:** Any changes in Procurement related policies, contract documents, bidding process, and all the transactions must be immutable and auditable by all the citizens. Public Auditability will reduce insider frauds like system-admin level modifications, log removal, and firewall misuse.
- **The Correctness of Evaluation:** The Bid evaluation criterion should be clear and transparent to everyone.
- **Bid Privacy and Anonymity:** Keeping the bids private and unlinkable to bidders, revealing only the maximum bid will help in building a trust-free and competent environment. Sealed bid auctions provide an advantage over open-cry counterparts where all the bidders submit their bids to the auctioneer and are assured that competitors do not get information about their bids. However, the bid values can be misused once all the bids are opened for deciding the winner.
- **Non-interactivity between Auctioneer and Bidders:** Most of the systems today depend either upon a trusted third party or a server node in order to decide the auction winner. Bid privacy, as mentioned in the previous point, can be of no use for fear of an untruthful auctioneer or the reluctance of bidders of reveling their real valuation. The auctioneer could easily expose the bid information to other bidders, declare a wrong auction winner, or announce the incorrect second-highest price in order to maximize his profit.
- **Centralized Environment:** Traditional systems use a centralized server and can be subject to infrastructure failures, hacking, or DDOS attacks. It may result in loss of data or can be manipulated in favour of a particular bidder.

Blockchain has the potential to be a disruptive technology for many industries and applications. Bitcoin [11], a highly popular digital currency, based on blockchain, is a value transfer technology that established trust between unknown users and automated the payments without any intermediaries. Blockchain is a distributed shared ledger build on top of a p2p network that maintains the history of all transactions rendering them immutable after verification. All the network peers agree on the transactions through a consensus. Bitcoin and other blockchain technologies also use cryptography techniques to secure the transactions and provide privacy to the stakeholders. Beyond payments, blockchain also supports storing and execution of contract code on top of them, commonly known as *Smart Contracts*. They reside on the blockchain, and execution is done using user transactions. The Consensus mechanism guarantees that the contract is executed as per the contract code and accepted by all nodes. There are two main types of blockchain systems. In public or permissionless blockchain, anyone can participate without a specific identity. Public blockchain typically involves a native cryptocurrency and often use consensus based on "proof of work" (PoW) and economic incentives. Permissioned blockchain, on the other hand, runs a blockchain among a set of known, identified participants who do not fully trust each other.

1.2 Our Contribution

In this paper, we propose a blockchain based solution adopting a bidder-resolved auction protocol from [3] utilizing cryptographic primitives to address the issues mentioned in the previous subsection for standard auction systems. The protocol presented in this paper does not require any trusted third party or any bulletin board and tries to obtain full privacy. Bidders jointly compute the auction result, and any subset of bidders will not be able to reveal any private information. To avoid excess interaction among the bidders, auditability, and low resiliency required by the system, we use the transaction immutability property of blockchain. The auction smart contract pseudo-code is provided for a better understanding of the solution.

1.3 Outline of Work

The Rest of the paper is organized as follows. Section 2 describes the current work done in the area of sealed-bid auctions, and current public procurement solutions based on blockchain. Section 3 describes the cryptographic primitives used in the protocol of the presented blockchain solution. In Sects. 4 and 5, design objectives and assumptions behind the solution are given. In Sect. 6, we provide the solution with the protocol to choose the bid winner and a way to verify the correctness of the result. Analysis of the presented solution against our design objectives is done in Sect. 7. Conclusion and future work are described in Sect. 8.

2 Current Work

Cryptographically secure e-Auctions have been of great research interest since 1990. We have gone through some of the representative papers that utilize different techniques for auction of single unit goods. One of the first efficient sealed-bid auctions was proposed by Franklin et al. [7]. It handled malicious bidders and auction service failures. A semi-trusted third party had to be present for the transaction even though it didn't learn anything from the protocol. It also lacked the secrecy because all the bids are opened to decide the winner. A garbled circuit-based approach was given by Naor et al. [12], resulting in the secure auction provided that Auction Issuer and Auctioneer do not collude. A circuit evaluation based non-interactive auction scheme was proposed by Baudron et al. [2], where a short proof of fairness was used to handle cheating players. However, it was limited to a logarithmic number of players and utilized a semi-trusted third party for deciding the winner. Omote et al. proposed a sealed-bid auction scheme [13], which employs an efficient homomorphic encryption algorithm with threshold distributed decryption to provide secrecy of bids. It shifts the computation complexity from bidder to auction managers. However, secrecy can be compromised if the two managers collude. Abe et al. too proposed an (M+1)st price auction using homomorphic encryption [1], which provides secrecy and public verifiability. However, each bidder must compute K+1 Zero-Knowledge Proofs in bidding, where K is the number of bidding points. In a recent paper [10], Montenegro et al. used bit commitment and circuit-based proof for their auction scheme to be secure and public verifiable, though still dependent on an auctioneer and a randomness server.

2.1   Bidder-Resolved Auctions

As per our survey, most of the sealed-bid auction proposals either use single semi-trusted auctioneer or multiple auctioneers to distribute trust. But bidders can not trust any number of third parties as they may share knowledge and give away to bidders. Only the schemes by Felix Brandt in [3] and [4], referred to as 'bidder-resolved auction', provide 'full privacy'. These schemes do not use auctioneer at all and selling price is calculated in a distributed manner among the bidders only. No information concerning the bids is revealed unless all the bidders share their knowledge. The Main downside of this approach is low resilience and relatively high computational complexity. However, given our use case of high profile auctions and a limited number of bidders, we think a private blockchain based system will work well.

2.2   Blockchain Based Public Procurement Solutions

Ethereum based auction/procurement solutions have been proposed recently. Galal and Youssef [8] proposed 'Trustee', a full-privacy preserving Vickrey Auction on Ethereum, which utilizes Intel SGX TEE (Trusted Execution Environment) along with zero-knowledge proof for verifiability. The protocol assumes a trusted setup of proof and verification keys. One of the issues with this paper is that bid evaluation is done on an off-chain host, prone to hacker attacks.

3   Definition/Preliminaries

In this section, we briefly describe the building blocks such as cryptographic primitives and efficient proof of correctness used in the auction protocol.

3.1   ElGamal Encryption System

ElGamal cipher [5] is an asymmetric key encryption algorithm for public-key cryptography based on the discrete logarithm problem for a group G_p^*. Let p and q be large primes so that q divides p–1. Let g be a generator of Z_p^*'s subgroup G_q of order q mod p. Let the private key be $x \in Z_q$ and the public key be $y = g^x$.

The encryption of a message m (already converted from plain text such that $m \in Z_q$) is given by

$$(\alpha, \beta) = (my^r, g^r)$$

where r is called ephemeral key in Z_q. Decryption of message is calculated using

$$\frac{\alpha}{\beta^x} = \frac{my^r}{(g^r)^x} = m$$

ElGamal encryption is also homomorphic over multiplication as the multiplication of two cipertexts $(\alpha\alpha', \beta\beta') = (mm' * y^{r_1+r_2}, g^{r_1+r_2})$ is same as the encryption of two plaintexts' product mm'.

3.2 Zero-Knowledge Proofs

Following three Schnorr Protocols are used for proofs of correctness.

Proof of Knowledge of a Discrete Logarithm. Prover A and Verifier B both know y and g but only A knows x, so that $y = g^x$. A proves knowledge of x in zero-knowledge by using following protocol.

1. A picks a random number $r \in G_q$, computes $a \equiv g^r (mod p)$ and sends to B.
2. B chooses a challenge random number c and sends it to A.
3. A sends $z \equiv r + cx (mod q)$ to B.
4. B verifies that $g^z = ay^c$.

Total bits sent by A is $\log p + \log q$.

Proof of Equality of Two Discrete Logarithms. Prover A and Verifier B both know y_1, y_2, g_1 and g_2 but only A knows x, so that $y_1 = g_1^x$ and $y_2 = g_2^x$.

1. A picks a random number $r \in G_q$, computes $a \equiv g_1^r (mod\ p)$ and $b \equiv g_2^r (mod\ p)$. He, then, sends both the values to B.
2. B chooses a challenge random number c and sends it to A.
3. A sends $z \equiv r + cx (mod q)$ to B.
4. B verifies that $g_1^z = ay^c$ and $g_2^z = by^c$.

Total bits sent by A is $2\log p + 2\log q$. Likewise, it can be shown that, for proving equality of discrete logarithm of n values, A needs to send $n \log p + n \log q$ bits.

Proof that an Encrypted Value is One Out of Two Values. Prover A proves that an ElGamal encrypted value $(\alpha, \beta) = (my^r, g^r)$ either decrypts to 1 or to a fixed value $z \in G_q$ (i.e. $m \in 1, z$) without revealing exactly which one is the case.

1. if $m = \begin{cases} 1 & :\text{A chooses random values } r_1, d_1, w \text{ and sends } (\alpha, \beta), a_1 = g^{r_1}\beta^{d_1}, \\ & b_1 = y^{r_1}(\frac{\alpha}{z})^{d_1}, a_2 = g^w \text{ and } b_2 = y^w \text{ to B} \\ z & :\text{A chooses random values } r_2, d_2, w \text{ and sends } (\alpha, \beta), a_1 = g^w, \\ & b_1 = y^w, a_2 = g^{r_2}\beta^{d_2} \text{ and } b_2 = y^{r_2}\alpha^{d_2} \text{ to B} \end{cases}$

2. B chooses a challenge random number c and sends it to A.

3. if $m = \begin{cases} 1 & :\text{A sends } d_1, d_2 = c - d_1 (\text{mod } q), r_1 \text{ and } r_2 = w - rd_2 (\text{mod } q) \text{ to B.} \\ z & :\text{A sends } d_1 = c - d_2 (\text{mod } q), d_2, r_1 = w - rd_1 (\text{mod } q) \text{ and } r_2 \text{ to B.} \end{cases}$

4. B verifies that $c = d_1 + d_2 (\text{mod } q)$, $a_1 = g^{r_1}\beta^{d_1}$, $b_1 = y^{r_1}(\frac{\alpha}{z})^{d_1}$, $a_2 = g^{r_2}\beta^{d_2}$ and $b_2 = y^{r_2}\alpha^{d_2}$

Total bits sent by A is $4 \log p + 4 \log q$.

4   Design Objectives

We are listing below all the required parameters of an electronic sealed-bid auction system including the prime objectives mentioned in Subsect. 1.1 and will analyze later how our proposed solution performs on each of these parameters.

– Public Auditability: Refer Subsect. 1.1
– Bid Privacy and Anonymity: Refer Subsect. 1.1
– Correctness of Evaluation: Refer Subsect. 1.1
– Non-interactivity between Auctioneer and Bidders: Refer Subsect. 1.1
– Trust-less environment: Refer Subsect. 1.1
– Public Verifiability: Anyone can verify that the winning bid is highest of all the bids, and the winner can provide proof that he has actually placed that bid.
– Robustness: Auction process is secure against the malicious bid.
– Non-repudiation: A winner may deny having submitted the winning bid. The protocol should be able to identify the winner on its own.
– Reserve Price: Seller should be able to specify the minimum price at which he will accept the winning bid.
– Efficiency: Computational and communication efficiency of the protocol is reasonable for conducting a regular bidding process.

5   Assumptions

1. The auction takes place with a small number of well-known bidders.
2. A permissioned blockchain framework supporting an in-built cryptocurrency is already deployed on the multiple nodes across various agencies representing government and companies.
3. All the bidders have completed their KYC verification in the blockchain system against their public/private keys and possess valid certificates.

6 Proposed Solution

Here we will describe the proposed solution and the auction protocol. We will be using the term smart contract for the user code written on the blockchain. Please refer to Fig. 1 for overall system design.

Table 1. Notations

n	:	Total no of bidders
i, h	:	Index of bidder
$\mathbf{p}$	:	Bid price vector
j	:	Index of bid price vector
k	:	Highest index of bid price vector
b_i	:	Bid price for bidder i
G_q	:	Z_p^*'s multiplicative sub-group of order q
g	:	Arbitrary generator of G_q
Y	:	Arbitrary value $\in G_q \setminus \{1\}$
x_{+i}	:	Private key of bidder i, $x_{+i} \in Z_q$
$y_{\times i}$	:	Public key of bidder i
y	:	Composite public key
α_{aj}, β_{aj}	:	j'th element of Bidder a's encrypted bid vector
$\gamma_{ij}^{\times a}, \delta_{ij}^{\times a}$	:	First-price Outcome of Bidder a
C	:	The Auction Smart Contract on blockchain

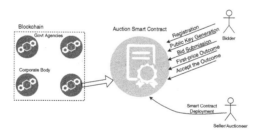

Fig. 1. Overview of blockchain based auction system.

6.1 Blockchain System

A permissioned blockchain framework that supports a native cryptocurrency and smart contract code or custom user services is suitable for our purpose. In public or permissionless blockchain, any user without a proper KYC can participate, and a "proof of work" (POW) based consensus is used which is not desirable. Native cryptocurrency is required for handling the penalties. Please refer to Table 1 for the notations used in this protocol.

6.2 Auction Protocol

We propose to use the auction protocol [4] based on secure multiparty computation (MPC) for our solution. It allows bidders to compute the auction outcome without revealing further information collaboratively. The MPC is based on ElGamal encryption [5], which is a multiplicative homomorphic encryption scheme. This scheme allows random number exponentiation of encrypted values efficiently.

Let $\mathbf{p}$ be a vector of k possible prices, $\mathbf{p} = (p_1, p_2, p_3...p_k)$ and bid vector b_i for bidder i, bidding at p_{bid_i}, is defined as $b_{i,bid_i} = 1$. All other components are 0, as shown below.

$$
\mathbf{b}_i = \begin{pmatrix} b_{ik} \\ \cdot \\ b_{i,bid_i+1} \\ b_{i,bid_i} \\ b_{i,bid_i-1} \\ \cdot \\ b_{i1} \end{pmatrix} = \begin{pmatrix} 0 \\ \cdot \\ 0 \\ 1 \\ 0 \\ \cdot \\ 0 \end{pmatrix}
$$

This allows efficient performance of certain operations. The correctness of bid vector is given by showing $\forall j \in \{1, 2, .., k\} : b_{ij} \in \{0, 1\}$ and $\sum_{j=1}^{k} b_{ij} = 1$.

Consider a group of n bidders that wants to compute the maximum of their secret bid values. The below first-price auction protocol is given for an arbitrary bidder b.

Generate Public Key

- choose a private key $x_{+i} \in Z_q$ and $\forall i, j : m_{ij}^{+a}, r_{aj} \in Z_q$ at random.
- Send $y_{\times i} = g^{x+i}$ along with a zero-knowledge proof of knowledge of $y_{\times i}$'s discrete logarithm (Subsect. 3.2)
- After all shares are set by all bidders, fetch other's key shares and computes the public key as $y = \prod_{i=1}^{n} y_{\times i}$.

Note that Exponentiation complexity of key generation step is $O(1)$.

Encrypt Bid. Let Y be an arbitrary value in $G_q \setminus \{1\}$ that is known to all bidders, for e.g., g.

- Compute $b_{aj} = \begin{cases} Y & \text{if } j = b_a \\ 1 & \text{else} \end{cases}$ and send the encrypted bid vector $\forall j : \alpha_{aj} = b_{aj} y^{r_{aj}}$ and $\beta_{aj} = g^{r_{aj}}$.
- A bid vector's correctness is given by showing that 1) Each bid element value is either Y or 1. 2) Product of all bid elements of a bid vector is Y.

- Provide proof of correctness of the bid in zero-knowledge $\forall j : 1) \log_g \beta_{aj}$
  equals either $\log_y (\alpha_{aj})$ or $\log_y (\frac{\alpha_{aj}}{Y})$ (Subsect. 3.2) and 2) $\log_y \left(\frac{\prod_{j=1}^{k} \alpha_{aj}}{Y} \right) =$
  $\log_g \left(\prod_{j=1}^{k} \beta_{aj} \right)$ (Subsect. 3.2). A non-interactive proof can also be generated
  using Fiat Shamir Heuristic [6].

Compute First-Price Outcome

- Compute and send $\forall i, j$:

$$\gamma_{ij}^{\times a} = \left(\left(\prod_{h=1}^{n} \prod_{d=j+1}^{k} \alpha_{hd} \right) \cdot \left(\prod_{d=1}^{j-1} \alpha_{id} \right) \cdot \left(\prod_{h=1}^{i-1} \alpha_{hj} \right) \right)^{m_{ij}^{\times a}} \quad \text{and}$$

$$\delta_{ij}^{\times a} = \left(\left(\prod_{h=1}^{n} \prod_{d=j+1}^{k} \beta_{hd} \right) \cdot \left(\prod_{d=1}^{j-1} \beta_{id} \right) \cdot \left(\prod_{h=1}^{i-1} \beta_{hj} \right) \right)^{m_{ij}^{\times a}}$$

with a proof of correctness (Subsect. 3.2).
Components of the first inner braces result in a vector where all elements corresponding to prices greater than or equal to the highest bid are zero. Components of the second inner braces transform the previously computed vector so that a single element remains zero if and only if bidder a bid the maximum bid. Components of the third inner braces resolve ties and results in vector with single 'zero' element for winning bidder with lowest index as it adds the bids of all users with the lower indices than that of bidder a.

Decrypt Outcome Share

- Compute and send the final outcome vector $\forall i, j : \varphi_{ij}^{\times a} = \left(\prod_{h=1}^{n} \delta_{ij}^{\times h} \right)^{x_{+a}}$ with a proof of correctness (Subsect. 3.2).

Determine Winner

- Compute the auction outcome function $\forall j : v_{aj} = \dfrac{\prod_{i=1}^{n} \gamma_{aj}^{\times i}}{\prod_{i=1}^{n} \varphi_{aj}^{\times i}}$
- If $v_{aw} = 1$ for any w, then bidder a is winner of the auction and p_w is the winning price.

Note that, all the vectors or matrices computed by a bidder can be compacted and set in a single transaction to avoid communication overhead.

6.3 Smart Contract Design

Here we present the pseudo-code of the auction smart contract.

Phase 1: Initial Setup and Registration. The seller (or auctioneer) deploys the auction smart contract C with all the auction parameters on the blockchain using procedure `Initialization` and publishes its address to the interested buyers. Interested bidders deposit the security money in form of cryptocurrency with the auction account and register their public key if not already done earlier using function `Registration` (Algorithm 1).

New Bidders are added to the back of the list so that early bidders have lower indices and it can be used in case of tie-breaking (Subsect. 6.2). We can use any other criterion such as bidder with the highest security amount for generating this index by sorting them accordingly and reinserting. Bidders can be registered only until the bid starts.

Algorithm 1. Auction Initialization and Registration

1: **procedure** INITIALIZATION($PubKeyGenStart, BidStart, BidEnd, PriceVector, BidSecAmt$)
    ▷ Initialization of Auction parameters
2:    $PubKeyGenerationStart \Leftarrow PubKeyGenStart$
3:    $BidSubmissionStart \Leftarrow BidStart$
4:    $BidSubmissionEnd \Leftarrow BidEnd$
5:    $BidPriceVector \Leftarrow PriceVector$
6:    $BidSecurity \Leftarrow BidSecAmt$
7:    $Bidders \Leftarrow [], Winner \Leftarrow None$
8: **end procedure**
9: **function** REGISTRATION($Bidder$)   ▷ Registration of a Bidder
10:    **assert** : $CurrTime < PubKeyGenerationStart$
11:    **assert** : Bidder's KYC details exist
12:    **assert** : Fund Received From Bidder = $BidSecurity$
13:    $Bidders.AddTail(Bidder)$
14:    **return** $BidderIndex_i$
15: **end function**

Phase 2: Public Key Generation. Each bidder generates the random numbers as per the protocol and updates the smart contract C using procedure `SetPublicKeyShare` and `IsAllPublicKeySharesSet`. After all the shares are set by all bidders, bidder a fetc.hes all other key shares using `GetPublicKeyShare` and computes the public key.

Phase 3: Bid Submission. As per the *Encrypt Bid* step in Subsect. 6.2, Bidder a computes his bid vector α_{aj}, β_{aj} for all j (all possible bid prices) and updates C using procedure `SubmitBidShare` (Algorithm 3). Zero knowledge proof of his bid validity can either be done interactively on demand or non-interactively [6].

Algorithm 2. Set and Fetch Public Key Share for a Bidder

1: **procedure** SETPUBLICKEYSHARE($BidderIndexi, y, PoKy$)
2:     **assert** : $CurrTime > PubKeyGenerationStart \wedge CurrTime < BidSubmissionStart$
3:     $Bidder \Leftarrow Bidders[i]$
4:     $Bidder.y \Leftarrow y, Bidder.PoKy \Leftarrow PoKy$
5:     $Bidder.PublicKeyShareSet \Leftarrow true$
6: **end procedure**
7: **function** GETPUBLICKEYSHARE($BidderIndexi$)
8:     $Bidder \Leftarrow Bidders[i]$
9:     **return** $Bidder.y$
10: **end function**
11: **function** ISALLPUBLICKEYSHARESSET   ▷ Check if all Public Key Shares are set
12:     $i \Leftarrow Bidders.Count$
13:     $AllSharesSet \Leftarrow true$
14:     **while** $i > 0$ **do**
15:         $Bidder \Leftarrow Bidders[i]$
16:         **if** $Bidder.PublicKeyShareSet$ is false **then**
17:             $AllSharesSet \Leftarrow false$
18:         **end if**
19:         $i \Leftarrow i - 1$
20:     **end while**
21:     **return** $AllSharesSet$
22: **end function**

Algorithm 3. Bid Submission

1: **procedure** SUBMITBIDSHARE($BidderIndexi, \alpha[,], \beta[,]$)   ▷ Bid Submission for Bidder with BidderIndex i
2:     $Bidder \Leftarrow Bidders[i]$
3:     $Bidder.\alpha[] \Leftarrow \alpha[], Bidder.\beta[] \Leftarrow \beta[]$
4: **end procedure**

Phase 4: Winner Determination. As per the protocol steps *Compute First-Price Outcome* and *Decrypt Outcome Share* in Subsect. 6.2, firstly the nk first-price outcome values ($\gamma_{ij}^{\times a}$ and $\delta_{ij}^{\times a}$ for each i and j) are computed by all bidders and updated at C using SetComputedOutcomeShare and IsAllComputedOutcomeSharesSet (Algorithm 4). Once every bidder has updated these values, decrypted outcome $\varphi_{ij}^{\times a}$ for every i and j are updated at C using GetComputedOutcomeShare and SetDecryptedOutcomeShare. Finally, auction outcome function v_{aj} is calculated for all j (all possible bid prices) by bidder a using GetDecryptedOutcomeShare so that he only learns whether he won the auction or not.

Algorithm 4. first-price outcome of each Bidder for winner determination

1: **procedure** SETCOMPUTEDOUTCOMESHARE($BidderIndexi, \gamma[,], \delta[,]$)   ▷ Set
    Public Key Share for bidder with index i
2:      $Bidder \Leftarrow Bidders[i]$
3:      $Bidder.\gamma[] \Leftarrow \gamma[], Bidder.\delta[] \Leftarrow \delta[]$
4:      $Bidder.ComputedOutcomeShareSet \Leftarrow true$
5: **end procedure**
6: **function** GETCOMPUTEDOUTCOMESHARE($BidderIndexi$)   ▷ Fetch Computed
    Outcome Share for bidder with index i
7:      $Bidder \Leftarrow Bidders[i]$
8:      **return** $Bidder.\gamma[], Bidder.\delta[]$
9: **end function**
10: **function** ISALLCOMPUTEDOUTCOMESHARESSET   ▷ Check if all Computed
    Outcome Shares are set
11:      $i \Leftarrow Bidders.Count$
12:      $AllSharesSet \Leftarrow true$
13:      **while** $i > 0$ **do**
14:          $Bidder \Leftarrow Bidders[i]$
15:          **if** $Bidder.ComputedOutcomeShareSet$ is false **then**
16:              $AllSharesSet \Leftarrow false$
17:          **end if**
18:          $i \Leftarrow i - 1$
19:      **end while**
20:      **return** $AllSharesSet$
21: **end function**
22: **procedure** SETDECRYPTEDOUTCOMESHARE($BidderIndexi, \varphi[,]$)   ▷ Set
    Decrypted Outcome Share for bidder with index i
23:      $Bidder \Leftarrow Bidders[i]$
24:      **assert** : $Verify the correctness of \varphi[,]$
25:      $Bidder.\varphi[] \Leftarrow \varphi[]$
26:      $Bidder.DecryptedOutcomeShareSet \Leftarrow true$
27: **end procedure**
28: **function** GETDECRYPTEDOUTCOMESHARE($BidderIndexi$)   ▷ Fetch Decrypted
    Outcome Share for bidder with index i
29:      $Bidder \Leftarrow Bidders[i]$
30:      **return** $Bidder.\varphi[]$
31: **end function**

Phase 5: Winner Disclosure. Once the bidder with the highest bid has confirmed his winning position, he can accept the auctioned item using `AcceptAuctionedItem` (Algorithm 5) and pay the bidding amount. Once the winner has paid the bidding amount (or equivalently accepted the auctioned item), C will refund the security amount to all bidders. If he does not accept, C can hold his security fund as a penalty The protocol can be restarted later by the seller after excluding him from the bidders' list as his identity is already known. If, during any phase of bidding, a malicious bidder does not respond within the given timeout period, the smart contract C will deduct his security money and refund others similar to the winner disclosure step.

Algorithm 5. Accept the auction item for the bid placed

1: **procedure** AcceptAuctionedItem($BidderIndex i$)   ▷ Accept the auction item
2:    $B \Leftarrow Bidders[i]$
3:    **assert** : B's outcome function value matches his claim
4:    $Winner \Leftarrow B$
5: **end procedure**
6: **function** GetWinner ▷ Get the Winner if the protocol is successfully completed
7:    **assert** : $Winner \neq None$
8:    **return** $Winner$
9: **end function**

---

7   Analysis

In this section, we will argue how the proposed system performs against the design objectives. We will provide communication and computation complexity as a part of *Efficiency*, one of the objectives.

Since every transaction is recorded immutably and change in every auction system parameter needs redeployment, the whole process can be checked and investigated later for any irregularities, thus providing *Public Auditability*. Bid evaluation criterion and possible bid prices are part of the smart contract. They can not be changed once the process has started, ensuring *Correctness of Evaluation* and the ability to fix a *Reserve Price*.

Each bid is encrypted using the bidder's private key and never decrypted. The security of underlying ElGamal cipher and zero-knowledge proofs is based on the intractability of decisional Diffie-Hellman assumption. The security of the distributed key generation is provided in [3]. Since the encryption keys are based on n-out-of-n secret sharing, the privacy of bids can not be broken unless all the bidders collude even in the case of tie-breaking. If a malicious bidder breaks away from the protocol, it gets restarted and hence preserves *Bid Privacy*. If multiple bidders bid for the same price, the bidder with the lowest index is declared the winner. Our Solution does not involve a seller for most of the bidding process besides deployment and restart, which minimizes the interaction, and thus corruption.

Having the same ledger replicated over all the blockchain nodes avoids issues with *Centralized Environment* and helps in creating an independent and semi-trusted consortium-like system. *Public Verifiability* follows from the fact that anyone can view the auction outcome. At each step, anyone can verify the correctness of the values provided by bidders using zero-knowledge proofs. Our solution is *Robust* against malicious bid as the computation can be verified at each step. However, it is not fully robust as the protocol will need to be restarted in case a bidder stops following the protocol. The protocol itself identifies the winner and the proof of the same can be used for *Non-repudiation*.

7.1   Efficiency

The total number of bits each bidder needs to communicate in the protocol (Subsect. 6.2) is $(6k(n+1)+5)\lceil \log p \rceil + (2k(n+2)+3)\lceil \log q \rceil$. For sufficiently large values of p and q, we will need 1024 and 768 bits, respectively. For an auction with 10 bidders and 500 possible prices, a bidder broadcasts about 5.1 MB of data. Considering the data is transferred in multiple phases and over a permissioned blockchain, we think our proposed solution can handle the complexity without any issues in today's infrastructure.

8   Conclusion and Future Work

In this paper, we presented a blockchain based first-price sealed-bid auction protocol that can be used in government organizations for public procurement of goods and services. The proposed solution provides full privacy such that 1) bidders do not learn any information about bids except the highest bid, 2)No subset of bidders can collude to find the bid amount of a particular bidder and 3) no dependency on any third party. The system exhibits a trust-less environment where all the protocol steps, including the auction outcome, can be publicly verified, and a consortium like distributed environment will bring security and competitive culture. The communication complexity and Partial robustness are the main challenges in this system, and we will continue to look into ways to overcome them. We also plan to implement a hyperledger based blockchain system for evaluation.

References

1. Abe, M., Suzuki, K.: $M + 1$-st price auction using homomorphic encryption. In: Naccache, D., Paillier, P. (eds.) PKC 2002. LNCS, vol. 2274, pp. 115–124. Springer, Heidelberg (2002). https://doi.org/10.1007/3-540-45664-3_8
2. Baudron, O., Stern, J.: Non-interactive private auctions. In: Syverson, P. (ed.) FC 2001. LNCS, vol. 2339, pp. 364–377. Springer, Heidelberg (2002). https://doi.org/10.1007/3-540-46088-8_28
3. Brandt, F.: Fully private auctions in a constant number of rounds. In: Wright, R.N. (ed.) FC 2003. LNCS, vol. 2742, pp. 223–238. Springer, Heidelberg (2003). https://doi.org/10.1007/978-3-540-45126-6_16
4. Brandt, F.: How to obtain full privacy in auctions. Int. J. Inf. Secur. **5**(4), 201–216 (2006). https://doi.org/10.1007/s10207-006-0001-y
5. Elgamal, T.: A public key cryptosystem and a signature scheme based on discrete logarithms. IEEE Trans. Inf. Theor. **31**(4), 469–472 (1985). http://ieeexplore.ieee.org/document/1057074/. https://doi.org/10.1109/TIT.1985. ISSN: 0018–9448
6. Fiat, A., Shamir, A.: How to prove yourself: practical solutions to identification and signature problems. In: Odlyzko, A.M. (ed.) CRYPTO 1986. LNCS, vol. 263, pp. 186–194. Springer, Heidelberg (1987). https://doi.org/10.1007/3-540-47721-7_12. ISBN: 9783540180470

7. Franklin, M.K., Reiter, M.K.: Design and implementation of a secure auction service. In: Proceedings of the IEEE Computer Society Symposium on Research in Security and Privacy, pp. 2–14. IEEE (1995). https://doi.org/10.1109/32.502223

8. Galal, H.S., Youssef, A.M.: Verifiable sealed-bid auction on the ethereum blockchain. In: Zohar, A., Eyal, I., Teague, V., Clark, J., Bracciali, A., Pintore, F., Sala, M. (eds.) FC 2018. LNCS, vol. 10958, pp. 265–278. Springer, Heidelberg (2019). https://doi.org/10.1007/978-3-662-58820-8_18

9. Graycar, A., et al.: Preventing Corruption in Public Sector Procurement (2013). https://www.oecd.org/governance/ethics/Corruption-Public-Procurement-Brochure.pdf. Accessed 11 June 2019. https://doi.org/10.1057/9781137335098_7

10. Montenegro, J.A., et al.: Secure sealed-bid online auctions using discreet cryptographic proofs. Math. Comput. Model. **57**(11–12), 2583–2595 (2013). https://doi.org/10.1016/j.mcm.2011.07.027. ISSN: 08957177. 027

11. Nakamoto, S.: Bitcoin: A Peer-to-Peer Electronic Cash System. Technical report. https://www.bitcoin.org/bitcoin.pdf

12. Naor, M., Pinkas, B., Sumner, R.: Privacy preserving auctions and mechanism design. In: ACM International Conference Proceeding Series, pp. 129–139 (1999). https://doi.org/10.1145/336992. ISBN: 1581131763. 337028

13. Omote, K., Miyaji, A.: A Second-price sealed-bid auction with public verifiability. Trans. Inform. Process Soc. Jpn. **43**, 1405–2413 (2002)

Comparison of Decentralization in DPoS and PoW Blockchains

Chao Li[1(✉)] and Balaji Palanisamy[2]

[1] Beijing Key Laboratory of Security and Privacy in Intelligent Transportation,
Beijing Jiaotong University, Beijing, China
li.chao@bjtu.edu.cn
[2] School of Computing and Information, University of Pittsburgh, Pittsburgh, USA
bpalan@pitt.edu

Abstract. Decentralization is a key indicator for the evaluation of public blockchains. In the past, there have been very few studies on measuring and comparing the actual level of decentralization between Proof-of-Work (PoW) blockchains and blockchains with other consensus protocols. This paper presents a new comparison study of the level of decentralization in Bitcoin and Steem, a prominent Delegated-Proof-of-Stake (DPoS) blockchain. Our study particularly focuses on analysing the power that decides the creators of blocks in the blockchain. In Bitcoin, miners with higher computational power generate more blocks. In contrast, blocks in Steem are equally generated by witnesses while witnesses are periodically elected by stakeholders with different voting power weighted by invested stake. We analyze the process of stake-weighted election of witnesses in DPoS and measure the actual stake invested by each stakeholder in Steem. We then compute the Shannon entropy of the distribution of computational power among miners in Bitcoin and the distribution of invested stake among stakeholders in Steem. Our analyses reveal that neither Bitcoin nor Steem is dominantly better than the other with respect to decentralization. Compared with Steem, Bitcoin tends to be more decentralized among top miners but less decentralized in general. Our study is designed to provide insights into the current state of the degree of decentralization in DPoS and PoW blockchains. We believe that the methodologies and findings in this paper can facilitate future studies of decentralization in other blockchain systems employing different consensus protocols.

1 Introduction

The evolution of Blockchain made Bitcoin the first cryptocurrency that resolves the double-spending problem without the need for a centralized trusted party [15]. From then on, rapid advances in blockchain technologies have driven the rise of hundreds of new public blockchains [12]. For most of these public blockchains, the degree of decentralization of resources that decide who generates blocks is the key metric for evaluating the blockchain decentralization [6,12,18]. This in turn facilitates further understanding of both security and scalability

© Springer Nature Switzerland AG 2020
Z. Chen et al. (Eds.): ICBC 2020, LNCS 12404, pp. 18–32, 2020.
https://doi.org/10.1007/978-3-030-59638-5_2

in a blockchain [11]. Intuitively, having only a few parties dominantly possess the resources indicates a more centralized control of blockchain, which is potentially less secure. This is due to the fact collusion among these few parties can be powerful enough to perform denial-of-service attacks against targeted blockchain users and even falsify historical data recorded in blockchain. More concretely, in a Proof-of-Work (PoW) blockchain such as Bitcoin [15], a miner possessing higher computational power has a better chance of generating the next block. In Bitcoin, a transaction is considered to be 'confirmed' after six blocks as it is estimated that the probability of creating a longer fork after six blocks to defeat the one containing the 'confirmed' transaction is negligible. However, the assumption is not held when a few miners possess over half of overall computational power in the network, in which case these miners are able to launch the commonly known 51% attack to control the blockchain and double-spend any amount of cryptocurrency. Through selfish mining [5], the difficulty of performing 51% attack could be further reduced to the demand of possessing 33% of overall computational power, indicating even weaker security in less decentralized blockchains.

Recent research pointed out that Bitcoin shows a trend towards centralization [1,6,12,17,18]. For the purpose of reducing the variance of income, the majority of Bitcoin miners have joined large mining pools and a small set of mining pools are now actually controlling the Bitcoin blockchain. Meanwhile, the use of PoW consensus protocol in Bitcoin requires the decentralized consensus to be made throughout the entire network and the throughput of transactions in Bitcoin is limited by the network scale. As a result, the 7 transactions/sec throughput in Bitcoin cannot satisfy the need of many practical applications [3]. Motivated by these concerns, recently, the Delegated Proof-of-Stake (DPoS) consensus protocol [13] is becoming increasingly popular and has given rise to a series of successful blockchains [12,14]. The key selling point of DPoS blockchains is their high scalability. In DPoS blockchains, blocks are generated by a small set of witnesses that are periodically elected by the entire stakeholder community. Thus, the decentralized consensus is only reached among the witnesses and the small scale of the witness set could boost the transaction throughput to support various types of real applications such as a social media platform [14]. However, there are disagreements over the level of decentralization in DPoS blockchains. The supporters believe that, in practice, the design of equally generating blocks among witnesses in DPoS blockchains is less centralized than the current PoW blockchains dominated by few mining pools. Others believe that, in theory, the very limited scale of the witness set naturally shows a low degree of decentralization. Existing research works have evaluated the degree of decentralization in Proof-of-Work (PoW) blockchains represented by Bitcoin and Ethereum [6,18]. However, there have been very few comparison studies on measuring the actual level of decentralization between PoW blockchains and DPoS blockchains.

This paper presents a comparison study of the level of decentralization in Bitcoin and in Steem [14], a prominent DPoS blockchain. Our study particularly focuses on analysing the power that decides the creators of blocks in the blockchain. We analyze the process of stake-weighted election of witnesses in DPoS and measures the actual stake invested by each stakeholder in Steem. Similar to the analyses in recent works [12,18], we quantify and compare the actual degree of decentralization in these two blockchains by computing the Shannon entropy of the distribution of computational power among miners in Bitcoin and that of the distribution of invested stake among stakeholders in Steem. Our results shows that the entropy in Steem among top stakeholders is lower than the entropy in Bitcoin among top miners while the entropy in Steem becomes higher than the entropy in Bitcoin when more stakeholders and miners are taken into computation.

Our analyses reveal that neither Bitcoin nor Steem is dominantly better than the other with respect to decentralization. Compared with Steem, Bitcoin tends to be more decentralized among top miners but less decentralized in general. Our study is designed to provide insights into the current state of the degree of decentralization in representative DPoS and PoW blockchains. We believe that the methodologies and findings in this paper can facilitate future studies on decentralization in other blockchains and consensus protocols.

The rest of this paper is organized as follows: We introduce the background in Sect. 2. In Sect. 3, we present the preliminary measurements for Bitcoin miners and for Steem witnesses. Then, in Sect. 4, we present the methodologies of measuring the impact of stakeholders in the process of stake-weighted witness election in Steem. In Sect. 5, we quantify and compare the degree of decentralization among Bitcoin miners, among Steem witnesses and among Steem stakeholders. Finally, we discuss related work in Sect. 6 and we conclude in Sect. 7.

2   Background

In this section, we introduce the background about the Steem-blockchain [2], including its key application *Steemit*, its implementation of the DPoS consensus protocol and its ecosystem in general.

The Steem-blockchain is the backend for *Steemit*, which is the first blockchain-powered social media platform that incentivizes both creator of user-generated content and content curators. *Steemit* has kept its leading position during the last few years and its native cryptocurrency, *STEEM*, has the highest market capitalization among all cryptocurrencies issued by blockchain-based social networking projects. Users of *Steemit* can create and share contents as blog posts. A blog post can get replied, reposted or voted by other users. Based on the weights of received votes, posts get ranked and the top ranked posts make them to the front page. *Steemit* uses the Steem-blockchain to store the underlying data of the platform as a chain of blocks. Every three seconds, a new block is produced, which includes all confirmed operations performed by users during the last three seconds. *Steemit* allows its users to perform more than thirty different types of operations. In Fig. 1, we display four categories of operations that are most relevant to the analysis presented in this paper. While post/vote and follower/following are common features offered by social sites, operations such as witness election and cryptocurrency transfer are features specific to blockchains.

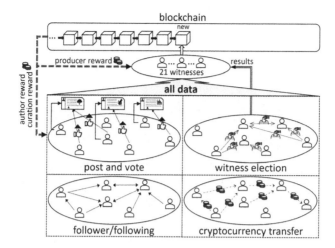

Fig. 1. Steem blockchain overview

Witnesses in *Steemit* are producers of blocks, who continuously collect data from the entire network, bundle data into blocks and append the blocks to the Steem-blockchain. The role of witnesses in *Steemit* is similar to that of miners in Bitcoin. In Bitcoin, miners keep solving Proof-of-Work (PoW) problems and winners have the right to produce blocks. With PoW, Bitcoin achieves a maximum throughput of 7 transactions/sec [3]. However, transaction rates of typical mainstream social sites are substantially higher. For example, Twitter has an average throughput of more than 5000 tweets/sec [10]. Hence, the Steem blockchain adopts the Delegated Proof of Stake (DPoS) [13] consensus protocol to increase the speed and scalability of the platform without compromising the decentralized reward system of the blockchain. In DPoS systems, users vote to elect a number of witnesses as their delegates. In *Steemit*, each user can vote for at most 30 witnesses. The top-20 elected witnesses and a seat randomly assigned out of the top-20 witnesses produce the blocks. With DPoS, consensus only needs to be reached among the 21-member witness group, rather than the entire blockchain network like Bitcoin, which significantly improves the system throughput.

We now present the process of stake-weighted witness election with more details. Any user in *Steemit* can run a server, install the Steem-blockchain and synchronize the blockchain data to the latest block. Then, by sending a *witness_update* operation to the network, the user can become a witness and have a chance to operate the website and earn producer rewards if he or she can gather enough support from the electors to join the 21-member witness group. A user has two ways to vote for witnesses. The first option is to perform *witness_vote* operations to directly vote for at most 30 witnesses. The second option is to perform a *witness_proxy* operation to set another user as an election proxy. The weight of a vote is the sum of the voter's own stake and the stake owned by other users who have set the voter as proxy. For example, Alice may set Bob to be her proxy. Then, if both Alice and Bob own \$100 worth of stake, any vote cast by Bob will be associated with a weight of \$200 worth of stake. Once Alice deletes the proxy, the weight of Bob's votes will reduce to \$100 worth of stake immediately.

The ecosystem in Steem is a bit complex. Like most blockchains, the Steem-blockchain issues its native cryptocurrencies called $STEEM$ and Steem Dollars (SBD). To own stake in $Steemit$, a user needs to 'lock' $STEEM/SBD$ in $Steemit$ to receive Steem Power (SP) at the rate of 1 $STEEM = 1\ SP$ and each SP is assigned about 2000 vested shares ($VESTS$) of $Steemit$. A user may withdraw invested $STEEM/SBD$ at any time, but the claimed fund will be automatically split into thirteen equal portions to be withdrawn in the next thirteen subsequent weeks. For example, in day 1, Alice may invest 13 $STEEM$ to $Steemit$ that makes her vote obtain a weight of 13 SP (about 26000 $VESTS$). Later, in day 8, Alice may decide to withdraw her 13 invested $STEEM$. Here, instead of seeing her 13 $STEEM$ in wallet immediately, her $STEEM$ balance will increase by 1 $STEEM$ each week from day 8 and during that period, her SP will decrease by 1 SP every week. In the rest of this paper, for ease of exposition and comparison, we transfer all values of $STEEM/SBD/SP/VESTS$ to VESTS, namely the stake in Steem, based on 1 $SBD \approx 0.4\ STEEM = 0.4\ SP \approx 800\ VESTS$ [9].

3   Data Collection and Preliminary Measurements

In this section, we describe our data collection methodology and present some preliminary measurements among Bitcoin miners and among Steem witnesses.

3.1   Data Collection

The Steem-blockchain offers an Interactive Application Programming Interface (API) for developers and researchers to collect and parse the blockchain data [8]. From block 24,671,073 to block 25,563,499, we collected 892,426 Steem blocks produced during a time period of one month. The Bitcoin blockchain offers similar API at [7]. From block 534,762 to block 539,261, we collected 4,499 Bitcoin blocks produced during the same one-month time period.

3.2   Preliminary Measurements

To understand the degree of decentralization in Bitcoin and Steem, we start measurements by parsing the collected blocks and counting the number of blocks produced by each generator, namely each Bitcoin miner or Steem witness. The results of distributions of blocks created by top-30 generators in Bitcoin and Steem are shown in Fig. 2 and Fig. 3, respectively.

We notice that 4,430 out of 4,499 Bitcoin blocks (98.6%) were generated by mining pools, which illustrates the domination of mining pools in current Bitcoin mining competitions. The top 5 mining pools mined 848 (18.9%), 661 (14.7%),

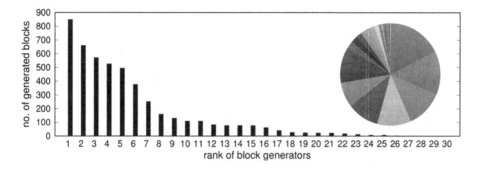

Fig. 2. Distribution of blocks generated by top-30 miners in Bitcoin

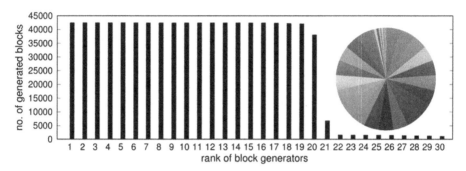

Fig. 3. Distribution of blocks generated by top-30 witnesses in Steem

571 (12.7%), 525 (11.7%) and 494 (11.0%) blocks, respectively. As revealed by the pie chart plotted in Fig. 2, the sum of blocks produced by the top 4 mining pools, namely 2605 (57.9%) blocks in total, has already exceeded the bar of launching 51% attack. The top 2 mining pools generated 1,509 (33.5%) blocks have been higher than the 33% bar suggested by the selfish mining research [5]. Intuitively, we see how fragile the security in the current Bitcoin blockchain is in practice. It is true that mining pools may not want to attack Bitcoin as it would decrease the market price of Bitcoin and damage the profit of themselves. However, the risk is still high because compromising two mining pools is much easier than attacking a large distributed network and it is also hard to quantify and compare the short-term profit of performing double-spend before Bitcoin gets crashed and the long-term profit of keeping honest.

Next, we notice that 844,390 out of 892,426 Steem blocks (94.6%) were gener-ated by the top-20 witnesses. Interestingly, as indicated by the pie chart plotted in Fig. 3, the mean and standard deviation of blocks generated by top 20 wit-nesses are 42,219 and 978 respectively, indicating that these top 20 witnesses continuously reserved 20 seats in the 21-member witness group and generated nearly the same amount of blocks in the selected month. Although we do not see that the seats were frequently switched among a larger set of witnesses, intuitively, the distribution of blocks among Steem witnesses shows a trend of a higher degree of decentralization. However, unlike mining pools in Bitcoin that possess computational power directly determining the number of blocks they could mine, witnesses in Steem do not own the similar resources themselves because their sears in the 21-member witness group are determined by the VESTS (i.e., stake) accumulated from the votes cast by stakeholders in the entire network. That is, block generation in Steem and other DPoS blockchains is actually controlled by stakeholders who possess the power of appointing and removing witnesses at any time. Therefore, in the next section, we investigate the impact of stakeholders in the process of stake-weighted witness election in Steem, which would facilitate the quantification of the actual level of decentralization in Steem.

4   Measurements on Impact of Stakeholders in Steem

In this section, we measure the actual impact of stakeholders in determining active witnesses in Steem, namely in actually controlling the Steem blockchain. We first present our measuring methodology and then the results.

4.1   Methodology

Each stakeholder could cast at most 30 votes and each vote is weighted by net VESTS, namely the sum of the stakeholder's pure VESTS and the VESTS received from other stakeholders who have set this stakeholder as proxy. Therefore, we first investigate pure VESTS that each stakeholder possesses and compute net VESTS belonged to each stakeholder in witness election by combining pure VESTS with VESTS received from other stakeholders.

However, computing the degree of decentralization in Steem based on net VESTS is inaccurate for two reasons: (1) stakeholders may not choose to vote for any witness and therefore, VESTS owned by this type of stakeholders has no contribution to witness election and these stakeholders have no actual control of the blockchain; (2) a stakeholder can cast at most 30 votes, but not all stakeholders cast 30 votes in full. For example, Alice may cast 20 votes to 20 witnesses and Bob may cast a single vote to a single witness. Assuming that Alice and Bob have the same net VESTS and all these voted witnesses generated the same amount of blocks, we consider that the impact of Alice in witness election is twenty times that of Bob. In other words, what determines the actual impact of a stakeholder in witness election is the accumulated VESTS from all his/her votes, namely the multiplication of net VESTS and the number of votes.

To do that, we need to collect the number of votes cast by each stakeholder. After that, we compute accumulated VESTS from votes cast by each stakeholder and accumulated VESTS from votes received by each witness. Finally, we re-allocate the 892,426 Steem blocks to the stakeholders based on accumulated VESTS of their votes and we investigate the distribution of blocks among stakeholders after the re-allocation.

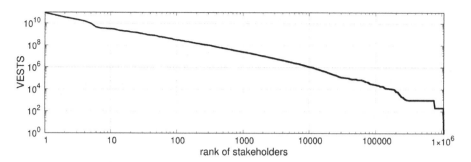

Fig. 4. Distribution of pure VESTS among stakeholders with at least 1 VESTS

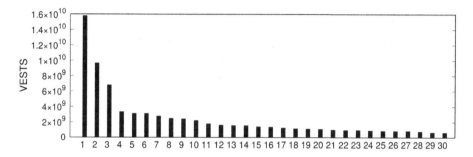

Fig. 5. Distribution of net VESTS among top-30 stakeholders

4.2 Measurement Results

Following the above-mentioned methodology, the measurements start by investigating pure VESTS that each stakeholder has in Steem at the moment of block 25,563,499. Figure 4 shows pure VESTS of 1,077,405 stakeholders who have at least 1 VESTS. Here, stakeholders are sorted based on their pure VESTS. The results indicate a heavy-tailed distribution. We find that the top-10 stakeholders possess 1.93E+11 VESTS, about 48.5% of overall VESTS. In contrast, the last 1,000,000 stakeholders possess only 4.83E+09 VESTS, about 1.2% of overall VESTS. The top-1, top-2 and top-5 stakeholders possess 9.00E+10 (22.7%), 1.26E+11 (37.5%) and 1.74E+11 (43.9%) VESTS, respectively. Therefore, the results here suggest a trend towards centralization in Steem, which is similar to that in Bitcoin.

Next, Fig. 5 presents the distribution of net VESTS among top-30 stakeholders who cast at least one vote and also set no proxy at the moment of block 25,563,499. Stakeholders here are ranked based on their net VESTS, namely the sum of pure VESTS and received VESTS. In the rest of this paper, for the ease of presentation, we use the same rank for stakeholders and the phrase 'top-30 stakeholders' refers to the top-30 stakeholders sorted by net VESTS. The net VESTS belonging to top-1, top-3 and top-5 stakeholders are 1.58E+10, 3.23E+10 and 3.87E+10 respectively, which are only 17.6%, 21.7% and 22.2% of the pure VESTS possessed by stakeholders with the same ranks. The main reason is that many stakeholders neither cast a single vote nor set other stakeholders as their proxy. Another interesting observation is that only seven stakeholder possessing top-30 pure VESTS also own top-30 net VESTS. One possible reason is that many stakeholders may want to isolate operations about witness election from other types of operations, so they create a new account to be their proxy for voting witnesses.

Fig. 6. No. of votes casted by top-30 stakeholders

After measuring both pure VESTS and net VESTS, we plot the number of votes cast by top-30 stakeholders ranked by net VESTS in Fig. 6. The results show that only 12 out of top-30 stakeholders have cast 30 votes in full. The number of votes is quite a personal option. The Steem team encourages the community to actively participate in witness election, but some stakeholders may have a strict standard in mind and believe in only less than 30 witnesses, so they do not aim at maximizing their impact in witness election by casting exact 30 votes.

We can now compute accumulated VESTS from votes cast by top-30 stake-holders by multiplying net VESTS and the number of cast votes. The results are shown in Fig. 7. As can be seen, the 12 stakeholders who cast 30 votes in full amplify their net VESTS by a factor of 30 and maximize their impact in witness election. In contrast, some stakeholders (i.e, rank-2, rank-4 and rank-7), who cast a few votes, amplify their net VESTS by a much smaller factor, which actu-ally reduces their impact in witness election. It is hard to comment whether the strategy of always casting 30 votes in full is healthy for Steem or not, but stake-holders who intend to maximize their control in the Steem blockchain would be incentivized to always follow this strategy and their impact in Steem may eventually overtake the impact of stakeholders who cast a personalized number of votes.

Following the same methodology, we can also compute accumulated VESTS from votes received by each witness, namely the sum of net VESTS of each vote received by a witness. The results are shown in Fig. 8. The mean and standard deviation of accumulated VESTS received by top-30 witnesses are 5.65E+10

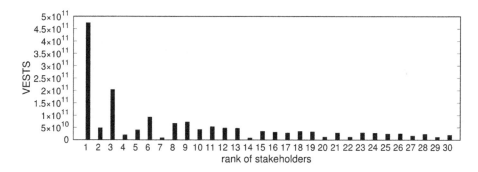

Fig. 7. Accumulated VESTS from votes cast by top-30 stakeholder

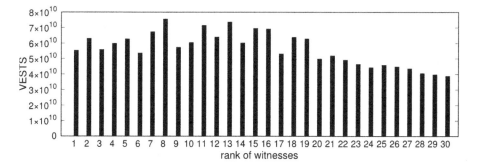

Fig. 8. Accumulated VESTS from votes received by top-30 witness

and 1.06E+10, respectively. The comparison between Fig. 8 and Fig. 7 thus tells us that the degree of decentralization among VESTS accumulated via witnesses tends to be much higher than that among VESTS accumulated via stakeholders. The relationship between stakeholders and witnesses is similar to that between shareholders and managers in a corporation. A corporation is actually controlled by its shareholders, especially the major ones, and likewise the Steem blockchain is actually controlled by shareholders, especially the ones possessing large amounts of net VESTS. Therefore, we consider that the actual degree of decentralization in Steem is expressed through that among stakeholders, rather than that among witnesses. Another interesting observation is that the amount of blocks generated by a witness is not exactly proportional to its accumulated VESTS. For instance, the rank-8 witness in Fig. 8 received the most VESTS from stakeholders. This scenario may be caused by the bias that we took the pure VESTS and votes as a snapshot at block 25,563,499 while some stakeholders may have changed their pure VESTS or votes during the one-month time period.

Finally, we can observe the actual degree of decentralization in Steem by reallocating the 892,426 Steem blocks to the stakeholders based on accumulated VESTS of their votes. The results are shown in Fig. 9, which is obviously more

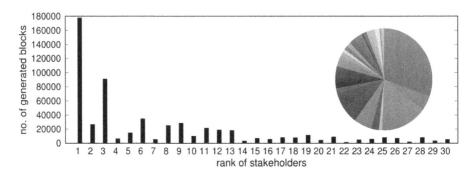

Fig. 9. Distribution of blocks re-allocated to top-30 stakeholders

skewed than the distribution we see in Fig. 3. From the pie chart, we can see that the majority of the 892,426 Steem blocks have been re-allocated to only a few major stakeholders. The amounts of blocks re-allocated to the rank-1 stakeholder and to rank-3 stakeholder are 177,698 and 91,207 respectively, namely 30.5% and 16.1% of blocks re-allocated to top-30 stakeholders or 20.0% and 10.1% of overall blocks.

We have measured the distribution of blocks among Bitcoin miners (Fig. 2), among Steem witnesses (Fig. 3) and finally among Steem stakeholders (Fig. 9). In the next section, we will quantitatively analyze the degree of decentralization in Bitcoin and Steem.

5   Quantitative Analysis of the Degree of Decentralization

In this section, similar to the analyses in recent works [12,18], we quantify and compare the degree of decentralization in Bitcoin and Steem by computing the Shannon entropy [16]. We first normalize the three distributions from Fig. 2, Fig. 3 and Fig. 9 to display a more intuitive comparison among the three distributions. We then quantify the Shannon entropy (or entropy for short) of the three distributions.

5.1   Normalized Comparison

We display the three normalized distributions at Fig. 10. Specifically, the normalized number of blocks at y-axis has the range $[0,1]$, where the upper bound indicates the number of blocks generated by the rank-1 Bitcoin miner in the Bitcoin (miner) distribution at Fig. 2, the amount of blocks generated by the rank-1 Steem witness in the Steem (witness) distribution at Fig. 3 and the amount of blocks re-allocated to the rank-1 Steem stakeholder in the Steem (stakeholder) distribution at Fig. 9.

Bitcoin (miner) vs. Steem (witness): The comparison between Bitcoin miners and Steem witnesses seems to support the opinion of supporters of Steem,

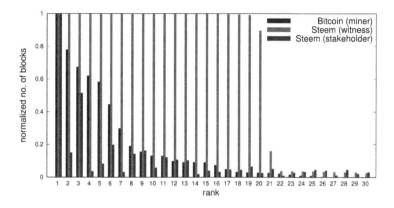

Fig. 10. Comparison of normalized distributions

who believe that the design of equally generating blocks among witnesses in DPoS blockchains is less centralized than the current PoW blockchains dominated by few mining pools. It is true that the distribution of Bitcoin miners is quite skewed while the distribution of Steem witnesses is quite flat before rank 20. It is also true that the miners/witnesses after rank 20 generate quite limited amounts of blocks. However, the fundamental problem of this opinion is that measuring witnesses is not the proper approach for understanding the actual degree of decentralization in Steem. In Bitcoin, miners possess computational power that determines their probability of mining blocks. In Steem, witnesses do not possess VESTS that determines their chance to join the 21-member witness group. As a result, collusion among the few top stakeholders can easily remove the majority of current top witnesses out of the 21-member witness group and control the seats in their hands. Therefore, to understand the actual situation, we need to compare Bitcoin miners with Steem stakeholders.

Bitcoin (miner) vs. Steem (stakeholder): The comparison between Bitcoin miners and Steem stakeholders can be analyzed in three ranges. From rank 1 to 7, we see that only three out of the top 7 stakeholders cast 30 votes in full, which indicates a significant advantage owned by these three stakeholders in controlling Steem blockchain. We also see that the distribution among top-7 stakeholders is much skewed than that among top-7 Bitcoin miners. From rank 8 to 13, the figure suggests no significant advantage between the two distributions. After rank 13, we see that the distribution of Bitcoin miners quickly drops to zero while the distribution of Steem stakeholders keeps a flat shape. Overall, intuitively, the degree of decentralization in Bitcoin seems to be higher among top miners than that among top Steem stakeholders but be lower among low ranking miners than that among low ranking Steem stakeholders.

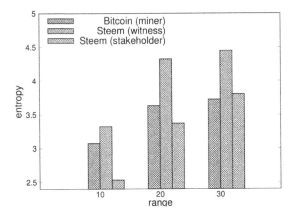

Fig. 11. Comparison of entropy

5.2 Quantitative Analysis

We compute the Shannon entropy *entropy* of the three distribution via:

$$p_i = \frac{b_i}{\sum_{i=1}^{r} b_i}$$

$$entropy = -\sum_{i=1}^{r} p_i \log_2 p_i$$

where b_i denotes the amount of blocks generated by miners/witnesses or re-allocated to stakeholders and r denotes the range of miners/witnesses/stakeholders that entropy is computed for. For instance, $r = 10$ indicates that entropy is computed based on blocks belonging to top-10 miners/witnesses/stakeholders.

We show the computed values of entropy for $r = 10, 20, 30$ in Fig. 11. We can see that the results well support our analysis in Sect. 5.1. First, the entropy among witnesses in all selected ranges keeps being the highest one, which suggests a higher degree of decentralization among witnesses because a group of witnesses has a close probability to be the generator of a block and the uncertainty of inferring the generator is quite high. Next, the entropy among Bitcoin miners is higher than that among Steem stakeholders in ranges $r = 10$ and $r = 20$ but turns to become lower in the range $r = 30$. The reason is that the impact of the few major Steem stakeholders is more significant in the sets of top-10 and top-20 stakeholders but is less significant when the computation counts more low ranking stakeholders. The results thus indicate that, compared with Bitcoin, Steem tends to be more centralized among top stakeholders but more decentralized in general.

6   Related Work

Most of related works on decentralization in blockchains have focused on Bitcoin [1,4,5,17]. These works pointed out that Bitcoin shows a trend towards centralization because of the emergence of mining pools. In [5], authors proposed the selfish mining, which reduces the bar of performing 51% attack to possessing over 33% of computational power in Bitcoin. Later, authors in [4] analyzed the mining competitions among mining pools in Bitcoin from the perspective of game theory and proposed that a rational mining pool may get incentivized to launch a block withholding attack to another mining pool. Besides Bitcoin, recent work has analyzed the degree of decentralization in Steem [14]. The work analyzed the process of witness election in Steem from the perspective of network analysis and concluded that the Steem network was showing a relatively low level of decentralization.

Recently, there have been a few studies on comparing the level of decentralization between different blockchains [6,12,18]. Specifically, the work in [6] compared the degree of decentralization between Bitcoin and Ethereum and concluded that neither Bitcoin nor Ethereum was performing strictly better properties than the other. The work in [18] also focused on investigating Bitcoin and Ethereum, but by quantifying the degree of decentralization with Shannon entropy. Their results indicate that Bitcoin tends to be more decentralized than Ethereum. The closest work to our study in this paper is the study in [12], where authors analyzed the degree of decentralization in dozens of blockchains including Bitcoin and Steem. However, the degree of decentralization in Steem in [12] was computed among witnesses rather than stakeholders, which in our opinion fails to reflect the actual degree of decentralization in a DPoS blockchain. To the best of our knowledge, our paper is the first research work that quantifies the degree of decentralization in a DPoS blockchain from the perspective of stakeholders after careful analysis and measurements of the witness election.

7   Conclusion

In this paper, we present a comparison study of the degree of decentralization in PoW-powered Bitcoin blockchain and DPoS-powered Steem blockchain. Our study analyzes the process of stake-weighted election of witnesses in the DPoS consensus protocol and measures the actual stake invested by each stakeholder in Steem. We then quantify and compare the actual degree of decentralization in the two blockchains by computing the Shannon entropy. Our measurements indicate that, compared with Steem, Bitcoin tends to be more decentralized among top miners but less decentralized in general. We believe that the methodologies and findings in this paper can facilitates future studies on decentralization in other blockchains and consensus protocols.

Acknowledgement. Chao Li acknowledges the partial support by the Fundamental Research Funds for the Central Universities (Grant No. 2019RC038).

References

1. Beikverdi, A., Song, J.: Trend of centralization in bitcoin's distributed network. In: 2015 IEEE/ACIS 16th SNPD, pp. 1–6. IEEE (2015)
2. Steem blockchain. https://developers.steem.io/. Accessed Oct 2018
3. Croman, K., et al.: On scaling decentralized blockchains. In: Clark, J., Meiklejohn, S., Ryan, P.Y.A., Wallach, D., Brenner, M., Rohloff, K. (eds.) FC 2016. LNCS, vol. 9604, pp. 106–125. Springer, Heidelberg (2016). https://doi.org/10.1007/978-3-662-53357-4_8
4. Eyal, I.: The miner's dilemma. In: 2015 IEEE Symposium on Security and Privacy, pp. 89–103. IEEE (2015)
5. Eyal, I., Sirer, E.G.: Majority is not enough: bitcoin mining is vulnerable. In: Christin, N., Safavi-Naini, R. (eds.) FC 2014. LNCS, vol. 8437, pp. 436–454. Springer, Heidelberg (2014). https://doi.org/10.1007/978-3-662-45472-5_28
6. Gencer, A.E., Basu, S., Eyal, I., van Renesse, R., Sirer, E.G.: Decentralization in bitcoin and ethereum networks. In: Meiklejohn, S., Sako, K. (eds.) FC 2018. LNCS, vol. 10957, pp. 439–457. Springer, Heidelberg (2018). https://doi.org/10.1007/978-3-662-58387-6_24
7. BTC.COM API V3. https://btc.com/api-doc. Accessed Oct 2019
8. Interactive Steem API. https://steem.esteem.ws/. Accessed Oct 2019
9. STEEM Price. https://coinmarketcap.com/currencies/steem/. Accessed Oct 2018
10. Twitter Usage Statistics. http://www.internetlivestats.com/twitter-statistics/. Accessed Oct 2018
11. Kokoris-Kogias, E., et al.: Omniledger: a secure, scale-out, decentralized ledger via sharding. In: 2018 IEEE Symposium on Security and Privacy (SP), pp. 583–598. IEEE (2018)
12. Kwon, Y., Liu, J., Kim, M. Song, D., Kim, Y.: Impossibility of full decentralization in permissionless blockchains. In: Proceedings of the 1st ACM Conference on Advances in Financial Technologies, pp. 110–123 (2019)
13. Larimer, D.: Delegated proof-of-stake (DPOS). Bitshare whitepaper (2014)
14. Li, C., Palanisamy, B.: Incentivized blockchain-based social media platforms: a case study of steemit. In: Proceedings of the 10th ACM Conference on Web Science, pp. 145–154 (2019)
15. Nakamoto, S.: Bitcoin: A Peer-to-Peer Electronic Cash System (2008)
16. Shannon, C.E.: A mathematical theory of communication. Bell Syst. Tech. J. **27**(3), 379–423 (1948)
17. Tschorsch, F., Scheuermann, B.: Bitcoin and beyond: a technical survey on decentralized digital currencies. IEEE Commun. Surv. Tutor. **18**(3), 2084–2123 (2016)
18. Wu, K., Peng, B., Xie, H., Huang, Z.: An information entropy method to quantify the degrees of decentralization for blockchain systems. In: 2019 IEEE 9th International Conference on Electronics Information and Emergency Communication (ICEIEC), pp. 1–6. IEEE (2019)

MULTAV: A Multi-chain Token Backed Voting Framework for Decentralized Blockchain Governance

Xinxin Fan$^{(\boxtimes)}$ (iD), Qi Chai, and Zhi Zhong

IoTeX, Menlo Park, CA 94025, USA
{xinxin,raullen,zhi}@iotex.io

Abstract. Governance is a critical component in cryptocurrency systems for their sustainable development and evolution. In particular, on-chain governance has attracted a lot of attention in cryptocurrency communities after the hard forks of Bitcoin and Ethereum. The on-chain governance mechanisms offered by the existing cryptocurrencies have been implemented on their own blockchains. This approach, while working well for the established cryptocurrencies, raises certain security concerns for newly launched cryptocurrency projects with small market capitalization and initial circulating supply. To mitigate potential attacks against on-chain governance, we present a multi-chain token backed voting framework named MULTAV in this contribution. The MULTAV framework is able to enhance security of the current on-chain governance practices by enabling token holders to vote on multiple established cryptocurrency systems. The instantiation of the MULTAV framework for electing block producers on the IoTeX network demonstrates its feasibility and effectiveness in practice.

Keywords: Cryptocurrency · Blockchain · On-chain governance · Voting · Multi-chain · Decentralization

1 Introduction

A blockchain is a distributed ledger that records all the transactions that take place within the system in a decentralized and immutable manner. As sophisticated and complex IT systems, blockchains contain multiple components (e.g., protocol, software, hardware, etc.) that are produced, operated and maintained by diverse group of people. How various entities come together to achieve long-term sustainability of the blockchain system as a whole has raised the question of governance in the cryptocurrency space. Although blockchain technology has received increasing attention during the past few years, the topic of blockchain governance often remains poorly understood. At a high level, blockchain governance refers to the mechanisms that enable the decentralized systems to adapt and change over time [1]. It is a rapidly evolving topic covering a wide spectrum

© Springer Nature Switzerland AG 2020
Z. Chen et al. (Eds.): ICBC 2020, LNCS 12404, pp. 33–47, 2020.
https://doi.org/10.1007/978-3-030-59638-5_3

of activities, including but not limited to changing protocol parameters, electing block producers, distributing subsidies, etc.

The existing blockchain governance mechanisms can be roughly classified into two primary categories [1]: on-chain governance and off-chain governance. In on-chain governance, token holders vote on whether a governance proposal encoded on the blockchain is accepted or rejected. The off-chain governance, on the other hand, requires informal coordination among stakeholders to decide whether certain changes on the blockchain should be made. Established cryptocurrencies such as Bitcoin [2] and Ethereum [3] utilize the off-chain governance model in which developers submit changes through formal improvement proposals (see [4] and [5] for examples) and stakeholders coordinate the corresponding activities among developers, node operators, miners and users through community channels. As pointed out in [6], the major criticism of the off-chain governance model is that it is relatively centralized among core developers and miners and excludes the mainstream token holders from the decision making process, which has led to slower technological advancement and conservatism.

To better balance decision making among token holders, a host of cryptocurrency projects [9–11,14,15,17] were launched with on-chain governance as one of the core functionalities. Depending on the system design of cryptocurrencies, the on-chain governance on these projects focus on different aspects such as block producer election [9–11], treasury fund distribution [14,15], block validation [15], protocol-level changes [11,15,17] and block state editing [17]. When compared to its off-chain counterpart, on-chain governance brings a number of advantages [19] such as decentralized voting, fast decision-making process, reduction in disagreement, etc. While many cryptocurrencies made announcements of on-chain governance, the actual development progress have been quite slow due to complex governance scenarios and blockchain integration.

We notice that all the existing cryptocurrency projects supporting on-chain governance implement the mechanisms on top of their own blockchains. While this strategy works for established cryptocurrencies, it poses potential security risk for newly launched blockchain projects due to their small market capitalization and initial circulating supply. As a result, it might not need to take great effort for well-funded adversaries breaking the security assumption of cryptocurrencies and controlling the governance process. To address this issue, we propose MULTAV, a multi-chain token backed voting framework for decentralized on-chain governance, in this work. With the distribution of token holders among multiple established cryptocurrencies, MULTAV is able to enhance security of on-chain governance effectively. Our instantiation of the MULTAV framework for block producer election on the IoTeX network [20] demonstrates the viability and effectiveness of the proposed on-chain governance solution in practice.

The rest of the paper is organized as follows. Section 2 gives a brief overview of blockchain and smart contract, followed by the detailed description and security analysis of the MULTAV framework in Sect. 3. In Sect. 4, we describe the instantiation of the MULTAV framework for block producer election in the IoTeX network. Sect. 5 presents the related work for on-chain governance. Finally, we conclude this paper in Sect. 6.

2   Preliminaries

2.1   Blockchain

A blockchain is a distributed data structure of a chronological, linked sequence of data blocks $(b_0, b_1, b_2, \cdots)$. These blocks are continuously appended to the chain by mutually distrustful peers through a so-called *mining* process. To initiate this process, clients broadcast transactions to specific nodes in the peer-to-peer network. Those nodes are miners that check the validity of received transactions, generate a new block with valid transactions and perform a consensus mechanism to append the block. The resulting chaining of blocks ensures the integrity of existing ones and results in an immutable distributed ledger without requiring a trusted central authority.

2.2   Account-Based Cryptocurrencies

A cryptocurrency is a tradable digital asset that is built on the blockchain and employs cryptographic protocols to control the creation of monetary units and to verify the transfer of funds. In such a system, the blockchain acts as a decentralized ledger and each block keeps a record of transactions that transfer values among participants. In particular, all the transactions can be settled without a need for a central clearing authority. Depending on the transaction models, cryptocurrencies can be classified into two categories: the unspent transaction outputs (UTXO) based model (e.g., Bitcoin [2]) and account-based model (e.g., Ethereum [3]).

An account-based cryptocurrency explicitly operates transactions with the accounts of participants, where each account is identified by an *address* derived from the participant's public key. A transaction, which transfers a certain amount of coins between two accounts, is represented by the following tuple:

$$\mathsf{tx} := (\mathsf{tx.sender}, \mathsf{tx.receiver}, \mathsf{tx.value}, \mathsf{tx.nonce}, \mathsf{tx.fee}, \mathsf{tx.data}),$$

where tx.value denotes the number of coins that are transferred from the sender's address tx.sender[1] to the receiver's address tx.receiver at the cost of tx.fee as a transaction fee. tx.nonce is a globally accessible nonce associated with each account to prevent replay attacks and tx.data $\in \{0,1\}^*$ is a data field that can store arbitrary non-transactional data. A transaction tx is valid if it is signed with the sender's private key and the corresponding account has sufficient balance. Upon validation of a transaction, the sender's account is debited by the (tx.value + tx.fee) coins, whereas the accounts of the receiver and the miner are credited with tx.value and tx.fee coins, respectively.

---

[1] tx.sender might be recovered by the receiver from the transaction signature and the hash of the transaction data in some account-based cryptocurrencies (e.g., Ethereum [3]). In those cases, tx.sender can be removed from tx.

2.3 Smart Contract

The term "smart contracts" refers to computer transaction protocols that execute the terms of a contract automatically based on a set of conditions, as first conceptualized by Szabo in 1996 [21]. In the context of blockchain, a smart contract represents a piece of code that is stored, verified and executed on a blockchain. The state of a smart contract, which consists of the contract's balance and the internal storage, is updated each time the contract is invoked. Users can invoke a smart contract by sending transactions to the contract address and each of them triggers the state transition of the contract, with data being written to the contract's internal storage. During the run-time, the smart contract performs predefined logic and may also interact with other accounts by sending messages (i.e., call other smart contracts) or transferring funds. The salient features of smart contracts such as computation and data storage facilitate the development of decentralized applications on the blockchain.

3 MULTAV: A Multi-chain Token Backed Voting Framework

In this section, we present MULTAV, a multi-chain token based voting framework for decentralized on-chain governance, in great detail.

3.1 Design Rationale

The security of all cryptocurrency systems is based on certain assumptions (e.g., the majority of nodes in the consensus group are honest). Once the security assumptions are violated, those systems might either stop working or controlled by adversaries. Under such circumstances, on-chain governance mechanisms that run on top of the cryptocurrency systems under attack fail as well. While the security assumptions have held true for the well-established cryptocurrencies such as Bitcoin [2] and Ethereum [3] throughout their history, it might not be the case for numerous new cryptocurrency systems.

We notice that the initial market capitalization and circulating supply for a new cryptocurrency are generally quite small, which renders them vulnerable to manipulation at the early stage. Furthermore, it usually takes some time (e.g., a few months or years) for a well-designed cryptocurrency system gaining popularity and value, thereby ensuring better attack resistance. As a result, in order to minimize the risk that on-chain governance mechanisms might be manipulated and provide disaster recovery capabilities for new cryptocurrency systems, it is desirable to realize those schemes with the aid of a number of established cryptocurrencies. This has motivated us to design a novel multi-chain token backed voting framework that enables token holders to conduct on-chain governance through the voting process across multiple cryptocurrency systems.

3.2   System Model

We consider a cryptocurrency system whose governance is based on the principle of token-holder voting and backed by multiple established cryptocurrencies, as illustrated in Fig. 1 (see Table 1 for the notations). In our system, we assume that a cryptocurrency system under governance (CSUG) is a new cryptocurrency with the consensus mechanism being performed by the miners in a consensus group (CG). A governance proposal for CSUG can be encoded on the blockchain with a governance smart contract $GC_j, j \in \{1, \dots, m\}$ and the community voting results directly determine whether the governance proposal will be executed. Moreover, the token holders of CSUG, who can participate in on-chain governance, are distributed across multiple cryptocurrency systems $CS_i, i = 1, \dots, n$. On each cryptocurrency $CS_i, i \in \{1, \dots, n\}$, the voting process for a governance proposal is managed by registration smart contracts $RC_{i,j}$ and voting smart contracts $VC_{i,j}, i \in \{1, \dots, n\}, j \in \{1, \dots, m\}$.

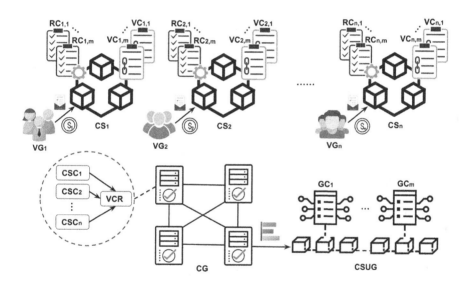

Fig. 1. A multi-chain token based voting framework for decentralized blockchain governance

3.3   The MULTAV Framework

In our multi-chain token based voting framework, token holders of CSUG are widely distributed across n established cryptocurrency systems $CS_i, i = 1, \dots, n$ and those token holders can cast votes for one or multiple governance proposals through the smart contracts $RC_{i,j}$ and $VC_{i,j}, i \in \{1, \dots, n\}, j \in \{1, \dots, m\}$. Based on the predefined rule in the governance proposals as well as the corresponding governance smart contract $GC_j, j \in \{1, \dots, m\}$, the nodes in CG fetch

Table 1. Notations

Notation	Description
CSUG	A cryptocurrency system under governance
CG	The consensus group of CSUG
$GP_i, i = 1, \ldots, m$	The i-th governance proposal for CSUG
$GC_i, i = 1, \ldots, m$	The i-th governance smart contract on CSUG
$CS_i, i = 1, \ldots, n$	The i-th well-established cryptocurrency system
$RC_{i,j}, i = 1, \ldots, n, j = 1, \ldots, m$	The registration smart contract on CS_i for the voting choices in the governance smart contract GC_j
$VC_{i,j}, i = 1, \ldots, n, j = 1, \ldots, m$	The voting smart contract on CS_i for the governance smart contract GC_j
$VG_i, i = 1, \ldots, n$	The voting group on CS_i that holds tokens of CSUG
$CSC_i, i = 1, \ldots, n$	The light client of CS_i
GPR	The governance proposal registry
VCR	The vote counting routine

the states of the voting smart contracts $VC_{i,j}, i \in \{1, \ldots, n\}, j \in \{1, \ldots, m\}$ with the light clients $CSC_i, i = 1, \ldots, n$, respectively. The votes from $CS_i, i = 1, \ldots, n$ are then aggregated using the vote counting routine (VCR) by each node in CG independently and the final voting result is obtained via a consensus process. Finally, the governance smart contract $GC_j, j \in \{1, \ldots, m\}$ is triggered by the voting result and the specific actions are taken. The proposed multi-chain token based voting framework is comprised of five phases as described in the following subsections.

Phase 1: Initial Token Distribution. In Phase 1, in order to support decentralized voting, the tokens of CSUG are offered across n established cryptocurrency systems $CS_i, i = 1, \ldots, n$ based on the specific token contracts. The project team will initially choose n well-established cryptocurrency systems and determine the corresponding token distribution on those blockchain platforms. Since the project team generally has sufficient knowledge on the state-of-the-art blockchain technologies, it is able to make sound decisions on the selection of n well-established cryptocurrency systems. In practice, the total token supply can be equally or proportionally[2] allocated to $CS_i, i = 1, \ldots, n$. In this way, the token holders of CSUG are widely distributed in n cryptocurrency systems.

---

[2] The tokens are allocated according to certain security metrics selected by the creators of CSUG.

Phase 2: Proposal Voting Preparation. In Phase 2, any token holder who wishes to submit a governance proposal $GP_j, j \in \{1, \ldots, m\}$ needs to deploy a governance smart contract GC_j on CSUG for acting on the voting results as well as a pair of smart contracts $RC_{i,j}$ and $VC_{i,j}$ on $CS_i, i = 1, \ldots, n$ for registering voting choices and managing votes, respectively[3]. Once the smart contracts are deployed, the contract creator kicks off the voting process by sending a transaction to a governance proposal registry (GPR) with the following tuple:

$$tx_{proposal} := (tx.addGC, tx.addRC, tx.addVC,$$
$$tx.period, tx.fee, tx.data),$$

where tx.addGC, tx.addRC and tx.addVC denote the addresses of the smart contracts $GC_j, RC_{i,j}$ and $VC_{i,j}$ on the corresponding blockchains, respectively. tx.period specifies a list of block heights on $CS_i, i = 1, \ldots, n$, which determines the start and end of the voting process on the respective blockchains. tx.fee is the transaction fee and tx.data contains metadata of the governance proposal GP_j such as title, subject, author, create date, URL, voting choices, etc. The GPR is a smart contract which manages the status of all the governance proposals deployed on CSUG. Besides storing the proposal related information received from $tx_{proposal}$, each entry in GPR also contains a 'stage' field which tracks the different stages (i.e., 'pre-voting', 'voting', 'valid', and 'invalid') of a governance proposal during its lifecycle, as detailed in the next subsections.

Phase 3: Proposal (Pre)-Voting in Action In Phase 3, the voting choices for the governance proposal GP_j of CSUG are first registered with the registration smart contract $RC_{i,j}$ on $CS_i, i = 1, \ldots, n$, respectively. The registration transaction is composed of the following fields:

$$tx_{registration} := (tx.sender, tx.addRC, tx.choices, tx.nonce, tx.fee),$$

where the governance proposal creator with the wallet address tx.sender sends the transaction to the address tx.addRC of the registration smart contract for registering voting choices tx.choices at the cost of tx.fee transaction fees. After completing the registration, token holders can vote for GP_j anytime during the voting period by sending voting transactions to the voting smart contract $VC_{i,j}$ on $CS_i, i = 1, \ldots, n$, respectively. The voting transaction is represented by the following tuple:

$$tx_{vote} := (tx.voter, tx.choice, tx.addVC, tx.votenum,$$
$$tx.fee, tx.data(optional)),$$

where tx.voter is the wallet address of the voter and tx.choice is the voting choice. The voting smart contract with the address tx.addVC records tx.votenum which

---

[3] To mitigate the limitation that some token holders cannot write the smart contracts on blockchains, the project team could create code examples for smart contracts used in the MULTAV framework and provide detailed user guide to explain how to change the sample smart contracts for different purposes.

is the number of votes cast by tx.voter. tx.data, which is optional, may contain any information related to the voting process. For example, if the governance proposal is incentive involved, tx.data might include relevant information (e.g., staking period, recurring staking, etc.) for reward calculation.

To prevent malicious token holders from abusing the MULTAV framework, an on-chain pre-voting phase has been introduced, which requires a governance proposal to collect a certain number of votes (e.g., 50% of the total votes) within a system-defined pre-voting period (e.g., one month from deployment of the governance contract). This pre-voting mechanism guarantees that only important governance proposal which has received significant attention will be further considered by the community.

Phase 4: Proposal Vote Counting. In Phase 4, based on the per-voting period defined in the system configuration as well as the voting period specified in $\mathsf{tx_{proposal}}$, the light clients $\mathsf{CSC}_i, i = 1, \ldots, n$ running on the nodes in CG read the states of smart contracts $\mathsf{VC}_{i,j}$ at certain heights of $\mathsf{CS}_i, i = 1, \ldots, n$, respectively. A vote counting routine (VCR) is then called to generate the voting results, which are validated and finalized through the consensus process conducted by the nodes in CG. In the case that the governance proposal offers incentives, the reward calculation can also be done by VCR in this phase. If a governance proposal does receive enough votes during the pre-voting period, its 'stage' field in GPR is changed from 'pre-voting' to 'voting', thereby continuously accepting votes until the end of the voting period. Otherwise, the 'stage' field is set to be 'invalid' after the pre-voting period. For a governance proposal entering into the voting stage, the voting results are deemed as 'valid' if a majority of votes (e.g., 70% of the total votes) have been cast.

Phase 5: Proposal Decision Execution. In Phase 5, the valid voting results are added to the blockchain and sent to the address of the governance smart contract GC_j by the nodes in CG. Depending on the predefined rule, the voting results are either accepted or rejected by the smart contract GC_j. If the proposal is accepted by the community, actions will be taken to make certain changes on CSUG. Otherwise, the proposal is rejected and nothing happens.

3.4   Security Properties of the MULTAV Framework

The trust of the proposed MULTAV framework is anchored to n established cryptocurrency systems, which effectively mitigates potential attacks against the on-chain governance scheme. Thanks to the distributed nature of our design, an adversary needs to break the security assumptions[4] of CSUG or a number of CS_i's, $i \in \{1, \ldots, n\}$ in order to take over the on-chain governance mechanism. We consider the following three attacking scenarios:

---

[4] For example, the adversary should control 51% of the mining power for a proof-of-work based cryptocurrency system.

- If the adversary can break the security assumption of CSUG, he/she is able to alter the voting results and create false blocks arbitrarily. Unfortunately, those blocks with wrong voting results cannot pass the validation by other full nodes equipped with the light clients $CSC_i, i = 1, \ldots, n$. As a result, the blockchain CSUG is stalled completely until other recovery mechanism is in place to reinstate the security assumption.
- If the adversary can break the security assumptions of $CS_{i_1}, \ldots, CS_{i_m}$, where $\{i_1, \ldots, i_m\} \subset \{1, \ldots, n\}$, he/she is able to collect enough votes for passing malicious governance proposals. Given that a single cryptocurrency system $CS_i, i \in \{1, \ldots, n\}$ is broken with p, the probability that m of which are broken is p^m. We would like to emphasize that p is generally quite small for established cryptocurrencies in practice and the adversary needs an enormous amount of funds to attack the system. For the well-established proof-of-work cryptocurrency systems such as Bitcoin and Ethereum, the relationship between the the success probability of 51% attack with varying hashing power and number of confirmations has been extensively analyzed in the literature [7,8]. Essentially, if an attacker is not able to attain the majority of the network's hash rate, the success probability of 51% attack approaches to zero with the increasing number of block confirmations. Therefore, the possibility of breaking m established cryptocurrency systems is negligible.
- While the MULTAV framework allows any token holder to submit a governance proposal, the proposal should pass both pre-voting and voting phases in order to be finally executed on CSUG, which requires one or a group of adversaries to collect a significant amount of votes (e.g., 50% and 70% of the total votes) from widely distributed token holders of CSUG.

The above analysis shows that by distributing token holders across multiple established cryptocurrencies the proposed MULTAV framework can improve the security of on-chain governance significantly.

4 Instantiation of the MULTAV Framework for Delegate Election

Delegated Proof of Stake (DPoS) is a blockchain consensus mechanism in which a fixed number of network entities (called block producers) are elected via community voting to create blocks in a round-robin manner. In this section, we describe how the block producer election, which is a typical governance task in DPoS-like blockchain platforms, is realized in the IoTeX network [20] using the MULTAV framework.

4.1 IoTeX Token Distribution

IoTeX tokens (IOTX) are offered via a token contract that is created following the ERC-20 token standard [22] on the Ethereum platform. The token contract maintains the state describing the number of tokens each account owns. Note that it is possible to extend the IOTX token offering to other account-based cryptocurrencies (e.g., EOS [11]) without altering the total supply. More specifically, a number of IOTX tokens are first burned on the Ethereum platform by sending them to an account no one has the private key. The same amount of tokens can then be minted on another account-based cryptocurrency system. For keeping the implementation simple, IOTX tokens are solely offered on Ethereum currently and all the token holders can participate in voting for electing block producers in the IoTeX network.

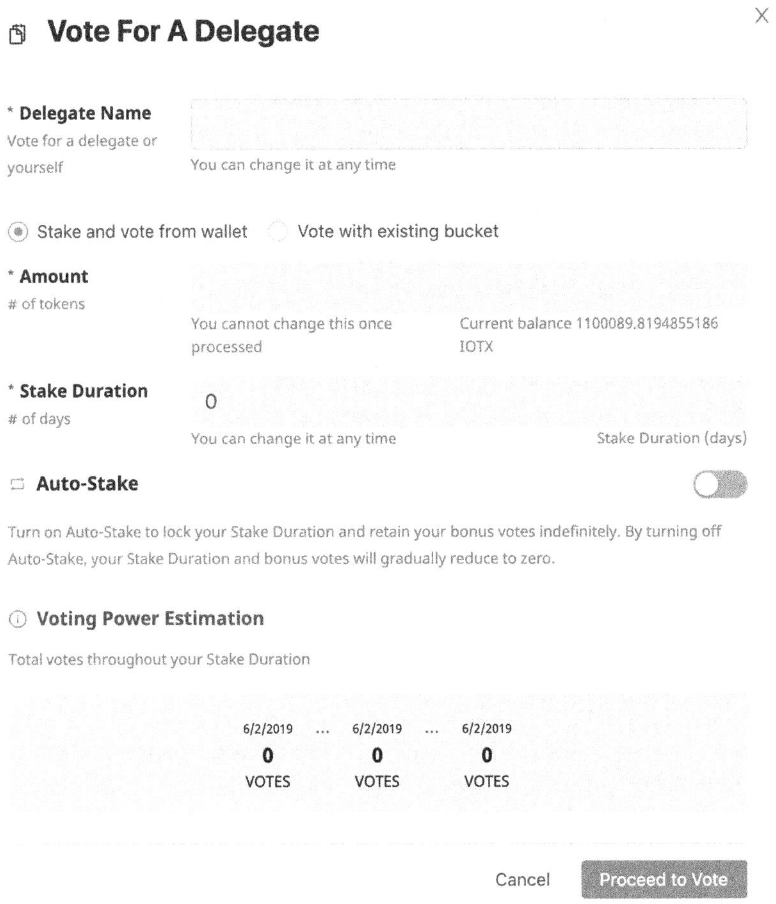

Fig. 2. The voting interface in the IoTeX's voting DApp

4.2   Block Producer Election with the MULTAV Framework

The consensus protocol in the IoTeX network, namely Roll-DPoS [23], is a randomized variant of DPoS, in which 24 block producers are randomly selected each epoch (i.e., one hour) from a candidate pool of 36 nodes. For electing block producers with the MULTAV framework, one smart contract is deployed on the IoTeX blockchain to manage the status of nodes in the candidate pool. In addition, two smart contracts are deployed on the Ethereum platform to deal with voter registration and vote management, respectively.

The election of block producers is a continuous process in Roll-DPoS and the candidate pool is refreshed after every epoch. A governance smart contract deployed on the IoTeX network records who are the block producers in each epoch based on the voting results. Once the nodes register with the registration contract, all the token holders can elect block producers at any time through the voting interface in the IoTeX's voting DApp as shown in Fig. 2. The tokens voted for block producers (i.e., one token for one vote) are locked in the voting contract for a certain period of time as specified by the token holder and block producers allocate a percentage of block rewards to their voters accordingly. At the end of the lock period, the token holder can get all the staked tokens back to his/her account.

A token holder first selects one of the registered nodes, followed by the specification of the number of the votes as well as the staking period. The token holder can also set the "Auto-Stake" for enabling the recurring voting. All the voting related information is then sent to the voting contract for processing. An Ethereum light client, which is run by each block producer, reads the state of the voting contract at the predefined height starting from the middle of the current epoch. The block producer proposes a new block that contains the transaction of the voting results for all the nodes. The block is finalized after passing the Practical Byzantine Fault Tolerance (PBFT) [24] consensus process in Roll-DPoS. The transaction of the voting results will update the state of the governance contact for the block producers in the next epoch. Figure 3 illustrates a partial list of active block producers and the number of votes they received in the epoch number 1010.

5   Related Work

On-chain governance has become a major topic in cryptocurrency community since the hard forks of Bitcoin and Ethereum happened. In particular, a number of projects have been focused on addressing this issue over the past years. In this section, we present related work and highlight the design considerations of the MULTAV framework for addressing this problem.

BitShares [9], Steem [10] and EOS.IO [11] are Graphene-based blockchains that leverage DPoS as a consensus mechanism. In BitShares, governance is conducted by the BTS token holders who can either directly vote with a special transaction on the blockchain or delegate their votes to one single account,

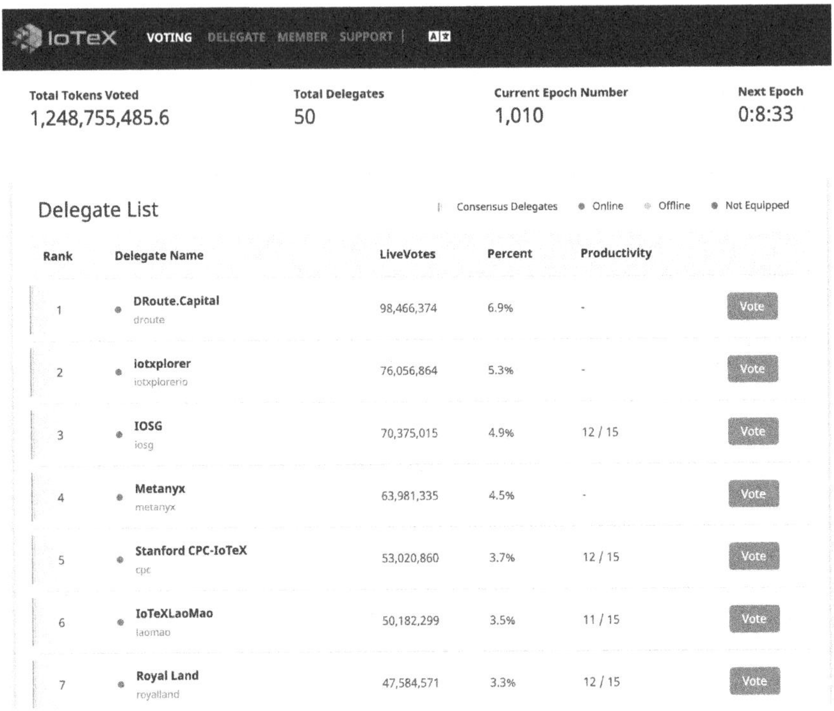

Fig. 3. The block producers elected by token holders in the 1010th Epoch

the proxy. The introduction of proxies aims to improve the efficiency of a governance system and keeps the decentralization and flexibility at the same time. The token holders in BitShares can vote for three entities: i) block producers that perform consensus and add new blocks; ii) committee members that manage a few blockchain parameters and determine the required transaction fees; and iii) workers that receive funding for the development of the BitShares Improvement Proposals (BSIPs).

In Steem, the STEEM token holders can only vote for block producers (called "witnesses"). The election of witnesses is based on sorting their stake in the form of STEEM Power (SP) that is STEEM locked in a 13 week vesting smart contract. After 21 witnesses have been elected, they are responsible for conducting various governance activities on behalf of STEEM token holders through on-chain voting. If a supermajority (i.e., 17/21) of the witnesses vote in favor of a governance proposal (e.g., hard fork), the change is going to take effect and the blockchain will update automatically. In the case that the token holders believe that witnesses do not perform their tasks properly, they can unvote them and vote in new witnesses.

As described in the latest EOS.IO technical white paper [12], the EOS governance aims to facilitate people in the EOS community to: i) reach consensus on subjective matters of collective action that cannot be captured entirely by software algorithms; ii) carry out the decisions they reach; and iii) alter the governance rules themselves via Constitutional amendments. EOS has a governing body, namely EOS Core Arbitration Forum (ECAF) [13], that resolves disputes filed by the EOS token holders with its own arbitrators. The block producers are responsible for executing the decisions that come out of the community voting or arbitrator orders. Moreover, it is also possible to alter the Constitution in EOS through a complicated process as detailed in [12].

In Dash [14], each token holder can submit a proposal to the Dash network and the built-in Decentralized Governance by Blockchain (DGBB) system enables the so-called Dash masternodes to vote for the proposal. To become a Dash masternode, one needs to stake at least 1000 DASH. Besides the common governance functionalities, the DGBB system also provides a mechanism for Dash funding its own development. More specifically, the highest-ranked proposal will be funded with the 10% of the block reward accumulated throughout the month. In addition, Dash does not utilize the DGBB system to implement protocol level changes.

Decred [15] implements a more complex governance mechanism based on the idea of distributing the power between token holders and miners. It features a hybrid proof-of-stake (PoS)/proof-of-work (PoW) consensus mechanism and the token holders participate in governance by staking DCR tokens to purchase tickets that can be used for on-chain and off-chain voting. While on-chain voting deals with validating blocks created by PoW miners and consensus rule changes, off-chain voting is managed by the Decred's Politeria system [16] and addresses high-level issues concerning the direction of the project. Similar to Dash, 10% of the block reward will go into the Decred's subsidies for funding project development.

DFINITY [17] introduces a novel decentralized decision-making system called the "Blockchain Nervous System" (BNS). BNS is an algorithmic governance mechanism aiming for protecting token holders from attacks and optimizing the on-chain governance. Once a token holder submits a proposal, it will be evaluated by BNS using votes made by human-controlled "neurons" that automatically follow each other. If the proposal is accepted, it will be executed by the BNS using privileged op codes in the Ethereuem Virtual Machine (EVM). A controversial feature of the DFINITY governance is that it allows roll back or rewrite the blockchain in addition to the rules of governance themselves.

Tezos [18] is a self-amending meta protocol for on-chain governance which takes a fundamentally different approach by creating a formal, multi-stage protocol modification process for token holders approving protocol upgrades that are then automatically deployed on the network. Tezos allows independent developers to submit proposals for protocol updates and receive compensations for their contributions upon approval and inclusion of the upgrades, thereby incentivizing user participation in the core development and ensuring smooth evolution of the platform. As a result, the Tezos platform is shaped by the community through democratization of development process.

While the aforementioned projects deal with the different facets of blockchain protocols regarding on-chain governance, the MULTAV framework does not focus on the specific governance activities. Instead, considering the small market capitalization and initial circulating supply of newly launched blockchain projects, the MULTAV framework aims to boost the security for the voting process on those blockchains with the aid of multiple established cryptocurrency systems.

6   Conclusion

In this paper, we present a multi-chain token backed voting framework for decentralized blockchain governance. The MULTAV framework allows token holders distributed across multiple established cryptocurrencies to vote for the governance proposal in an efficient and secure manner. The proposed framework improves security of the existing on-chain governance practices by anchoring trust on established cryptocurrency systems. Our instantiation of the MULTAV framework on the IoTeX network demonstrates that electing block producers for DPoS-like cryptocurrencies can be efficiently done under the multi-blockchain setting in practice. As our future work, we plan to implement other more complex governance activities with the proposed framework.

Acknowledgement. The authors would like to thank the anonymous reviewers for their insightful comments and suggestions.

References

1. Curran, B.: What is Blockchain Governance? - Complete Beginner's Guide, 21 September 2018. https://blockonomi.com/blockchain-governance/
2. Bitcoin. https://bitcoin.org/
3. Ethereum. https://www.ethereum.org/
4. Bitcoin Improvement Proposals. https://github.com/bitcoin/bips
5. Ethereum Improvement Proposals. http://eips.ethereum.org/
6. Ehrsam, F.: Blockchain Governance: Programming Our Future, 27 November 2017. https://medium.com/@FEhrsam/blockchain-governance-programming-our-future-c3bfe30f2d74
7. Saad, M., et al.: Exploring the Attack Surface of Blockchain: A Systematic Overview, CoRR abs/1904.03487 (2019)
8. Ramezan, G., Leung, C., Wang, Z.J.: A strong adaptive strategic double-spending attack on blockchains. In: Proceedings of iThings/GreenCom/CPSCom/SmartData 2018, pp. 1219–1227. IEEE Computer Society (2018)
9. BitShares. https://bitshares.org/
10. Steem. https://steem.com/
11. EOS.IO. https://eos.io/
12. EOS.IO Technical White Paper v2. https://github.com/EOSIO/Documentation/blob/master/TechnicalWhitePaper.md
13. ECAF - The EOSIO Core Arbitration Forum. https://www.eoscorearbitration.io/
14. Dash. https://www.dash.org/

15. Decred. https://decred.org/
16. Politeia. https://proposals.decred.org/
17. DFINITY. https://dfinity.org/
18. Tezos. https://tezos.com/
19. Frankenfield, J.: On-Chain Governance, 4 April 2018. https://www.investopedia. com/terms/o/onchain-governance.asp
20. IoTeX. https://iotex.io/
21. Szabo, N.: Smart Contracts: Building Blocks for Digital Markets (1996). http:// www.fon.hum.uva.nl/rob/Courses/InformationInSpeech/CDROM/Literature/ LOTwinterschool2006/szabo.best.vwh.net/smart_contracts_2.html
22. ERC20 Token Standard. https://theethereum.wiki/w/index.php/ERC20_Token_ Standard
23. Fan, X., Chai, Q.: Roll-DPoS: a randomized delegated proof of stake scheme for scalable blockchain-based internet of things systems. In: Proceedings of the 15th EAI International Conference on Mobile and Ubiquitous Systems: Computing, Networking and Services - MobiQuitous 2018, pp. 482–484. ACM Press (2018)
24. Castro, M., Liskov, B.: Practical byzantine fault tolerance and proactive recovery. ACM Trans. Comput. Syst. **20**(4), 398–461 (2002)

Reducing Storage Requirement in Blockchain Networks Using Overlapping Data Distribution

Md. Touhidul Islam and Muhammad Abdullah Adnan[⊠]

Bangladesh University of Engineering and Technology (BUET), Dhaka, Bangladesh
touhidul.shohan@gmail.com, abdullah.adnan@gmail.com

Abstract. Blockchain technology first gained attention via public blockchain platforms like Bitcoin and Etherium. Over the years, researchers have continuously explored the potential of blockchains in a more restricted environment, which in turn has paved the way for the creation of many private blockchain platforms. In a private blockchain system, the identity of every entity is known and thus, the issue of trust is less prominent. In addition to the added customizability of permissions regarding who gets to do what, private blockchains also reduce the resource requirement as no proof-of-work is needed here. However, each node in a private blockchain network still needs to store the whole blockchain consisting of all the transactions from the beginning. If the number of transactions in a private blockchain network rises to a very large number, the storage requirement can rise proportionately. In addition to that, public blockchain platforms like Bitcoin and Etherium are already in need of storage optimizations because of their size. We propose a method to divide the whole blockchain of transactions into some non-overlapping shards and make multiple copies of them. Then, we distribute these shards uniformly across the nodes in the network. We show theoretically that this approach not only improves the storage requirement but also ensures the integrity of the data in blockchain in case of node failures.

Keywords: Blockchain · Consensus · Cryptographic hash

1 Introduction

Blockchains first came into consideration as the public transaction ledger for Bitcoin cryptocurrency [9]. Introduction of blockchain solved the long overdue double spending problem [12] in digital currency systems. Blockchain is a chain of immutable blocks where each block usually contains the necessary information about a certain transaction. Each block in a blockchain contains a cryptographic hash of the previous block and thus modifying any block in a blockchain requires the modification of all the subsequent blocks in the system, which is computationally expensive. For this reason, data stored in a blockchain is usually considered secure and immutable.

© Springer Nature Switzerland AG 2020
Z. Chen et al. (Eds.): ICBC 2020, LNCS 12404, pp. 48–60, 2020.
https://doi.org/10.1007/978-3-030-59638-5_4

1.1   Public Blockchains

Public blockchains do not have any restrictions over who joins the network. The identities of the users in the network thus remain hidden and so, the trust issue in public blockchain is prominent. In case a new transaction request arrives, some nodes in the network (known as miners) engage in a competition on who gets to complete the proof-of-work first by calculating a computationally demanding cryptographic hash. The miner who completes the proof-of-work first receives some incentives for completing the work and the new transaction gets into the blockchain in the form of a new block. Examples of public blockchains include Bitcoin [9] and Etherium [13]. The main advantage of public blockchains is that they are extremely secure. Without compromising at least 51% of the nodes (known as the 51% attack), it is nearly impossible to modify the existing data and get it validated. The disadvantages mainly include lack of scalability and more time to verify and add a transaction in the blockchain.

1.2   Private Blockchains

Private blockchains operate in a more restricted manner by allowing only the users that are supposed to be in the network. As the identities of all the users in the network are known, the trust issue among the users is non-existent here. In fact, most scenarios associating private blockchains assume that the users in the network will not go rogue. Even if someone does go rogue and makes a change, the record will always tell exactly what has been altered and who altered that. There is no proof-of-work concept in private blockchains and every node in the network can be assigned some specific role. Two parties in a private blockchain can take part in private transactions that are only visible to them and not to anyone else in the network and hence, the privacy is preserved. The main advantages of private blockchains include the facility of private transactions and good scalability. The disadvantage arises from the fact that private blockchains do not keep the identities of their users private. Examples of private blockchain platforms include Hyperledger-fabric [3] and Corda [2].

1.3   The Storage Problem in Blockchains

The main problem we are trying to address in this paper comes from the storage requirement at each node in a blockchain network, public or private. In a blockchain network, each node stores one copy of the entire blockchain. If the number of existing blocks is high enough, the required storage to store the whole blockchain can get very large. For example, the Bitcoin network takes up around 242 GB of space as of September 2019 [1] and this number is continually increasing by around 0.1 GB per day. Estimations say that Bitcoin blockchain will take up around 40 TB in 20 years from now. This will put outrageous load on required storage at each node. Things can get equally bad for private blockchains with large number of blocks.

1.4 Our Proposed Solution

To reduce the amount of storage needed in the network, we propose to store only a portion of the blockchain at each node. First, we gather information about the number of nodes or make an estimation if needed. We divide the blockchain into some non-overlapping shards after making multiple copies of the blockchain to ensure fault tolerance. Then, we put a certain number of shards at each node in the network and thereby reduce the amount of storage needed. In the process, we also make sure to provide fault tolerance by having multiple copies of a shard across the nodes in the network. Mathematical analysis show that our proposed method can not only reduce the storage requirement greatly but also ensure fault tolerance based on the selected parameters.

The rest of this paper is organized as follows: first, we discuss the existing methodologies that attempts to reduce space requirement in blockchains. After that, we propose our method, discuss a few cautions while using our method, explain some of the complications that may arise after deploying such a distributed storage system, and possible solutions to some of these complications. Later on, we show mathematically that our method improves storage requirement greatly. We finish the paper by presenting possible future directions of this work.

2 Related Works

Database systems have been using distributed data methodologies for a while now [7,10]. The main motivation behind using distributed data sources instead of a central one has always been to increase throughput and reduce latency. Distributed data implementations in database systems has inspired many researchers to try and import this technique into blockchain based systems.

Some researchers focused on creating clusters using the nodes in the network and then distribute the data among them for faster response time and quicker consensus; while other groups have focused on dividing the data only and not on making clusters of nodes.

An example of the former is [6], which proposes an efficient shard formation protocol to assign nodes into groups. The reasoning behind their choice is to minimize the inter-group communication when validating transactions. If a transaction requires the nodes in a group to only communicate within themselves, extra communication overheads are greatly reduced. They also design a general distributed transaction protocol to ensure safety and liveness even if some of the coordinators are corrupt. [8] proposes a service-oriented sharded blockchain protocol to increase scalability. Like [4,6] proposes to form clusters of nodes first. Each cluster contains a certain number of nodes and is isolated from the other clusters. Then, the whole data is divided into some data shards (one for each cluster) and assigned to each of the node clusters. However, each node in a cluster has a copy of the data shard that has been assigned to that cluster. They allow intra-shard and cross-shard transactions. In intra-shard transactions, the data shard of only one cluster is needed. However, cross-shard transactions account for the scenarios where we need to access more than one data shard across multiple clusters.

[16] proposes a sharding-based public blockchain protocol which they claim to be fault tolerant for up to $\frac{1}{3}$ fraction of all the nodes in the system. They also achieve complete sharding of communication, storage overhead, and computation.

Examples of the later approach (dividing data only) includes the work of Mingjin Dai et al. in [5] that introduces Network-Coded Distributed Storage (NC-DS) for blockchain platforms. They propose to divide the blockchain into some shards and then encode them using linear transformations or bit wise operations. These encoded blocks are then stored at the nodes in the network. They show theoretical improvements in storage requirement as well as bandwidth consumption within the blockchain network.

[11] addresses the problem of running out of storage in portable devices. They specifically address the issue of limited storage in mobile devices and explain how large storage requirements can be problematic for them. Other research efforts like [15] and [14] attempts to build a file storage system without the use of Network Coding.

We take the later approach in our proposed method. We keep our focus on reducing the storage needed at each node and not on forming clusters of nodes. Our work was greatly inspired by the work of Mingjin Dai et al. in [5] but we offer some major improvements. Firstly, their method uses encoding before distributing shards to the nodes in the blockchain. This results in added overhead of fetching all the parts and decoding them when a query is made. We do not use any encoding and save quite a bit of computational power in the process. Secondly, their method does not offer any fault tolerance as they do not use overlapping. On the other hand, our approach allows customizable levels of fault tolerance to serve the needs of any system. People willing to use our method will have the liberty to choose between very low storage requirement or very high fault tolerance. In most cases, choosing a good balance between the two is the ideal option.

3   Our Solution

To address the ever increasing storage requirement problem, we propose to divide the whole blockchain into some shards where each shard can contain one or more blocks from the blockchain. Then, we distribute the shards across the nodes in the blockchain network. We will show with mathematical analysis that this technique can reduce the storage requirement immensely while ensuring data integrity in case of node failures.

3.1   Procedure

Without using any data sharding, each node in the blockchain network needs to store the entire chain of blocks as displayed in Fig. 1. Here, the total storage requirement is $m * B$ when m denotes the number of nodes in the network and B denotes the blockchain size.

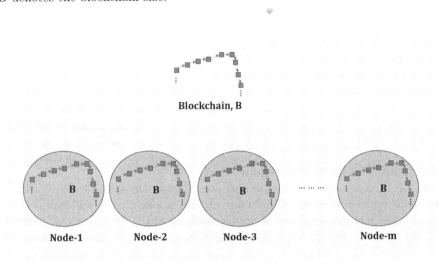

Fig. 1. Blockchain network before using data sharding

To ensure fault tolerance, we need to make sure that there are multiple copies of a block in the network. Thus, we need to make a number of copies (n) of the initial blockchain first. This number should go up there we expect more fault tolerance from a system. The replication technique for $n = 3$ is shown in Fig. 2.

Let us consider that we generate k shards from each copy of a blockchain. This will leave us with a total of $n * k$ shards in the system ($3k$ in the example). Now, we have to distribute these $n * k$ shards across m nodes. Let us consider that we put p shards at each of the m nodes to use up all the $n * k$ shards. Figure 3 shows the distribution process for $p = 3$.

As we place $n * k$ shards at m nodes with each node containing p shards, we can say that the following relation holds:

$$n * k = m * p$$

or,

$$k = \frac{m * p}{n}$$

Algorithm 1 shows the process we just described. We collect or estimate the value of m and take input the possible values of n, p. Then, we calculate k and create the shards that we need to distribute. We keep distributing these shards as long we have them available. For the last node, we just assign all the remaining shards there.

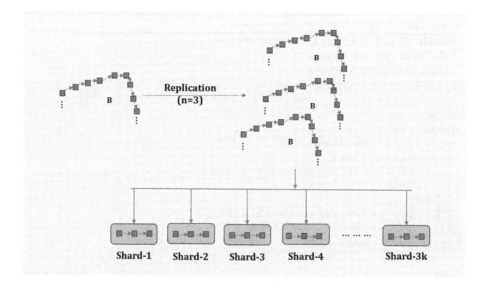

Fig. 2. Dividing the blockchain into shards

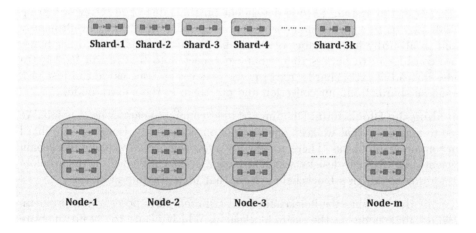

Fig. 3. After distributing shards to nodes with overlap

3.2   Probable Issues and Solutions

The Value of m: In our method, we need to know the value of the number of nodes (m) beforehand. We select our values of n and p based on m. In private blockchains, this is no big issue as the number of nodes is limited and often kept track of. In public blockchains however, the number of nodes is changing continuously and in most cases, we cannot know the specific value of m.

One possible solution is to make an estimation on the value of m. For public blockchains, it is safer to assume a lower bound on m. Because, the total number

---

Algorithm 1: Sharding and Distribution

Result: Shards distributed among all the nodes
Take input the value of **n, p**;
Collect or estimate the value of **m**;
$k = \frac{m*p}{n}$; [as $n*k = m*p$]
$k = Floor(k) + 1$;
total $= n*k$;
nodes $= m$;
while $total > 0$ and $nodes > 0$ **do**
$\quad$ **if** $nodes == 1$ **then**
$\quad\quad$ put all the remaining shards in the last node;
$\quad\quad$ break;
$\quad$ **else**
$\quad\quad$ Take p shards and put them in a node ;
$\quad\quad$ $total = total - p$;
$\quad\quad$ $nodes = nodes - 1$;
$\quad$ **end**
end

---

of shards in the system $n*k$ is dependent on the value of m. Overestimating m will lead us to a higher number of shards in the system that can ultimately result in absurdly high number of shards in the last node. On the other hand, if we consider m to be less than what we expect it to be, we will have extra nodes instead of extra shards. Extra nodes is never an issue as we can just pick p random shards from our collection and put them in these extra nodes.

Dividing the Blockchain: Dividing the blockchain into parts is no easy job. We need to make sure that we keep one block in one shard only. However, one shard can contain many blocks. There are already a few works on dividing a blockchain efficiently [4]. System designers should have a good knowledge on them before attempting to design a blockchain system that uses distributed blocks.

Overheads: Keeping the blockchain in distributed parts poses a new problem. Now, no single node has the entire blockchain. Which means, to obtain an entire copy of the blockchain, we have some overheads like fetching the shards and then joining them in order.

There is no solution that completely solves the problem here. This is an old-fashioned balancing problem. If low response times and less overheads are more important to one particular system than storage, this probably will not be the ideal technique to use.

The Values of n and p: Proper selections of n and p are very crucial are determining what combination of values works the best for one's need. We recommend going through a few test runs with different combinations of k, n, p to find out which one is the most suitable for a specific system. For example, systems that demand strong fault tolerance should opt for higher values of n. On the other hand, if a system opts to minimize storage, choosing small n would be the wiser route to go. The value of p, on the other hand, is dependent on the value of n. The more copies we want of a certain shard to exist, the more storage we need to use in a single node, and that is what p denotes.

To summarize the above paragraph, we can say that a higher value of n is desirable for higher fault tolerance. In addition to that, a higher n also means that we have to put more shards in every node (denoted by p). Putting more shards increases the storage requirement at each node. So, finding a suitable point where both fault tolerance and acceptable storage requirement is ensured is a mandatory prerequisite of designing such a system.

Management of New Blocks and Shards: The data on the blockchain is always increasing and so is the number of blocks. We use a dynamic method for adding these new blocks to the already existing shards which will be easier to explain with a real example. Let us consider that we are allowing 10 blocks per shard. We already have 80 blocks in the system and thus 8 shards in total. Now, when a new block arrives, we need a new shard. So, we will create a new shard and mark this shard as the *shard in use*. Initially, this shard will have 9 empty slots which will be filled up by later blocks. Once a new shard is created, it is given to a certain number of nodes in the system. To determine which nodes will get the new shard, we use simple round-robin method.

Finding the Data on the Blockchain: In our proposed method, each node on the blockchain stores a certain number of shards. We keep track of these shards via a separate data structure. When one of our peers encounters a query that requires the traversal of the whole blockchain, we use this data structure to find the shards, and then traverse.

4   Solution Analysis

4.1   Mathematical Analysis

Let us consider a total of m nodes in the blockchain network where each of these m nodes had to store the whole blockchain without our proposed method. Now, let us divide the whole blockchain into k non-overlapping shards. If the size of each shard is s and the whole blockchain size is B then,

$$B = k * s \tag{1}$$

and if the total storage requirement without our method is T_1,

$$\begin{aligned} T_1 &= m * B \\ &= m * k * s \end{aligned} \tag{2}$$

Let us consider that we make n copies of each of these k shards and distribute them to m available nodes. If we decide to place p shards at each node, then the following condition is true.

$$n * k = m * p \tag{3}$$

or,

$$p = \frac{n * k}{m} \tag{4}$$

or,

$$\frac{k}{p} = \frac{m}{n} \tag{5}$$

Thus, we can calculate the total storage requirement T_2 as follows:

$$T_2 = m * p * s \tag{6}$$

Comparing the total storage requirement before and after applying our method,

$$\frac{T_1}{T_2} = \frac{m * k * s}{m * p * s} = \frac{k}{p} \tag{7}$$

In almost all the cases, $k >> p$ and thus the total storage requirement is reduced greatly. We call the fraction $\frac{k}{p}$ compression ratio, η

$$\eta = \frac{k}{p} \tag{8}$$

using Eq. 5, we get:

$$\eta = \frac{m}{n} \tag{9}$$

One extremely important point to keep in mind is that we need to make sure we select p and k in a away such that each of the k shards is available in at least one node. Thus, the condition must be true in order for a valid distribution.

$$mp >= k \tag{10}$$

or,

$$\frac{k}{p} <= m \tag{11}$$

or,

$$\eta <= m \tag{12}$$

Equation 10 defines an upper limit for our compression ratio. As a matter of fact, there is also a lower limit, which is 1. In this case, the values of p and k are equal and no extra storage is saved.

Putting η within proper limits, we get:

$$1 <= \eta <= m \tag{13}$$

4.2 Real Case Examples

To better illustrate our approach, we take into consideration some real data and see how much improvement we can actually make.

When $\eta = m$ ($n = 1$): As consider $n = 1$ in this scenario, we will have no fault tolerance here. Let us consider a blockchain network with 100 nodes (m). We divide the whole blockchain network into $100,000$ shards (k) each having 1MB of size (s). To apply our proposed method, we need to distribute the shards to the nodes. Let us say that we choose to distribute 1000 shards to each node in the network (p).

Our choice of k and p is valid as, $p * m = 10^3 * 10^2 = 10^5$, which is equal to k and thus satisfies Eq. 10

Using Eq. 2, we can calculate the storage requirement before applying our method.

$$T_1 = m * k * s$$
$$= (100 * 100,000 * 1)MB$$
$$= 10^7 MB$$

And, after applying our method, the storage requirement T_2 becomes,

$$T_2 = m * p * s$$
$$= (100 * 1000 * 1)MB$$
$$= 10^5 MB$$

From 10^7 MB to 10^5 MB is a 99% reduction in storage requirement. We can also calculate the compression ratio, η

$$\eta = \frac{k}{p}$$
$$= \frac{10^5}{10^3}$$
$$= 100$$

When $\eta = 1$: If we put 10^5 shards at each node (p) in the above example, we achieve no storage gain. Thus, the compression ratio is 1 according to Eq. 8. However, this mode will give us maximum fault tolerance.

Graph Illustrations: We understand from the discussion so far is that we want the compression ratio to be higher for reducing the needed space. One thing we need to keep in mind is the importance of a large n. What n basically means is the number of copies of a certain shard in the system. We can achieve maximum compression ratio by having $n = 1$ (according to Eq. 9), but it will give the possession of one particular shard to only one node in the system and thereby, compromising one of the most important characteristics of blockchain based systems. Moreover, even if we rule out the possibility of a node going rogue, it can still fail. With $n = 1$, failure in even only one node is going to create problem

Compression ratio, η

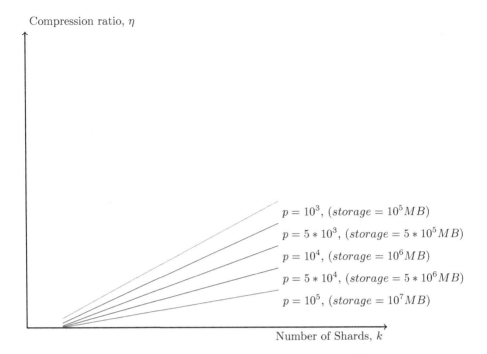

$p = 10^3$, ($storage = 10^5 MB$)

$p = 5 * 10^3$, ($storage = 5 * 10^5 MB$)

$p = 10^4$, ($storage = 10^6 MB$)

$p = 5 * 10^4$, ($storage = 5 * 10^6 MB$)

$p = 10^5$, ($storage = 10^7 MB$)

Number of Shards, k

Fig. 4. η vs. k for different values of p (Using equation $\eta = \frac{k}{p}$, Not drawn to scale)

as the copy of the shard contained in the failed node is not available anywhere else. Thus, $n = 1$ leaves us with an extremely efficient system in terms of storage with absolutely zero fault tolerance, in case of both crash and byzantine faults. So, we need to find a good middle ground.

We use the example of Sect. 4.2 to draw Fig. 4. We plot number of shards, k along X-axis and compression ratio, η along Y-axis. From Fig. 4, we observe what we discussed before. The red line ($p = 10^3$) denotes the maximum possible storage efficiency with least possible fault tolerance. As we increase the value of p, we start to see the decline in our compression ratio, with steady increase in fault tolerance. For each line, we keep the values of m and p constant. However, as we change k along the line, we adjust n to make sure Eq. 3 holds.

The green line shows the end of the line with the increment of p. Here, p reaches the value of k, and compression ratio becomes 1. We gain no storage efficiency along or beneath this line. In most cases, the task of the system designer will be to figure out a suitable value of p that ensures storage efficiency and fault tolerance at the same time. For this specific example, the limit of p is: $10^3 <= p <= 10^5$.

4.3   Storage Efficiency vs. Fault Tolerance

Let us recall Eq. 13. The minimum value of compression ratio (1) indicates that we are saving no space; which means, all the nodes contain k shards. This allows for maximum fault tolerance and minimum latency in queries. The maximum value of compression ratio is achieved when we take p to be as small as possible while not violating the condition $mp > k$. If $k = m$, we can have as little as one shard per node ($p = 1$), but this leaves us with no fault tolerance as discussed before. So, we need to find an optimal point based on use cases.

For example, if we make only one copy of each shard ($n = 1$), then the possibility that we lose a certain shard of the blockchain is equal to the probability of failure in a single node (say, $f\%$). If we make just 10 copies of each shard, then this probability drops dramatically as shown in the following calculation:

If, the probability of losing a shard with $n = 1$ is P_1

$$P_1 = \frac{f}{100}$$

And, the probability of losing a shard with $n = 10$ is P_2

$$P_2 = \frac{f}{100} * \frac{f}{100} * \frac{f}{100} * ...... * \frac{f}{100}; [10 fractions]$$
$$= (\frac{f}{100})^{10}$$

5   Conclusion and Future Directions

Storage problem in blockchain networks has become prominent in recent time with the growth of public blockchain networks like Bitcoin [9] and Etherium [13]. There have been a few works in trying to minimize the storage required at each node in the network. In this paper, we have proposed an overlapping distributed data storing method to reduce the storage requirement in different blockchain networks. We show mathematically that our method manages to reduce the storage requirement while also ensuring fault tolerance in case of node failures. Our method was easier to use in private blockchains because of the prior knowledge on the number of nodes in the system. However, in case of public blockchains, we need to make an assumption on the number of nodes. In our opinion, there is not exact value of number of shards, shards per node, and copies of each shard that will produce the best results for all systems. Rather, we suggest experimenting with several combinations of values to determine which one works the best.

There are a few possible future directions of this work. Implementing distributed data storing mechanisms in private blockchain framework like hyperledger-fabric is something to look at. Most functionalities in blockchain based systems do not assume the data to be distributed. Thus, optimal querying and data fetching should be of special interest in the future. Storing shards instead of the whole blockchain also presents the problem of keeping track of which block belongs exactly where in the chain and this can be another major problem of interest.

Acknowledgements. This research is supported by ICT Division Innovation Fund, Government of Peoples' Republic of Bangladesh.

References

1. Bitcoin statistics (2020). https://www.statista.com/statistics/647523/worldwide-bitcoin-blockchain-size/. Accessed 5 Feb 2020
2. Corda framework (2020). https://www.corda.net/. Accessed 5 Feb 2020
3. Hyperledger fabric (2020). https://www.hyperledger.org/projects/fabric. Accessed 5 Feb 2020
4. Amiri, M.J., Agrawal, D., Abbadi, A.E.: Sharper: sharding permissioned blockchains over network clusters. arXiv preprint arXiv:1910.00765 (2019)
5. Dai, M., Zhang, S., Wang, H., Jin, S.: A low storage room requirement framework for distributed ledger in blockchain. IEEE Access **6**, 22970–22975 (2018)
6. Dang, H., Dinh, T.T.A., Loghin, D., Chang, E.C., Lin, Q., Ooi, B.C.: Towards scaling blockchain systems via sharding. In: Proceedings of the 2019 International Conference on Management of Data, pp. 123–140 (2019)
7. Fetterly, Y.Y.M.I.D., Budiu, M., Erlingsson, Ú., Currey, P.K.G.J.: Dryadlinq: A system for general-purpose distributed data-parallel computing using a high-level language. In: Proceedings of LSDS-IR 8 (2009)
8. Gencer, A.E., van Renesse, R., Sirer, E.G.: Short paper: service-oriented sharding for blockchains. In: Kiayias, A. (ed.) FC 2017. LNCS, vol. 10322, pp. 393–401. Springer, Cham (2017). https://doi.org/10.1007/978-3-319-70972-7_22
9. Nakamoto, S.: Bitcoin: a peer-to-peer electronic cash system. Technical report, Manubot (2019)
10. Rodríguez-Martínez, M., Roussopoulos, N.: MOCHA: a self-extensible database middleware system for distributed data sources. In: Proceedings of the 2000 ACM SIGMOD International Conference on Management of Data, pp. 213–224 (2000)
11. Wang, K., Mi, J., Xu, C., Zhu, Q., Shu, L., Deng, D.J.: Real-time load reduction in multimedia big data for mobile internet. ACM Trans. Multimedia Comput. Commun. Appl. (TOMM) **12**(5s), 1–20 (2016)
12. Wikipedia contributors: Double-spending – Wikipedia, the free encyclopedia (2019). https://en.wikipedia.org/w/index.php?title=Double-spending&oldid=923712604. Accessed 5 Feb 2020
13. Wikipedia contributors: Ethereum – Wikipedia, the free encyclopedia (2020). https://en.wikipedia.org/w/index.php?title=Ethereum&oldid=938839249. Accessed 5 Feb 2020
14. Wilkinson, S., Boshevski, T., Brandoff, J., Buterin, V.: Storj a peer-to-peer cloud storage network (2014)
15. Wilkinson, S., Lowry, J., Boshevski, T.: Metadisk a blockchain-based decentralized file storage application. Technical report (2014)
16. Zamani, M., Movahedi, M., Raykova, M.: Rapidchain: scaling blockchain via full sharding. In: Proceedings of the 2018 ACM SIGSAC Conference on Computer and Communications Security, pp. 931–948 (2018)

BBM: A Blockchain-Based Model for Open Banking via Self-sovereign Identity

Chengzu Dong[1], Ziyuan Wang[1(✉)], Shiping Chen[2(✉)], and Yang Xiang[1(✉)]

[1] Swinburne University of Technology, Melbourne, Australia
{chengzudong,ziyuanwang,yxiang}@swin.edu.au
[2] CSIRO Data61, Eveleigh, Australia
Shiping.Chen@data61.csiro.au

Abstract. Open banking technology is an emerging data-sharing paradigm that can facilitate and inspire new businesses vie efficient data-sharing with banks, such as quick approval of loan applications and finding a better investment return. However, the majority of customers are reluctant to use the open banking service, because they feel unsafe to share data with third-party service providers. In this paper, we proposed (BBM) a blockchain-based self-sovereign identity system model for open banking. The model provides a reliable secured communication network between users and third-party service providers and enables users to control their own identities and data. Through a comparison with the existing related work, the superiority of the BBM model has been demonstrated and analysed.

Keywords: Blockchain · Self-sovereign identity · Open banking

1 Introduction

In the present, open banking gives either consumers or customers more privilege of access and control their financial data and transactions [1]. Also, banks provide APIs to third-parties, who utilise these APIs to provide a variety of potential benefits to businesses and clients. They can integrate consumer account information and various financial product information from different banks to enable a single view of account transactions, balance and other data [2]. The consumer can get suggestions on how to control their personal finances more efficiently from third-parties data analytics. When the consumer wants to apply for a loan, they can be evaluated more accurately and efficiently to avoid the risk of taking on unaffordable debt [3].

However, users do not want their data being used without their permission. And people do not trust banks because there is a risk of privacy leakage and personal information misconduct. BBM model provides a self-sovereign identity feature through using Uport as middleware. When banks or other institutions want to use data of a consumer, they must request permission from the consumer. And users only need to show their credential instead of revealing detailed personal information.

© Springer Nature Switzerland AG 2020
Z. Chen et al. (Eds.): ICBC 2020, LNCS 12404, pp. 61–75, 2020.
https://doi.org/10.1007/978-3-030-59638-5_5

The BBM model via self-sovereign identity (SSI) technology to allows customers use their digital identities in the off-line world as same as they use physical identities (e.g. driving license, passport). To avoid privacy leakage risk like Facebook-Cambridge Analytica data scandal [3]. Our BBM model empowers user to control their own identities instead of administrative third-party tracking access or granting to these sensitive credentials.

According to the investigation result from J. Xu [4], blockchain keeps cryptographic transactions in the public ledger, which is extremely hard to modify and hack due to the decentralised consensus. The BBM model is based on the blockchain technology. As a consequence, it can prevent from hacking, DDOS attacks and protect users from identity theft and fraud. Also, the BBM model is based on Ethereum, which is a blockchain-based platform and it has the same features with traditional blockchain. Also, the BBM model takes advantage of Ethereum to provide more functionalities like building decentralised applications and writing smart contracts.

To enable users to control their own identities while protecting their privacy in the data sharing process of open banking services. We develop the BBM model to provide a reliable solution to open banking services by using blockchain-based self-sovereign identity technology. Also, We create a scenario that users apply for a car loan service based on the BBM model. The scenario shows users can control their own identities to apply for a car loan service while their personal data are protected. It demonstrates the BBM model meets the requirement of open banking service. In addition, we improved Uport registry and recovery smart contracts, users can easily recover their identities if their identity device lost.

In Sect. 2, we describe the existing work in the current research filed. In Sect. 3, the design of the BBM model is explained in details. In Sect. 4, we provide a real-life scenario based on the BBM model. In Sect. 5, we did the comparative analysis between the BBM model and the existing work. Also, we evaluate the BBM model based on its features. In Sect. 6, we sum up this paper and propose our future work.

2   Related Work

2.1   Self-sovereign Identity

As C. Allen described the evolution of identity [7], there are four phases of evolution of self-sovereign identity below.

- **Phase1: Centralised identity.** Administrative control by a single authority
- **Phase2: Federated identity.** Administrative control by multiple, federated authority
- **Phase3: User-centric identity.** Administrative control by multiple authority without federation
- **Phase4: Self-sovereign identity.** Individual control across any number of authorities

The self-sovereign identity is the next generation of user-centric identity. It is entirely user-controlled identity management technology. Also, C. Allen proposed ten principles about self-sovereign identity below, these principles enable users at the central of self-sovereign identity.

- **Existence:** Users must have an independent existence.
- **Control:** Users must control their identities.
- **Access:** Users must have access to their own data.
- **Transparency:** Systems and algorithms must be transparent.
- **Persistence:** Identities must be long-lived.
- **Portability:** Information and services about identity must be transportable.
- **Interoperability:** Identities should be as widely usable as possible.
- **Consent:** Users must agree to the use of their identities.
- **Minimalization:** Disclosure of claims must be minimized.
- **Protection:** The rights of users must be protected.

2.2   KYC2

KYC2 framework is an improved version of existing KYC (Know your Customer) framework. The existing KYC framework is typically running slow, costly and usually accomplished in person. Also, the existing identity management framework takes away the digital identity and data control right from users. And user's data and identities are stored on different centralized identity management systems, which may cause a risk of privacy misconduct. KYC2 framework relies on Hyperledger Indy (a permissioned blockchain) to build a self-sovercign identity-based framework. In KYC2 framework, they improved the previous problems (e.g. privacy protection) in KYC framework [9]. In comparison with the BBM model, KYC2 framework did not consider the recoverability and flexibility.

2.3   Tradle

Tradle is a Know Your Customer (KYC) service provider, the Tradle framework use the self-sovereign identity techniques to put users in charge of their own identities stored in different platform or organisations. And users can share their identities and other data to one or multiple organisations. Also, Trade framework provides a serverless could platform to swap KYC properties to replace traditional complicated and costly back-end server [10]. In comparison with the BBM model, Tradle did not use blockchain to store data, they stored the user data in third-party cloud storage, the user privacy may be misused by third-party during the data sharing process.

2.4   Q.Stokkink

Q.Stokkink proposed a purely academic model for users to control their own identities. This model use blockchain consensus features to deal with the trust problem. With their model, users are tied to the claims, and they are not able to cheat the system. If users did malicious behaviour, they might be caught committing identity fraud and be punished by law.

As they claimed, they are the first decentralised permissionless digital passport and a authenticate peer to peer identity management model. And this model is created for the Netherlands government. The Netherlands citizen can become the first citizen to control their own digital identities. They do not need federated authority in charge of their own identities. Furthermore, they want to prompt their model into the global network. Each global citizen can have a unique legally digital passport [11]. To comparison with the BBM model, Q.Stokkink is not open-sourced. It only allows the authorised developer to write and deploy smart contract into their government-controlled system.

2.5 SCARAB

SCARAB first proposed the decentralised secure access control model to deal with the issue of accountability for self-sovereign identity featured blockchain system, by logging each request to allow data access publicly. SCARAB introduced the on-chain secrets method, which uses secret verifiable sharing to enable managed secrets collectively under Byzantine adversary. Also, SCARAB introduces identity skipchains, which will allow the access control policies identity management dynamically and enable users to use self-sovereign identity to manage their identities [12]. In comparison with the BBM model, SCARAB store everything on-chain, which can dramatically impact the system performance. Also, the sensitive data cannot be on-chain, on-chain data can be visible to the public.

2.6 Onename.io

Onename.io provide self-sovereign identity service based on blockchain technology, user can create blockstack ID (like a digital passport) through Onename.io platform. With the blockstack ID, user can connect their social media accounts (e.g. SpringRole, an application integrated Twitter, GitHub on their decentralised platform) and other productive tools (e.g. Dmail, an email application built on their decentralised platform).

Furthermore, Onename.io is like a platform that allows users to control their own identities in the decentralised network. However, users have to use the applications built on their platform, and users have limited selection range in this platform [13]. To comparison with the BBM model, Onename.io lack of portability and Interoperability. The onename.io has its own platform and not compatible with others.

3   BBM Model

3.1   Design Goals

- **Privacy and data protection during data sharing process.** The bank data and user personal data is very sensitive during the data sharing process.

The BBM model provides a reliably secured peer to peer network to keep the data safe. We also store the on-chain data and off-chain data separately to remain the user data private.

– **User-controlled identity and data.** Users should be able to control their own identities and data. The BBM model using self-sovereign identity techniques to enable user control their own data and identities.

– **New identity recovery solution.** The BBM model uses new registry and recovery smart contracts to replace the default registry and recovery smart contracts in Uport. The new smart contracts enable users to recover their identities more conveniently and easily.

3.2 Overview of BBM

The BBM model contains four layers (see Fig. 1), which are application layer, uport layer, blockchain network layer and the data layer. We orchestrated the data layer for storing client data off-chain and remain the client data private, invisible to the public. We used the blockchain peer to peer network to provide a trustworthy network.

In the Uport layer, we combined Uport as one part of the BBM model, and we modified the Uport default smart contracts to improve the recoverability. Also, we store on-chain data on the Ethereum in Uport layer. In the application layer, we provide API to regulate third-party. Only the authorized third-party can access the data from API.

3.3 Application Layer

In the application layer, the BBM model put banks APIs, integrated bank product, integrated bank service and integrated financial product application in this layer. This layer is close to users and regulator. User can easily access to these integrated open banking service and the regulator can regulate these third-party provided services and bank APIs. Also, the application layer provides the communication interface between users and BBM architecture.

3.4 Uport Layer

In the application layer, the BBM model put banks APIs, integrated bank product, integrated bank service and integrated financial product application in this layer. This layer is close to users and regulator. User can easily access to these integrated open banking service and the regulator can regulate these third-party provided services and bank APIs. Also, the application layer provides the communication interface between users and BBM architecture.

3.5 Uport Layer

In Uport layer, we present four key components, which are data component, mobile component, server component and the smart contract component.

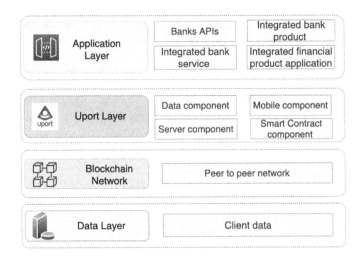

Fig. 1. System structure

The data component contains insensitive on-chain data (e.g. username, public key). The mobile component enables users to interact with their mobile Uport application. The Uport application has the user's private key. In the server component, users are able to scan the QR code to connect with the server by using a smartphone.

In a smart contract component, there are proxy contract and controller contract. The proxy contract is only for transfer transactions to the external address and swaps out the owner for another one. The controller contract provides main features (e.g. access control, registry, recovery) [13].

Uport has its own recovery contract to handle the account lost issue. However, their contract need two or three witnesses (e.g. Uport mobile app contacts or organisations like a bank) to prove the owner of the identity in the lost device, it does not make sense for a newly registered user to have two or three witnesses (e.g. Jack has registered his Uport account for half years but he did not add any individual or institutions to his Uport contact list). Therefore, we adopt a new recovery contract to replace the Uport default recovery smart contract. Also, to facilitate the new recovery contract, we deploy a new registry smart contract to replace the default registry contract. To deploy a smart contract on Uport platform, the deployment instruction [14] must be followed.

There is not pre-request to register a new account with Uport default registry smart contract. User can register their account by using a nickname with the default registry contract. The BBM model proposed a new registry smart contract, the new registry smart contract working process can be seen in the Fig. 3. To register a new Uport account through a new registry smart contract, users must provide their physical identities (e.g. passport or driving license) to the identity issuer (e.g. Government department of home affairs). If their physical identities are approved, the identity issuer will grant them an identity credential, and then their Uport account is activated.

By using the new recovery smart contract, once users lost their device, they can simply recover their lost identity with five steps (see Fig. 2).

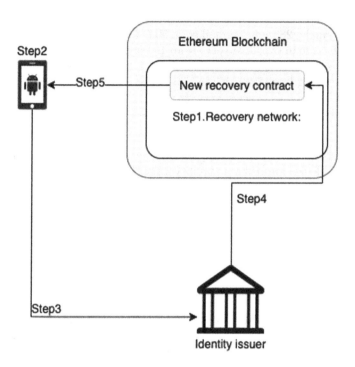

Fig. 2. Recovery contract working process

1. Having a recovery network stored in the recovery smart contract
2. Prepare the new phone
3. Inform recovery network about your new device public key to the recovery contract
4. Identity issuer verify the new device public key to the recovery contract
5. The recovery smart contract updates your public key and your identity is recovered.

3.6   Network Layer

The BBM model is based on Ethereum decentralised public blockchain network, It is a widely used network that provides consistency, security and smart contract feature. With the Ethereum network, the BBM model allows developers to use Solidity language writing a smart contract [18]. Also, the BBM model has a peer to peer network for transferring on-chain transaction data [19].

3.7   Data Layer

In the data layer, we store the sensitive data listed below in commercial DBMS for off-chain storage [16].

1. User sensitive information: The user sensitive information including user real name, sex, age, email address, income and the detailed transition history (e.g. peter, male, 28, peter@gmail.com, 50,000 salary p.a. applied for a 6.99% 30,000 dollars loan over five years from Bank A).
2. Financial service or product: The financial service or product that banks offered including bank deposit rate, loan rate, long or short term saving plan and so on.
3. Account data: the wallet data including user account balance and account number.

There are two reasons that we applied off-chain storage in our model. The first reason is that blockchain has a scalability issue that impacts on-chain data storage and computational power. If the BBM model store everything in blockchain, the scalability issue can significantly impact the performance of the BBM model. The second reason is that blockchain is public and transparent. However, the user sensitive data should not be revealed to the public. Therefore, we provide off-chain storage to remain the user sensitive data private.

4   Case Study

4.1   Real-World Open Banking Scenario: User Apply for a Car Loan

Banks provide application programming interface (API) to authorised third parties, third parties build the integrated application or platform to provide comparable financial products from different banks. The integrated application or platform benefit user to find the best deal from various banks products. For example, a client wants to apply a personal loan to buy a brand new car. A client finds there are two banks provide similar loan product with different annual interest rate. bank A provide a 6.99% p.a. Interest rate based on a 30,000 dollars loan over five years, bank B give an 8.05% p.a. Interest rate based on a 30,000 dollars loan over five years. Undoubtedly, the client requests the product that bank A offered.

Traditionally, the client needs to submit his identity proof, income statement, address, previous debt status to the bank A. Then the bank evaluate the client, if the client meets their requirement, they can provide the car loan to the client. However, the traditional method can cost plenty of time and efforts to the client and bank. The client has to prepare related documents. Bank have to verify these documents. Also, the client submitted information can only apply for a loan in bank A, he cannot use his documents provided to bank A in another bank. If the client wants to purchase a financial product from another bank or financial institutions. He has to submit the documents and wait for the verification process again.

4.2   Registration Phase

With our BBM model, we use Uport as middleware to provide self-sovereign identity service. When the client requests the car loan product from Bank A through integrated third-party application or platform. Firstly the client needs to download Uport mobile app to his smartphone and register his Uport account in Uport for further usage (see Fig. 3).

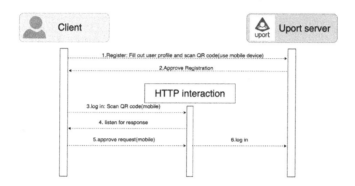

Fig. 3. Registration phase

4.3   Verification Phase

Secondly, the client need to submit his physical ID (e.g. passport, driving license) to an identity provider (e.g. Government department of Home Affairs). If an identity provider verifies the documents. The Uport server can receive a verified claim from an identity provider. Then the Uport server can generate a digital ID credential, which is displayed in Uport mobile app credential list. The client can use the ID credential to prove his identity (see Fig. 4).

4.4   Authorization Phase

Thirdly, the client needs to submit his income statement, previous debt status to another identity provider (e.g. Reserve Bank of Australia). If the documents are verified by this identity provider, the Uport server can receive a verified claim from this identity provider. Then the Uport server can generate a credit loan credential, which is also displayed in Uport mobile app credential list. The client can use the credit loan credential to prove his financial status (see Fig. 5).

Finally, the client only needs to show the digital credentials stored to the Bank A. If Bank A think the client is eligible to apply for the loan, they can provide the loan to the client directly. If not, Banks A would ask more credentials from the client. By using BBM model to provide service, client does not need to reveal their private information such as date of birth. And they only need to show

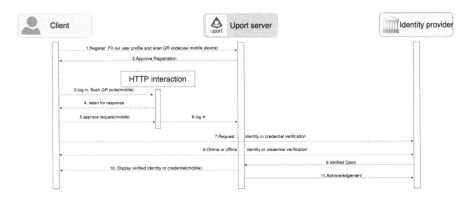

Fig. 4. Verification phase

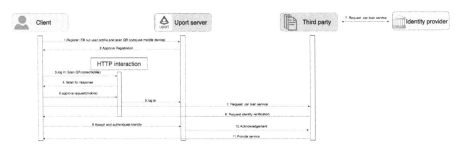

Fig. 5. Authorization phase

the credentials that the identity provider issued to the verifier (e.g. Bank A). As a consequence, the BBM model provides reliable privacy protection during the data sharing process of the scenario.

5   Discussion

The simply self-sovereign identity solution is not enough to provide trustworthy privacy protection during the data sharing process. For example, when users want to use their digital identities or credentials, users should find a verifier who has an existing trust relationship with the issuer to verify their digital identities and credentials. Then users are able to use their digital identities and credentials. However, how to identify and verify the issuer has become an issue.

The blockchain has a public decentralised consensus network, it also known as Distributed ledger technology (DLT). With the evolution of blockchain technology, Ethereum was introduced by Vitalik Buterin in 2015. Ethereum is an open-sourced platform based on blockchain technology, which provides programmable smart contract function. The developer can build smart contract and decentralised applications through Ethereum. The smart contract is irreversible and immutable after deployed [8].

Traditionally, the certificate authority (CA) is treated as the root of trust. The CA sign using their private key and issue the public key certificate. However, the traditional solution is very costly and still centralized. The latest solution is using blockchain technology to solve this problem. The blockchain can be treated as the root of trust. It is because of the public blockchain that using consensus protocol. The consensus protocol enables all nodes (stands for different entities) have replicated ledgers to record transactions in the blockchain network. It makes impossible to alter existing transactions in the decentralised blockchain network. With combing the features of blockchain technology, the issue of self-sovereign identity is solved.

However, there are many existing solutions using blockchain-based self-sovereign identity technology. To demonstrate the superiority of the BBM model, we present a comparative analysis between the BBM model and other related works with supporting evidence. Also, we evaluate the BBM model based on the features of the BBM model.

5.1 Comparative Analysis

The KYC2 framework has not covered the recoverability and flexibility. The recoverability stood for when users lost their device that contains their digital identities, they are able to recover their digital identities through specific recovery algorithm or contract. And the flexibility means users can easily and conveniently control and use their own digital identities. To achieve the recoverability, the BBM model adopts new registry and recovery smart contract that deployed in Uport layer smart contracts, which can help users to recover their identities easily. To achieve flexibility, the Uport layer of the BBM model store user digital credentials on-chain, users can show their digital credentials directly to the verifier instead of physical documents.

Tradle is not using blockchain to store any data, they saved the user data in the third-party storage, which cannot provide transparent and secure protection to user data. Also, the user data may have the risk of data misconduct. The BBM model is based on blockchain, which provides transparency, fairness privacy protection to users.

Q.Stokkink is designed as private instead of open-sourced. It only allows the authorised developer to write and deploy a smart contract on their system. The BBM model is open-sourced, which enable developers to write and deploy the custom smart contract. Everyone can contribute and add their own smart contract into the platform by following the deploy guideline [20].

SCARAB store all data on-chain, which can dramatically impact its performance because of the blockchain scalability issue. Also, the sensitive data cannot be stored on-chain, the on-chain data is visible to the public. The BBM model promise on-chain and off-chain storage, which can separate on-chain data (e.g. transactions) and off-chain data (e.g. name, gender, age) while stores off-chain data in the commercial DBMS.

Onename.io lack of portability and Interoperability. The Onename.io is based on their own platform (Blockstack [13]) and not compatible with others.

The BBM model enables all information, identities and services are transportable from one organization to others. Trough the Interoperability and portability, users can improve the persistence of their digital identities and use their digital identities in different platforms and geographical locations [15].

To summarise the comparative analysis of the BBM model compared to the existing work. We present the comparison table (see Fig. 6) among the BBM model with current related models.

Compare with existing works						
Property name	KYC 2	Tradle	Q.Stokkink	SCARAB	Onename.io	BBM
Recoverability	NO	NO	NO	NO	NO	YES
Flexibility	NO	NO	YES	YES	NO	YES
Portability	YES	YES	YES	YES	NO	YES
Programmable Smart contract	YES	NO	NO	NO	YES	YES
Interoperability	YES	NO	YES	YES	NO	YES
Privacy protection	YES	YES	YES	YES	YES	YES
Integrity and confidentiality	YES	YES	NO	NO	YES	YES
Accountability	YES	NO	NO	YES	NO	YES

Fig. 6. Comparison table

5.2 Evaluation of BBM Model

We summarise the features of the BBM model below, and we evaluate these features based on the real-life case.

- **Recoverability.** The BBM model adopts the new registry and recovery smart contract that deployed in Uport layer smart contracts. As mentioned in Sect. 3.2, the default Uport recovery smart contract need stringent requirement. It may cause the new user unable to recover their identities in case if they lost their device. With our BBM model, the new registry smart contract force user to prepare their physical identities (e.g. passport, driving license) ready. Then they can successful registered their identities on Uport. While their identities record is kept in identity issuer. To recover the lost identity with our new recovery smart contract, users only need to take five steps to recover their identities.
- **Flexibility.** The BBM model combined Uport as middleware to provide a flexible service by using Uport mobile application. User can show their credentials that authorised issuer acknowledged to verifier directly instead of providing plenty of material. For example, if a user wants to rent a car, he only needs to show his driving license credential to the verifier.

- **Portability.** The BBM model provides a standard interface to enable users to transports their identities across different platform and organisations.
- **Programmable smart contract.** The BBM model brings the smart contract component for developers to deploy their customized smart contract. The developer can deploy their own smart contract by following the guideline [20].
- **Interoperability.** The BBM model enable multi identity standards and platforms compliance. Also, the BBM model gives users a long-lived digital identity while enabling users to use their identities in different geographical locations.
- **Integrity and confidentiality.** The BBM model uses peer to peer network to ensure data integrity and confidentiality in the data sharing process.
- **Privacy Protection.** The BBM model uses blockchain technology to protect on-chain data, which provide a transparent and trustworthy mechanism based on blockchain consensus protocol.
- **Accountability.** The BBM model introduced the data right regulator, which regulate the organisation who used user data. If the regulator detects any data breach behaviours, the people who used the user data is accountable for their illegal behaviour.

6 Conclusion and Future Works

The BBM model is an up to date and complicated model. This paper demonstrates the groundwork for improving open banking service by using blockchain-based self-sovereign identity technology. Through this work, this paper is aim to solve the privacy issue happened in the data sharing process and consider how to recover the user's identity once their identity device lost. The Uport does not have a perfect solution to identity recovery. We propose a new recovery controller contract to replace Uport default recovery controller contract. With the BBM model, users can manage and control their own digital identities and credentials while their privacy and data are protected.

Future research work can be divided into two parts. In the first part, we will adopt Uport platform as middleware in BBM model. It is because we can technically improve our BBM model while we are developing it into a visible platform. And we can find more research challenges that we should resolve when developing the BBM model-based platform. Also, we are going to make a standard interface to adopt other platforms to improve the portability and interoperability of the BBM model.

In the second part, we will develop a new registry contract and recovery controller contract to replace Uport default registry smart contract and recovery smart contract. It is because the existing Uport recovery contract needs at least two or three witnesses to prove the user's identities if the user's identity device lost. The new user is almost impossible to have two or three Uport contacts or organisation to prove their identities. Therefore, they may lose their registered identities permanently. Nevertheless, with our new registry contract and recovery contract, The issue will be fixed.

References

1. Ma, S., et al.: Nudging data privacy management of open banking based on blockchain. In: International Symposium on Pervasive Systems, Algorithms and Networks, pp. 72–79 (2018)
2. Deloitte: Open Banking (2019)
3. van Bokkem, D., Hageman, R., Koning, G., Nguyen, L., Zarin, N.: Self-sovereign identity solutions: the necessity of blockchain technology. CoRR, vol. abs/1904.12816 (2019). http://arxiv.org/abs/1904.12816
4. Xu, J.J.: Are blockchains immune to all malicious attacks? Financ. Innov. **2**(1), 1–9 (2016). https://doi.org/10.1186/s40854-016-0046-5
5. Consumer data standard. Version 1.2.0 (2020)
6. Tobin, A., Reed, D.: The Inevitable Rise of Self-Sovereign Identity. The Sovrin Foundation (2016)
7. Allen, C.: The path to self-sovereign identity (2016). http://www.lifewithalacrity.com/2016/04/the-path-to-self-sovereignidentity.html
8. Wood, G.: A secure decentralised generalised transaction ledger. Ethereum Project Yellow Paper (2014)
9. Soltani, R., Nguyen, U.: A New Approach to Client Onboarding Using Self-Sovereign Identity and Distributed Ledger. Cybermatics 2018.2018.00205 (2018)
10. De Feniks, R., Reverelli, R.: Tradle: KYC on blockchain (2019). http://www.digitalinsuranceagenda.com/108/tradle-kyc-on-blockchain/
11. Stokkink, Q., Pouwelse, J.: Deployment of a blockchain-based self-sovereign identity. In: 2018 IEEE International Conference on Internet of Things (iThings) and IEEE Green Computing and Communications (GreenCom) and IEEE Cyber, Physical and Social Computing (CPSCom) and IEEE Smart Data (SmartData) Halifax, NS, Canada, pp. 1336–1342 (2018)
12. Kokoris-Kogias, E., et al.: Hidden in Plain Sight: Storing and Managing Secrets on a Public Ledger. IACR Cryptology ePrint Archive (2018)
13. OneName.io: The Bridge Between Physical & Digital Identity & Blockchain for the Billions on WordPress.com (2015). https://rywalk.wordpress.com/2015/02/13/onename-the-bridge-between-physical-digital-identity/
14. Lundkvist, C., et al.: Uport: a platform for self-sovereign identity (2017). https://whitepaper.uport.me/uPortwhitepaperDRAFT20170221.pdf
15. Matadium. Introduction to Self-Sovereign Identity and Its 10 Guiding Principles (2019). https://medium.com/metadium/introduction-to-self-sovereign-identity-and-its-10-guiding-principles-97c1ba603872
16. Xu, Z., et al.: PPM: a provenance-provided data sharing model for open banking via blockchain. In: Proceedings of the Australasian Computer Science Week Multiconference (2020)
17. Eberhardt, J., Tai, S.: Zokrates-scalable privacy-preserving off-chain computations. In: 2018 IEEE International Conference on Internet of Things (iThings) and IEEE Green Computing and Communications (GreenCom) and IEEE Cyber, Physical and Social Computing (CPSCom) and IEEE Smart Data (SmartData) (2018)
18. Yavuz, E., et al.: Towards secure e-voting using ethereum blockchain. In: 2018 6th International Symposium on Digital Forensic and Security (ISDFS) (2018)

19. Gencer, A.E., Basu, S., Eyal, I., van Renesse, R., Sirer, E.G.: Decentralization in bitcoin and ethereum networks. In: Meiklejohn, S., Sako, K. (eds.) FC 2018. LNCS, vol. 10957, pp. 439–457. Springer, Heidelberg (2018). https://doi.org/10.1007/978-3-662-58387-6_24
20. Uport. Contract contribution guideline. https://github.com/uport-project/uport-identity

ProvNet: Networked Blockchain for Decentralized Secure Provenance

Changhao Chenli and Taeho Jung$^{(\boxtimes)}$

Department of Computer Science and Engineering, University of Notre Dame,
Notre Dame, IN 46556, USA
`tjung@nd.edu`

Abstract. Data sharing is increasingly popular especially for scientific research and business fields where large volume of datasets are usually required. People benefit from data sharing, but keeping track of the history of the shared data (i.e., provenance records) for monitoring and protecting them is not easy. On one hand, due to the decentralized nature of data sharing nowadays, it is impractical to have a centralized entity who collects all the provenance records. Some previous works that combined the data sharing with blockchain can store the provenance records of data sharing in a blockchain system. On the other hand, previous works focus on the scenario where malicious users will not modify the shared datasets and re-share them as the owner of these changed datasets. Besides, maintaining the correctness of collected records in the presence of malicious attackers is challenging. In this paper, we present ProvNet, a decentralized data sharing platform which can provide a secure and correct provenance record using a networked blockchain. All the valid sharing records will be collected and stored in a tamper-proof networked blockchain, named *blocknet*. Furthermore, ProvNet can also discover and detect the misbehaviors with the stored provenance records.

1 Introduction

Data sharing plays a very important role in both scholarly research as well as industrial collaboration and business. On one hand, in the past years, the development of big data provides adequate raw data for research and business areas. By leveraging data sharing, cooperation among different institutions is enhanced and the usability of the collected data is also enlarged. There are many real-world scenarios that can benefit from data sharing, including but not limited to medical institutions, e-commerce companies, supply-chains, etc. On the other hand, some problems have come into people's eyesight, such as how to protect privacy of the shared data, how to securely capture the provenance during the sharing process, how to define and detect the corruption on data ownership, etc. Moreover, data sharing among different fields or regions may also lead to some disputes in terms of service (TOS). These concerns exist all because attacks occur frequently in the cyberspace (e.g., a study [11] shows that 29.6% of the companies experience data breaches). To further assist such needs, it is imperative that

© Springer Nature Switzerland AG 2020
Z. Chen et al. (Eds.): ICBC 2020, LNCS 12404, pp. 76–93, 2020.
https://doi.org/10.1007/978-3-030-59638-5_6

technical solutions which protect data security during data sharing be developed. The key to mitigating this concern is to introduce **control** and **tracking** in the data propagation *after* its initial release. Allowing data owners/producers to keep track of how their data are accessed, used, and further shared with others will greatly enhance the data security as well as the accountability during the data sharing. It is challenging to achieve such control and tracking during the data sharing because the sharing often occurs in a decentralized environment (e.g., internet) without any party controlled/monitored by any other party, and the parties may even be compromised and become malicious in real world (e.g., hackers compromising internal accounts and gaining escalated privileges).

Secure provenance (or secure data provenance [5,36,37]) is the technology used to capture the history of data (i.e., *provenance of data*) in an adversarial environment where attackers may attempt to tamper the records. Unfortunately, secure provenance is achieved mainly by enforcing strong controls and logging to the environment, e.g., one needs to deploy kernel-level software (e.g., software in the kernel of operating system) on others' host devices [19,37] to collect sufficient provenance records, which is impossible in a decentralized environment like the internet. In fact, such a software deployed at the kernel level may do more harm than good since it leads to more damage once it is compromised. There have been efforts in recording data sharing by utilizing blockchain systems [3,8,34,35]. MedRec [3] and MedShare [35] aim at electronic medical record (EMR) sharing. FairSwap[8] is designed for protecting fairness of data exchanging and Van Hoye et al.[34] proposes a logging mechanism to keep data exchange records.

Our work differs from existing works in two aspects. (1) Compared with existing works, we focus more on the scenarios where shared datasets can be modified and re-shared in the system. Specifically, we propose a more general way to track the shared datasets and such scenario is realistic and challenging because tracking mutable data is non-trivial. (2) We consider different attacker models. Besides the attacks considered in previous works, attackers we considered may attempt to actively deviate from the specified protocols and inject errors into the protocols in the real world. We present how to thwart the active attackers who try to perturb the tracking mechanism and deviate from it.

In this paper, we propose ProvNet, a decentralized data sharing platform that can protect data ownership, capture and store correct data sharing provenance. For each data sharing operation, ProvNet provides a framework for verifying whether the sharing is allowed by the owner. Besides, ProvNet can collect the provenance records during each approved data sharing process, such as the information of the data, the flow of the data and the relationship between datasets. To keep such records, ProvNet proposes a networked structure of blockchain, namely *blocknet*, to store and represent the provenance records (i.e., the records showing the origin and propagation of data). Unlike in existing secure provenance approaches, the capturing of provenance records in ProvNet is secured by a set of protocols followed by honest entities who maintain the blocknet. Moreover, with the blocknet, ProvNet enables users to detect misbehaviors in the data sharing. The contributions of this paper can be summarized as follows:

- ProvNet achieves secure provenance in the data sharing occurring in decentralized environments without needing to deploy kernel-level software.
- We propose a novel networked blockchain (denoted as *blocknet*) to store the provenance records, which makes the stored records tamper-proof.
- Besides the tamper-proofness of the collected records, ProvNet detects incorrect provenance records, and unallowed data sharing defined in this paper.
- We further extend our blocknet into a bi-directional directed graph, which can provide both forward and backward tracking with ProvNet for tracking the footprint of shared data in our blocknet.
- We formally define the completeness and correctness of decentralized secure provenance, and these properties are analyzed rigorously with theoretic proofs and large-scale simulations in ProvNet using real-world data.

The rest of the paper will be as follows: Sect. 2 will introduce some related works. Sect. 3 will introduce our assumptions and attack models. Then, Sect. 4 will describe ProvNet's protocols in detail and perform theoretical proofs as well as large-scale simulations. The conclusion will be made in Sect. 6.

2   Background and Related Works

Permissioned Blockchain: There are two types of blockchains, namely permissionless blockchains and permissioned blockchains. Permissionless blockchains such as Bitcoin [20] usually leverage some mechanisms (such as PoW and PoS) to reach the consensus of the global ledger. On the other hand, permissioned blockchains, such as Hyperledger Fabric [1], are those blockchains where users are not allowed to join or leave the system freely and must be pre-authenticated before participating in the system. Fabric aims at cross-industry cooperation and its modular architecture is flexible in different scenarios.

Blockchain-Based Data Sharing: Several works have also been proposed to provide a better application of data sharing by leveraging the use of blockchain. MedRec [3], MeDShare [35], HDG [18] and Medblock [9] are all aiming at using blockchains to improve the problems during electronic medical record sharing. Other scenarios, such as sharing data generated by IoT devices [29] or intelligent vehicles [14,31] are also combined with blockchains to provide a better solution. Besides, FairSwap [8] also leverages the use of smart contracts and aims at large-size file sharing where fair data transactions are protected.

Blockchain-Based Secure Provenance: Provenance record is meaningful to accountability and forensics, so the storage of provenance record is important for supporting correct references in such scenarios. As is mentioned above, blockchain systems are featured by its tamper-proofness. Therefore, many related works [2,17,21,26,35] have been proposed to address this problem and focus on different scenarios of provenance, such as medical records, supply-chains or designed under some regulations. Besides, LineageChain [28] was another work that collects the provenance during the execution time of smart contracts. They proposed Merkle DAG to store the collected provenance record and an append-only skip list to build an index for quick search. Van Hoye et al. [34] proposed a logging mechanism for the records generated during the data exchange processes in a cross-organizational data sharing scenario. Their mechanism leverages four functions related to data request and response as well as their confirmations. BlockIPFS [22] combines the IPFS with blockchain to gain the traceability attribute but they do not consider the problem of similarity detection.

Different from these works, ProvNet focuses on a more general scenario and considers more types of attacker models which may violate the data sharing in the system. Besides, the system will provide provenance records that stored on a blockchain-like structure, and such records can both turn back for future provenance collection and be beneficial for forensic usage.

3 Definitions and Assumptions

3.1 System Overview

ProvNet is a decentralized data sharing platform that can protect the data ownership and provide correct secure provenance records for potential use. It defines several system rules that should be followed by the entities, and the protocols are designed such that the entities not following the rules will be detected. By following the system rules, users in ProvNet can share data with each other and the trails of their data sharing will be captured and recorded. To store the provenance records, we present a new data structure, blocknet, which is a networked blockchain similar to a DAG. In a blocknet, each block can have one or more predecessors and successors. There are three types of entities in ProvNet:

- **Verifiers.** The verifiers in ProvNet are those entities who are in charge of verifying data sharing processes and updating the blocknet.
- **Publishers.** The publishers are those users who will share their datasets with other users. Publishers can be further divided into two types, *owners* and *senders*. Owners are those publishers whose datasets never shared before and senders are those publishers whose datasets are either a direct re-share of other datasets or derived from previously shared ones. (Note that there are many kinds of derivation, including simply addition, deletion and modification or performing complex calculation such as deep learning training, etc.) Besides, owners can also self-define the *Terms of Services (TOS)* of her/his dataset. TOS are those restrictions originally set by the owners of the datasets which can regulate how the dataset can be propagated in the network (e.g., the access control of the shared datasets or the limit of shared times). Here in ProvNet, senders can only comply with the previous TOS and perform *append-only* modifications on them when sharing with other users, which means the TOS in ProvNet can be defined by the owners and will be inherited in an append-only way by the senders. Note that if the sender is going to share a dataset which is derived from multiple datasets, s/he will need to inherit the terms which satisfy all the previous TOS and optionally append her/his own TOS.

– **Receivers.** The receivers are the users who receive the shared datasets from publishers and are another important party during the data sharing process.

To share a dataset, a publisher needs to send a sharing request to the verifiers. The verifiers will validate the request and approve the request if it is valid. With the approval from the verifiers, the publisher can share the dataset with the receivers. After ensuring that all the receivers have received the data, the verifiers will append a block storing this data sharing process into the blocknet. The detailed workflow of ProvNet is described in Sect. 4.

3.2 Assumptions

As aforementioned, there are two types of publishers during a data sharing process, either an owner claiming publishing a new data or a sender re-sharing published data. We assume that there is a validation function ϕ which can be used during the verifiers' validation process to verify whether an owner's data sharing request is valid or not. More specifically, in ProvNet, we assume such validation function ϕ can be used to decide whether an owner is true or not. Similar assumption can also be seen in FairSwap [8] where buyer would like to pay for some data x if x satisfies some function/predicate Φ. In reality, this validation function ϕ can be implemented in different forms depending on different use cases. For instance, if ProvNet is used for text files sharing, deciding whether a claimed owner is true or false will thus highly relevant to the plagiarism detection technology, where much previous research has been done, such as document plagiarism detection [30] and cross-language plagiarism detection [25]. Therefore, in such scenarios, both schemes mentioned above can be considered as a potential validation function ϕ. Then, the system can verify whether a *new* text file sharing is valid or not. Note that the plagiarism detection scheme is only one example of the validation function ϕ, under the scenario of text files sharing and the exact implementations may vary based on different scenarios.

In ProvNet, the provenance records are stored in a blocknet, which is a variant of permissioned blockchain (e.g., Hyperledger Fabric [1]). Such choice is made because our scenario is about data sharing among different users/organizations who do not trust each other, and the permissioned blockchain systems allow their nodes to distrust each other. However, due to the consensus mechanism in the permissioned blockchain, e.g., the Raft [23] used by Hyperledger Fabric, we assume the number of attackers is no more than $1/2$ of the total users. This is reasonable because all users are authenticated in the permissioned blockchain.

3.3 Attack Models

We assume that the publisher and the receiver will not be the attacker at the same time, which means that they will not collude with each other. This assumption is trivial because if collusion happens, both entities can share data offline without using our platform. We consider several types of possible attacks in ProvNet which are related to the correctness of provenance record.

- **Ownership Corruption:** A publisher will be considered compromising the ownership of a dataset if s/he claims as its owner but is not the real owner.
- **Propagation Violation:** A publisher will be considered violating the propagation of a dataset if s/he (1) does not correctly inherit the previous TOS, (2) corrupts the previous TOS, or (3) claims as a sender but there is no such record showing that the s/he received the relevant dataset from other users previously.
- **Sharing Inconsistency:** A sharing inconsistency is considered happened when the publisher and the receivers have a dispute on whether the dataset has been shared properly, e.g., the publisher claims having sent the dataset to the receivers while the receivers declare not having received the claimed dataset.
- **Data Leakage:** A data leakage is a scenario where a dataset is found compromised externally. In such case, the leaked dataset may be revealed by some users in the platform to some entities outside ProvNet.

Compared with previous works [8,34,35], the attackers in ProvNet may generate fake information (e.g., claim the wrong ownership or perturb the TOS) to deviate the system protocols and are therefore more active.

3.4 Security Definitions

If the ownership corruption occurs, ProvNet must be able to detect it. As aforementioned, the function ϕ can be used to detect the ownership corruption. Then, we use the following (ε, ϕ)-completeness to quantify how much ownership corruption ProvNet can detect.

Definition 1 ((ε, ϕ)-completeness). *We say our ProvNet's verification on the data propagation in the networks is (ε, ϕ)-**complete** if, for the chosen ϕ, it holds that*

$$\mathbf{Pr}[I^*_{\text{corrupt}} = I_{\text{corrupt}} \leftarrow \phi] \geq 1 - \varepsilon$$

where $\leftarrow$ is a standard notation denoting the output of a protocol, and I^*_{corrupt} is the ground truth of whether ownership corruption occurred.

Note that the (ε, ϕ)-completeness is given for ownership corruption only. Although other possible attacks, such as propagation violation and sharing inconsistency may also influence the completeness of the blocknet, they can be verified without running ϕ, e.g., to verify whether the TOS is correctly inherited, the verifiers can refer to the previous records about the dataset's TOS.

Correct provenance records acquisition is the necessary condition of achieving trackability in ProvNet. We use the following δ-correctness to quantify the quality of ProvNet's trackability in data sharing platforms.

Definition 2 ((δ_1, δ_2)-correctness). *We say our ProvNet's trackability in the data-oriented networks is (δ_1, δ_2)-correct if, for every propagation graph $\mathbb{G}$, it holds that*

$$\frac{|\mathbb{E}^* \cap \mathbb{E}|}{|\mathbb{E}^* \cup \mathbb{E}|} \geq 1 - \delta_1 \quad , \quad \frac{|\mathbb{V}^* \cap \mathbb{V}|}{|\mathbb{V}^* \cup \mathbb{V}|} \geq 1 - \delta_2$$

where V denotes the set of nodes in G and each node represents a block in blocknet. E denotes the set of edges in G and reveals the dependency between two datasets in two blocks. Both $\mathbb{V}$ and $\mathbb{E}$ are from $\mathbb{G}$ and $\mathbb{E}^*, \mathbb{V}^*$ are the ground truths of them, i.e., the set of edges and the set of vertices would have been in the provenance records if all TOS had been enforced without propogation violation.

The fractions at the left sides of the inequalities are Jaccard Index [10,27] of two sets of edges/vertices, which characterizes the similarity between two sets.

The ultimate goal is to achieve designs for ProvNet such that both $(\varepsilon, \phi) - completeness$ and $(\delta_1, \delta_2) - correctness$ are achieved with low ε, δ_1, and δ_2.

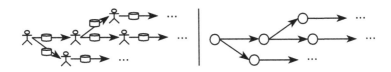

Fig. 1. Overview of ProvNet.

4   System Design

As is shown in Fig. 1, users share data with each other and their sharing records will be stored in a blocknet. To address those possible attacks analyzed above, we propose three protocols. Before a dataset can be shared, the verifiers will follow the protocol of **TOS-enforced and Ownership-protected Data Sharing** (Sect. 4.1) and give approval to those acceptable sharing requests. This protocol can address the ownership corruption and the propagation violation by detecting all the wrong ownership claims or false TOS inheritance in the data sharing request. After the datasets are successfully shared, another protocol called **Bidirectional Blocknet Construction** (Sect. 4.2) will be used to construct a blocknet where the trial of each data sharing process will be considered as a provenance record and stored as a block in the blocknet. Besides, since the verifiers have built the correct blocknet based on the collected records, ProvNet can further provide a **Backward and Forward Tracking for Accountability** (Sect. 4.3) function for tracking and forensic scenarios and we show an example where the provenance records stored in ProvNet can be used to detect the suspicious users in a data leakage attack.

A brief workflow of ProvNet is described in Fig. 2. A publisher will send a sharing request, which is denoted as *ShrReq* hereafter, to the verifiers and include some necessary terms for validation (step 1 and 2). The verifiers will give approval to the request or reject it based on the validation results (either the real owner of the data or sender who correctly inherits the TOS) (step 3). After receiving the approval from the verifiers, the publisher will share the dataset with receivers (step 4) and receivers will send an acknowledgement, denoted as *Ack* hereafter, as a declaration of receipt of the dataset to the verifiers (step 5). Note that it is the idea of sending some confirmation of receipts is a common idea in such data sharing scenarios [8,34]. The verifiers will update the blockchain after successfully validating the acknowledgements sent by the receivers or reject the sharing otherwise (step 6 and 7).

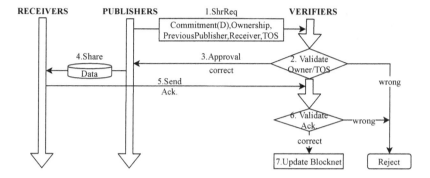

Fig. 2. Workflow of ProvNet.

4.1 TOS-enforced and Ownership-Protected Data Sharing

To describe our protocol, we will start from a simple case where a publisher P is going to share a dataset D. At the beginning of a data sharing, P will generate a *ShrReq*, which will include the following entries:

$$ShrReq = \{Commitment(D), IsOwner, Pre.P, R, TOS\}$$

Commitment(D) denotes the validation information that P generates for validation purpose, which can be applied to (or as an input of) the validation function ϕ so that the verifiers can verify whether P has claimed the correct ownership of D. (The *Commitment(D)* must be filled even if P claims as the sender of D.) *IsOwner* is P's claim on the ownership of D, where the value can be either owner or sender. *Pre.P* denotes the set of previous publisher(s) of D, which represents from whom P received the datasets that have relationship with D. As aforementioned, D may be derived from more than one dataset so there could be more than one publisher inside *Pre.P* and each previous publisher will be represented by the hash value of their own blocks. If P claims as the sender of D, then *Pre.P* must be filled. Otherwise, if P claims as the owner of D, it can be left empty. R represents the set of receivers who will receive D. *TOS* represents the Terms-of-Service that is defined by the original owner of the data, which describes the rules all users need to follow regarding this data. There can be many different and complex TOS examples. Here in ProvNet, we use a simple black list as an implementation of TOS to define who should not gain access to

---

Algorithm 1. Pseudocode for $ShrReq$ Validation

Require: $\{Commitment(D), IsOwner, Pre.P, R, TOS\}$

  if $IsOwner = sender$ **then**

    verifiers refer to the claimed $Pre.P$'s receiver list $(R_{Pre.P})$ and TOS $(TOS_{Pre.P})$

    if $P \in R_{Pre.P}$, $R \not\subset TOS_{Pre.P}$ and $TOS = \bigcup TOS_{Pre.P}$ **then**

      verifiers **return** an *approval* of the $ShrReq$

    else

      verifiers **reject** the $ShrReq$

    end if

  else if $IsOwner = owner$ **then**

    verifiers validate the $Commitment(D)$ using ϕ

    if ϕ returns *true* **then**

      verifiers **return** an *approval* of the $ShrReq$

    else

      verifiers **reject** the $ShrReq$

    end if

  else

    verifiers **reject** the $ShrReq$

  end if

---

the data. For simplicity, we assume the TOS is an *append-only* structure. In case D is derived from multiple datasets, the TOS must be the **union** of all the previous black lists, which has been defined at the beginning of Sect. 3.

As shown in Algorithm 1, upon receiving the sharing request from P, the verifiers will verify the request in two ways based on P's claim on the ownership.

If P claims as the sender of D, the verifiers will verify the $ShrReq$ in the following aspects: (1) check the receiver lists of all the previous publishers (denoted as $R_{Pre.P}$) and see whether P belongs to them, (2) check the all the TOS of the previous publishers (denoted as $TOS_{Pre.P}$) and make sure that P's receiver list R is not a subset of any of them, and (3) check that P's TOS is the union set of all the $TOS_{Pre.P}$. The reason for these check processes has been mentioned and explained in Sect. 3.2. Verifiers will approve P's $ShrReq$ if all these three aspects are checked without any fault. Otherwise, verifiers will reject this $ShrReq$ and therefore we can realize the **TOS-enforced Data Sharing** in ProvNet.

If P claims as the owner of D, then the verifiers will verify $Commitment(D)$ using the validation function ϕ. As is explained in Sect. 3.2, there can be different ϕ based on different scenarios when verifying whether P is the real owner of D or not. Here we use the similarity between two datasets to help make such decision. There are many methods to measure the similarity between two sets, one of which is the *Jaccard Index* (JI). The JI between two sets A and B can be calculated using the following equations: $J(A, B) = \frac{|A \cap B|}{|A \cup B|}$. In case two sets have a very large difference in their size (e.g., A is a subset of B), the JI between two sets will be very small but A should actually be considered relevant/similar to B. Therefore, we further use the following equation to measure the similarity between them: $S(A, B) = J(A, B) \cdot \frac{max(A,B)}{min(A,B)}$. It is obvious that A will be considered different from B when the result is 0 while both sets are the same when the result is 1. Other results will be considered as the similarity between two sets, namely the closer to 1 the more similar two sets are. To efficiently estimate the similarity between two datasets, we can use their MinHash values [4, 7] instead of comparing the original datasets. For each dataset, one way to calculate its MinHash values can be described as follows: (1) dividing the dataset into multiple subsets, (2) calculating the hash value of each subset using some hash functions, (3) choosing the smallest hash values among all the hash values calculated by the same hash functions as one MinHash value, (4) selecting another hash function (e.g., the same hash function with different seeds) and repeating step 2 and 3 for multiple times. After finishing these steps, a set of MinHash values will be generated and we can use the following equation to estimate the similarity between two datasets A and B: $Pr[h_{min}(A) = h_{min}(B)] = S(A, B)$, where $h_{min}(A)$ denotes the all the MinHash values that belong to A. We choose MinHash values in our scenario because users may not want to make their datasets public to the whole system, and more importantly, the size of datasets can be too large to perform efficient comparison on two datasets. Therefore, generating MinHash values for validation purpose is suitable in ProvNet. Similar choice can be seen in other work [12] and there are other ways to calculate the MinHash values [7, 15, 32]. Specifically, in ProvNet, we use SHA-256 as the exact hash function and for each file and according to some existing works that using similar MinHash method [6, 33], we calculate 200 MinHash values for each file. The extra calculation time of MinHash values of a 5 Mb file is less than 20 s on a Intel Core i5 CPU with 16 GB memory. Note that this can be easily accelerated if parallel computing is used as in existing works [12, 13].

With the example of ϕ's implementation in ProvNet, we can describe how do verifiers in ProvNet validate the ownership of datasets as follows. P claims as the owner of D and is required to generate the MinHash values of D (as the $Commitment(D)$). After receiving the $ShrReq$ from P, the verifiers will estimate the JI by comparing the MinHash values with all the MinHash values of published datasets that have been stored in the blocknet. If the JI exceeds some pre-defined threshold, then the verifiers will consider D is similar to some existing dataset and will reject the $ShrReq$ due to its wrong ownership declaration. Otherwise $ShrReq$ will be considered as valid and accepted. The exact threshold settings are left to the exact users.

By leveraging the validation function ϕ, we can also realize **Ownership-protected Data Sharing** in ProvNet. Therefore, any misbehaviors that corrupt the ownership or the TOS inside ProvNet can be detected with this *TOS-enforced and Ownership-protected Data Sharing* function/protocol.

After getting the approval of the $ShrReq$, P can share D with the claimed receivers. Receivers will broadcast their acknowledgements of receiving D from P to the verifiers as $Acks$, the commitment (e.g., MinHash values in our case) of the received dataset and the receiver's id. The verifiers will collect all the $Acks$ that represent the receipts from P. Since P has claimed all the receivers in the $ShrReq$ and share the dataset with them, verifiers will accept it if and only if all

Table 1. Block Contents

Term	Contents
Commitment(D)	MinHash values of D
IsOwner	O (owner) or S (sender)
Pre.P	All the previous blocks' hash values
R	Receivers' ids
TOS	The union of all the previous black lists
Acks	MinHash values of received dataset, ids and signatures

the claimed receivers have broadcast their *Acks* of D. Verifiers will not only need the correct number of *Acks*, namely they need to receive one *Ack* from each one in R, but also verify the correctness of all received *Acks*. To verify the correctness of the *Acks*, verifiers will have two steps, (1) comparing the *Commitment(D)*s that generated by both P and R are the same or not and (2) validating the receivers' signatures. The validation of signature is straightforward since it can prevent attackers from forging fake signatures. The comparison of the *Commitment(D)*s generated by P and R is a necessary step to address the sharing inconsistency mentioned in Sect. 3.3. This is because a block will not be added until verifiers have received and verified all the relevant *Acks*. If the *Acks* are not correct or received within some time, which means there is a dispute between the publisher and receivers, this block will not be accepted and such dispute will be detected. The solution to this dispute can be found in previous works [8] and will not be discussed in our paper. Upon verifying both the *ShrReq* and all the *Acks*, the verifiers will store them in a block-like structure as the items shown in Table 1.

4.2 Bi-directional Blocknet Construction

After capturing the data sharing records by checking the data sharing requests, verifiers will store such records in a novel data structure based on the blockchain – *blocknet*. Blocknet is designed by combining the blockchain structure and the idea of directed graphs, where it allows each block to have multiple predecessors and multiple successors. In other words, each block has multiple hash values of multiple predecessor/successor blocks. We use such a network of blocks on top of the hash chaining to store the provenance records because (1) the records are then tamper-proof and (2) the directed graph structure reveals the relationship of data flow among different users, which directly shows the provenance of data. This is a natural extension on the blockchain because one user may receive data from multiple other users, and one user may share data with multiple other users too. Note that this idea is similar to the that of *Merkle DAG* proposed in LineageChain [28] and Tangle of IOTA [24] but different from them. LineageChain stores each state as a node in their Merkle DAG to keep the provenance record and each transaction in the Tangle of IOTA can (directly) refer at most two previous transactions. Each block in ProvNet denotes a sharing of a dataset and connections among blocks reveal the dependencies among data.

Furthermore, our blocknet is bi-directional where a block will store both its predecessor and successors' hash values. Such attribute of bi-directional is specifically designed for those cases where both the predecessors and the successors of some block are needed. When a new block is generated, its predecessors already exist but its successors are not decided yet. Therefore, blocks in our blocknet are divided into two parts, the determined part, which is determined and does not change at the time of block creation, and the undetermined part, which is not determined at the time of block creation and will change in the future. An example is shown in Fig. 3. The determined part stores those entries included in *ShrReq* and the *Ack*s from the receivers while the undetermined part is saved for storing successors' hash values. The idea of traversing to future blocks from the past ones can also be seen in LineageChain [28] and the Tangle of IOTA [24].

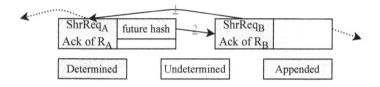

Fig. 3. Block structure of ProvNet.

As is shown in Fig. 3, sender B would like to share data D_1 to receiver C. D_1 was derived from D_0, which was received from B's predecessor A. When verifiers find that B is a receiver of A by checking A's block and C does not belong to the black list defined by A's TOS, then B's request will be approved and her/his block will also be added into the whole blocknet after C has sent her/his *Ack* of receiving D_1. To add B's block, two "arrows" (or pointers) will be added:

Previous hash is the same as the that of most common blockchains, such as storing the previous block's hash value in the block header. The *preivous hash* is stored in the *Pre.P* entry of B's block and points to the determined part of the A's block (Fig. 3), which has been described in Sect. 4.1.

Future hash is a new structure of our blocknet, which is an append-only entry stored on the undetermined part of A's block. After B's determined part is stored in the blocknet, the hash value of B's determined part will be decided and used to update A's *future hash* entry. Both B and its receiver will sign on the appended future hash using their private keys and others can verify the signature using their public keys provided by the CA in Fabric network. Note that the consensus of updating previous blocks can also be ensured by BFT and the signatures can protect the tamper-proofness of the future hash entry.

When it comes to multiple publishers and receivers, the provenance records among different data sharing will form a networked structure. Each block contains the information shown in Fig. 3, and we still use the publisher of the corresponding dataset to denote the block. In the example in Fig. 4, the dataset that

$R_{1,2}$ shares depends on three previous datasets shared by S_2, $S_{2'}$, and $S_{2''}$ while S_2 shares her/his dataset to four receivers $R_{2,1}$, $R_{2,2}$, $R_{2,3}$, and $R_{2,4}$. With such structure applied, we can construct our *Bi-directional Blocknet* and the exact update process of our blocknet can follow Hyperledger Fabric's workflow [1].

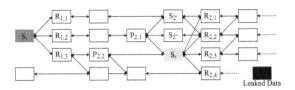

Fig. 4. An example of blocknet.

4.3   Backward and Forward Tracking for Accountability

After the construction of our bi-directional blocknet for provenance record storage, ProvNet can provide both backward and forward tracking to address the data leakage. In most common blockchain-based structures, it is easy to provide the function of backward tracking since each block will always include its previous block's hash value. (Note that here we consider the hash value of a block as a pointer that can be directed to the block itself.) However, it is not easy to keep another pointer which can be directed to its successor's block. The reason for this difficulty is trivial and the analysis has been presented in the previous section. Besides, in some cases, a backward tracking may not be sufficient enough to fulfill the requirements of tracking. For instance, a user would like to know who will refer to her/his data within the next three hops so that s/he can know the data's flow in the sharing platform. In other cases, if a published dataset is found containing wrong information sometime after its sharing, the system should be able to provide a list of nodes who may be affected by the fake data. The function of tracking the forward dependencies is necessary in such scenarios.

Here we show another example where our blocknet can be used to find out suspicious users when a data leakage happens. As is shown in Fig. 4, suppose the black block is a dataset which is found leaked outside of ProvNet and we want to find out the potential suspect in the platform. The verifiers will firstly calculate the MinHash values of the leaked dataset and then estimate its similarities with all the other datasets by using the MinHash values stored in the blocknet. For simplicity, we use the grayscale to demonstrate the similarity, namely the darker a block is, the more similar it is to the leaked dataset. For instance in Fig. 4, S_1 and S_2 are two senders whose datasets are very similar to the leaked one where S_1 is considered more similar since it is darker. In a straightforward approach, we can directly choose the most similar one, S_1, and perform a BFS(Breadth-First-Search) on both its predecessors and successors. However, this will cause a huge overhead since the whole blocknet may be traversed in the worst case.

To mitigate this, we can limit the number of hops during our search (e.g., up to k-hop predecessors/successors). This strategy reduces the overhead but also leads to incomplete search. Therefore, we further let verifiers choose the top-m similar blocks and perform k-hop BFS on each of their predecessors and successors. By doing so, the most relevant blocks (with both dependencies and similarities considered) are examined and their corresponding users will be added to a suspect list. Then, the verifiers report the suspect list to official institutions (e.g., law enforcement) for further investigation. Note that ProvNet does not find out who is the malicious user. Instead, we detect the occurrence of misbehavior and provide a list of suspicious users, which narrows down the search space.

5 Analysis of Completeness and Correctness

Lemma 1. *All ownership corruption will be detected if all claimed ownership is genuine.*

This lemma is straightforward since we explained in Sect. 3.3 that with all the previous ownership claimed properly, there will be no chance for a fake owner to be accepted in ProvNet.

Lemma 2. *Assume that* ProvNet *is given a validation function ϕ which always returns correct validation results on whether a given data sharing request is legitimate or not and* ProvNet *always queries the validation results to the function for a submitted dataset D. For each publisher P,* ProvNet *can guarantee that no one can claim as the owner if D is derivative, and that no one can successfully claim that a dataset D is derived from D' if it is not the receiver of D' in fact.*

Proof. The Lemma can be proved by induction. In a set of datasets $\mathbb{D}_1 = \{D_1\}$, D_1 must have been shared by the first publisher and s/he must be the owner of D_1 (since s/he is the first one who shared data). Then in the inductive step for a set $\mathbb{D}_k = \{D_1, D_2, ..., D_k\}$, we will have two cases where (1) if some publisher P claims as the owner of a new dataset D_{k+1}, or (2) P claims as the sender of a new dataset D_{k+1}. In the former case, the verifiers can leverage ϕ to verify whether D_{k+1} is acceptable or not. Since we assume ϕ can always return the correct validation results, D_{k+1} will be accepted by the verifiers if P is the real owner or rejected otherwise. For the latter case, since the set of $\mathbb{D}_k$ is well-stored and P has declared that D_{k+1} is derived from D', the verifiers can verify whether D is acceptable by checking the record of D's receiver. In conclusion, it is impossible that $\mathbb{D}_k$ increases to $\mathbb{D}_{k+1}$ if P wrongly claims as the owner/sender of D_{k+1}.

Theorem 1. *With the same assumption in Lemma 2, if* ProvNet *examines every sharing and every retrieval, all misbehavior is detected and the provenance records are correct.*

Theorem 1 has similar proof steps to Lemma 2 where proof by induction can be used. Note that up to this point, all the theoretic conclusions are drawn based on the perfect application of the validation function ϕ. However, in the real-world scenarios, it is possible that the function may have some error. Therefore, we have the following theorem.

Theorem 2. *The proposed design of* ProvNet *guarantees ε_0-completeness, where $\varepsilon_0 = err_\phi$ and err_ϕ, refers to the errors incurred by the validation function ϕ.*

Proof. The theorem can be easily shown by an induction starting from an empty blocknet. Lemma 2 conjunction with Lemma 1 show that all the fake ownership claims and fake re-share requests will be rejected by using the validation function ϕ or referring to all the predecessors. Therefore, the proposed ProvNet can detect all types of misbehaviors during the data sharing process. Inductively, in the blocknet, if a new node is added, its corresponding publisher P must either be a valid owner or sender; if an edge is added, it must be a valid retrieval from the platform. Therefore, at any time, only the valid data sharing are allowed, and all the provenance records must reflect the ground truth.

Unfortunately, it is not possible to give upper bounds for δ_1, δ_2 as we do in the completeness. δ_1, δ_2 will be both 1 as long as $\varepsilon > 0$ no matter how small it is, because then the probability that validation fails at all sharing will be greater than 0, which leads to a worst case where we have (1,1)-correctness (e.g., every node and edge in the blocknet is wrong). However, this is an extremely rare case and it is unlikely that δ_1, δ_2 will be high in reality. Thus, we estimate the values of δ_1, δ_2 via large-scale simulations, which appears to be negligible as well.

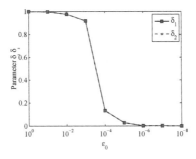

Fig. 5. δ_1 and δ_2 of ProvNet with simulated attackers

As aforementioned in Sect. 3.4, it is theoretically impossible to give a small upper bound for δ_1 and δ_2. Therefore, we simulated malicious entities' misbehavior using real-world social networks describing message exchanges [16]. Such graphs are highly cyclic, but since the provenance records in ProvNet are stored in a blocknet which has a strict time order between each two connected nodes, we first turned the blocknet to forests with BFS so that the structure fits better as a propagation way. Then, for each tree in the forests, we consider the network as the ground truth of a propagation graph $\mathbb{G}^*$. Since ProvNet has an upper bound of the error rate in the corruption detection ε_0, we let each entity in the network successfully become malicious with certain probability $p \leq \varepsilon_0$. Once an entity e_{mal} becomes malicious, all entities that are reached by e_{mal} as well as e_{mal} himself are marked as *undetected entities* since e_{mal} successfully moved to another blocknet $\mathbb{G}'$. Due to the same reason, all edges from undetected entities are also marked as *undetected edges*. This will give an upper bound of the disparity between constructed blocknet and the ground truth, because some entities that reachable from e_{mal} is also reached from another honest entity, and they may or may not further relay the data in $\mathbb{G}'$, but we moved them to $\mathbb{G}'$. Then, at the end, we can use the number of undetected entities $|\mathbb{V}_{inv}|$ and edges $|\mathbb{E}_{inv}|$ to calculate δ_1 and δ_2. Note that δ_1 and δ_2 are equal as they are used to describe the probability of wrongly detecting the vertices and the edges. We repeated the simulation for 100 times, where the average number of nodes in each tree is 81,306, and present the resulting δ_1, δ_2 with different ε in Fig. 5. The results show that δ_1 and δ_2 converge to 0 quickly when $\varepsilon_0 < 10^{-4}$.

6   Conclusion

In this paper, we present ProvNet, a decentralized data sharing platform which can provide secure and correct provenance records stored on a bi-directional networked blockchain. By choosing the appropriate validation function ϕ and enforcing the TOS, users in ProvNet can share data in a regulated manner. We also analysed that the correctness of the stored provenance records can be bounded by the choice of ϕ. Besides, the newly-proposed blocknet can also be used in forensic scenarios where useful evidence can be provided to account for the breaches occurred during data sharing in decentralized environments.

References

1. Open source blockchain technologies. https://www.hyperledger.org/
2. Abeyratne, S.A., Monfared, R.P.: Blockchain ready manufacturing supply chain using distributed ledger (2016)
3. Azaria, A., Ekblaw, A., Vieira, T., Lippman, A.: MedRec: using blockchain for medical data access and permission management. In: OBD, pp. 25–30. IEEE (2016)
4. Broder, A.Z.: On the resemblance and containment of documents. In: SEQUENCES, pp. 21–29. IEEE (1997)
5. Buneman, P., Khanna, S., Tan, W.-C.: Data provenance: some basic issues. In: Kapoor, S., Prasad, S. (eds.) FSTTCS 2000. LNCS, vol. 1974, pp. 87–93. Springer, Heidelberg (2000). https://doi.org/10.1007/3-540-44450-5_6
6. Cohen, E., et al.: Finding interesting associations without support pruning. IEEE Trans. Knowl. Data Eng. 13(1), 64–78 (2001)
7. Datar, M., Immorlica, N., Indyk, P., Mirrokni, V.S.: Locality-sensitive hashing scheme based on p-stable distributions. In: SoCG, pp. 253–262. ACM (2004)
8. Dziembowski, S., Eckey, L., Faust, S.: FairSwap: how to fairly exchange digital goods. In: CCS, pp. 967–984. ACM (2018)

9. Fan, K., Wang, S., Ren, Y., Li, H., Yang, Y.: MedBlock: efficient and secure medical data sharing via blockchain. J. Med. Syst. **42**(8), 136 (2018). https://doi.org/10.1007/s10916-018-0993-7

10. Hamers, L., et al.: Similarity measures in scientometric research: the Jaccard index versus Salton's cosine formula. Inf. Process. Manag. **25**(3), 315–18 (1989)

11. IBM: Cost of a data breach study. https://ibm.co/39rj6I3

12. Jung, T., et al.: AccountTrade: accountable protocols for big data trading against dishonest consumers. In: IEEE INFOCOM, pp. 1–9. IEEE (2017)

13. Jung, T., et al.: AccountTrade: accountability against dishonest big data buyers and sellers. IEEE Trans. Inf. Forensics Secur. **14**(1), 223–234 (2018)

14. Kang, J., et al.: Blockchain for secure and efficient data sharing in vehicular edge computing and networks. IEEE IoT J. (2018)

15. Kulis, B., Grauman, K.: Kernelized locality-sensitive hashing for scalable image search. In: ICCV, vol. 9, pp. 2130–2137 (2009)

16. Leskovec, J., Krevl, A.: SNAP datasets: Stanford large network dataset collection, June 2014. http://snap.stanford.edu/data

17. Liang, X., Shetty, S., Tosh, D., Kamhoua, C., Kwiat, K., Njilla, L.: ProvChain: a blockchain-based data provenance architecture in cloud environment with enhanced privacy and availability. In: CCGRID, pp. 468–477. IEEE Press (2017)

18. Liang, X., Zhao, J., Shetty, S., Liu, J., Li, D.: Integrating blockchain for data sharing and collaboration in mobile healthcare applications. In: PIMRC, pp. 1–5. IEEE (2017)

19. Muniswamy-Reddy, K.-K., Holland, D.A., Braun, U., Seltzer, M.I.: Provenance-aware storage systems. In: USENIX 2006, pp. 43–56 (2006)

20. Nakamoto, S., et al.: Bitcoin: a peer-to-peer electronic cash system (2008)

21. Neisse, R., Steri, G., Nai-Fovino, I.: A blockchain-based approach for data accountability and provenance tracking. In: ARES, p. 14. ACM (2017)

22. Nyaletey, E., Parizi, R.M., Zhang, Q., Choo, K.-K.R.: BlockIPFS-blockchain-enabled interplanetary file system for forensic and trusted data traceability. In: 2019 IEEE Blockchain, pp. 18–25. IEEE (2019)

23. Ongaro, D., Ousterhout, J.: In search of an understandable consensus algorithm. In: USENIX ATC, vol. 14, pp. 305–319 (2014)

24. Popov, S.: The tangle. cit. on, p. 131 (2016)

25. Potthast, M., Barrón-Cedeño, A., Stein, B., Rosso, P.: Cross-language plagiarism detection. Lang. Resour. Eval. **45**(1), 45–62 (2011)

26. Ramachandran, A., Kantarcioglu, et al.: Using blockchain and smart contracts for secure data provenance management. arXiv preprint arXiv:1709.10000 (2017)

27. Real, R., Vargas, J.M.: The probabilistic basis of Jaccard's index of similarity. Syst. Biol. **45**(3), 380–385 (1996)

28. Ruan, P., Chen, G., Dinh, T.T.A., Lin, Q., Ooi, B.C., Zhang, M.: Fine-grained, secure and efficient data provenance on blockchain systems. Proc. VLDB Endow. **12**(9), 975–988 (2019)

29. Shafagh, H., Burkhalter, L., Hithnawi, A., Duquennoy, S.: Towards blockchain-based auditable storage and sharing of IoT data. In: CCSW, pp. 45–50. ACM (2017)

30. Si, A., Leong, H.V., Lau, R.W.H.: Check: a document plagiarism detection system. In: SAC, vol. 97, pp. 70–77 (1997)

31. Singh, M., Kim, S.: Blockchain based intelligent vehicle data sharing framework. arXiv preprint arXiv:1708.09721 (2017)

32. Slaney, M., Casey, M.: Locality-sensitive hashing for finding nearest neighbors [lecture notes]. IEEE Sig. Process. Mag. **25**(2), 128–131 (2008)

33. Teixeira, C.H.C., Silva, A., Meira, W.: Min-hash fingerprints for graph kernels: a trade-off among accuracy, efficiency, and compression. J. Inf. Data Manag. **3**(3), 227–227 (2012)
34. Van Hoye, L., Maenhaut, P.-J., Wauters, T., Volckaert, B., De Turck, F.: Logging mechanism for cross-organizational collaborations using hyperledger fabric. In: ICBC, pp. 352–359. IEEE (2019)
35. Xia, Q.I., et al.: MeDShare: trust-less medical data sharing among cloud service providers via blockchain. IEEE Access **5**, 14757–14767 (2017)
36. Zhang, O.Q., Ko, R.K.L., Kirchberg, M., Suen, C.H., Jagadpramana, P., Lee, B.S.: How to track your data: rule-based data provenance tracing algorithms. In: TrustCom, pp. 1429–1437. IEEE (2012)
37. Zhou, W., Fei, Q., Narayan, A., Haeberlen, A., Loo, B.T., Sherr, M.: Secure network provenance. In: SOSP, pp. 295–310. ACM (2011)

On the Verification of Smart Contracts: A Systematic Review

Mouhamad Almakhour[1,3], Layth Sliman[2(✉)], Abed Ellatif Samhat[3], and Abdelhamid Mellouk[1]

[1] Paris-Est Creteil University, LISSI-TincNET Research Team,
Créteil and Vitry-sur-Seine, France
mouhamad.almakhour@univ-paris-est.fr, mellouk@u-pec.fr
[2] EFREI Engineering School-Paris, Villejuif, France
layth.sliman@efrei.fr
[3] Faculty of Engineering-CRSI, Lebanese University,
Univ. Campus, Hadath, Lebanon
samhat@ul.edu.lb

Abstract. Ensuring the correctness of smart contracts is of paramount importance to achieve trust and continuity in the Blockchain-based business process execution. Due to the immutable nature of distributed ledger technology on the blockchain, a smart contract should work as intended before using it. Any bugs or errors will become permanent once published and could lead to huge economic losses. To avoid such problems, verification is required to check the correctness and the security of the smart contract. In this paper, we consider the smart contracts and we investigate the verification of the correctness of the Blockchain-based smart contracts using formal verification methods. We provide an overview of the formal verification of smart contracts and we present the used methods, tools and approaches. We show a description of each method as well as its advantages and limitations.

Keywords: Smart contracts · BlockChain · Model checking · Theorem proving · Correctness · Formal verification

1 Introduction

After being introduced by the Satoshi Nakamoto [1], blockchain technology has recently gained a lot of interest from a variety of sectors such as government, finance, industry, health and research. Blockchain can be defined as a continuously growing ledger of transactions, distributed and maintained over a peer-to-peer network [2]. Based on several well-known core technologies, including cryptographic hash functions, cryptographic signatures and distributed consensus, it offers some key functionalities such as data persistence, anonymity, fault-tolerance, auditability, resilience, and execution in a trust-less environment among others. Its applications field goes far beyond cryptocurrency, its initial

© Springer Nature Switzerland AG 2020
Z. Chen et al. (Eds.): ICBC 2020, LNCS 12404, pp. 94–107, 2020.
https://doi.org/10.1007/978-3-030-59638-5_7

purpose. For instance, blockchain can be applied to various asset management use cases (e.g. supply chain management) [3] or data notarization (e.g. record, identity management) [4]. More recently, introduction of smart contract has extended the functionalities of blockchains. A smart contract is a computer program intended to enforce the execution of a deal between two or more parties. In the context of blockchain, a smart contract is a computer program stored in the blockchain and executed by some of its nodes. The correctness and security of the smart contracts are required as smart contract failures may cause millions of dollars of lost funds. Thus, a blockchain application based on smart contracts should be checked and verified to ensure the correctness, security and safety of smart contracts implementations. The smart contract is usually written in a high-level language such as Solidity or Vyper, and then it is compiled down to the Ethereum Virtual Machine (EVM) bytecode that runs on the blockchain. We can consider two aspects of verification of smart contracts, the first is related to the security assurance of smart contracts, the second one focuses in the correctness of smart contracts. The verification can be done on a source code level, bytecode level or both. Research papers that focused on the security issues of smart contracts are out of scope of this paper. The correctness verification is about respecting the specifications that determine how users can interact with the smart contracts and how the smart contracts should behave when used correctly. There are two ways to ensure the correctness of smart contracts, programming correctness and formal verification. In programming correctness we prove that the correct output is produced if the program successfully completes and that the program will always successfully complete. Verifying smart-contract using programming correctness helps in increasing security level and avoiding mistakes. However, formal verification methods [5] are more rigorous and reliable since they are based on formal methods (mathematical methods) [6]. This survey focuses on the formal verification approach, as it becomes a trend recently in the verification of smart contracts. Hence, we will present the used methods, tools and approaches based on formal verification. We show a description of each method as well as its advantages and limitations. The rest of this chapter is organized as follows. In Sect. 2, we give some background about smart contracts and the verification requirements. Then we present the formal verification concept and the verification methods in Sect. 3. In Sect. 4, we summarize the most used platforms and approaches in formal verification for smart contracts today. Finally, Sect. 5 gives a discussion and Sect. 6 concludes the paper.

2   Blockchain and Smart Contracts

2.1   Blockchain Smart Contracts

Blockchain technology allows a distributed computing architecture where the transactions are publicly announced and the participants agree on a single history of these transactions (or ledger) [7]. The transactions are grouped into blocks, given timestamps, and then published. The hash of each block includes the hash of the previous block to form a chain, making published blocks difficult to alter [8]. Blockchain technology is changing the way in which computer systems can regulate the interaction between real-world parties in a variety of ways. The requirements of the participation of trusted central authorities or resource managers were a limitation for the use of smart contracts [7,9]. Blockchain based smart contracts enforced implicitly by certain Blockchain architectures have opened wide opportunities. A smart contract is a computer program represented by its source code. It can implement automatically the content of a separate agreement, expressed in natural language. Smart Contracts are often written using dedicated languages and are then compiled into bytecode and embedded in self-contained and self-enforced virtual machines or containers that can be deployed in any node in the Blockchain. Due to the losses caused by uncorrected smart contracts, the verification of smart contracts is mandatory to avoid the failures and vulnerabilities. In the next section, we present several reasons to show why smart contracts should be verified before the deployment on Blockchain.

2.2 Verification Needs for Smart Contracts

The concept of smart contracts in distributed ledger systems has been considered as a safe way of enforcing agreements between participating parties. However, unlike legal contracts, which talk about the behavior to be conducted and the consequences of behaving differently, the executable code embedded in smart contracts give explicit instructions on how to achieve compliance. Consequently, ensuring correctness of the executable codes is an important, challenging task because incidents may lead to huge financial losses due to bugs, breaches and flaws in smart contracts. For instance, as mentioned in [10], an attacker managed to drain more than 3.6 million Ether by exploiting a flaw in the Distributed Autonomous Organization (DAO) smart contract's source code. In September 2017, the multi-signature wallet Parity was attacked in Ethereum, which had resulted in more than 150,000 Ether (about \$30 million) embezzlement. In April 2018, because of the BEC attack, about \$900 million were stolen. Facing these losses, the verification of smart contracts before the deployment on blockchain has attracted extensive attention. We can identify at least three reasons to apply formal specifications and verifications to smart contracts: First, smart contract vulnerabilities, due to the immutable nature of smart contracts, any bugs or errors will become permanent once published and could lead to huge losses. For this, we need to ensure the safety and security of smart contracts. Vulnerabilities in smart contracts have resulted in several high-profile exploits in the blockchain technology. Second, smart contracts are often low-level implementations of a high-level workflow that comprises a state machine with different actions predicated by suitable access control to determine who has the permission to execute a given action [11]. The lack of knowledge at the programmers for the semantics of programming that reflects the high-level workflows may lead to many misconception issues. As a result, we obtain "unfair contracts", which are syntactically technically correct but do not implement the desired business logic. Therefore, there is a strong need for a high-level specification language to express the intent of the workflow in a smart contract. Third, with regard to correctness, many programming paradigms used to write smart contract are not designed to be used in the context of the blockchain environment [12], resulting in many problems during execution time.

3   Formal Verification of Smart Contracts

Based on the formal methods, the formal verification of smart contracts provides the correctness of smart contracts in a rigorous and reliable mathematical model [5, 6]. In order to perform formal verification, formal specifications could be used. By using mathematical methods, formal verification can attest that the final program behaves exactly as described in its specification. Formal verification is used in the fields where errors can be quite significant as it eliminates human error. The basic steps in formal verification as given in [13]:

- Formally model the system
- Formalize the specification
- Prove that the model satisfies the specification. In the case of smart contracts verification, we can also improve smart contracts security by ensuring the correctness of contracts using formal verification. There are several projects aimed at creating formally specified execution environments (virtual machines) for various networks such as (Implementations in F* [14], Formal Ethereum Virtual Machine semantics in the K Framework [15]). Formal verification uses many approaches, here we will limit our discussion to those which are widely used in smart contract context, mainly Theorem Proving and Model Checking.

Theorem Proving in [16], the system is modeled mathematically, and the desired properties to be proven are specified. Then, the verification is performed. Theorem proving uses well-known axioms and simple inference rules. These are used to derive the new theorems, lemmas as needed for the proof [17]. Theorem proving is a very flexible verification method and it can be applied to different kind of systems as long as they can be expressed mathematically. Theorem proving can be interactive, automated or a hybrid [13]. Interactive theorem proving requires some human input. In contrast, the automated ones performs the theorem proving automatically. Hybrid theorem proving works on verification of the complex parts with interactive theorem proving while the rest parts can be verified with automated theorem proving. For theorem proving, the most expressive logic is higher-order logic (HOL) [18]. Theorem proving suffers from two main limitations: the massive human investment to prove theorems and the need of a deep understanding of the method [17].

Model Checking given a finite-state model of a system and a formal property, model checking is an automated technique that systematically checks whether this property holds for that model [19]. The verification is done with model checking software like NuSMV, SPIN, etc. The model checker checks automatically if each state of the model satisfies the specifications given by the user. In case that there is a property not satisfied, the model checker provides a counterexample that can help us to identify mistakes and to correct bugs. On the other hand, if each state of the model satisfies the specification, the model is formally verified for that specific property. The Fig. 1 shows the procedure of the model checker. We can summarize the procedure of the model checking by the following steps [19]:

i. modeling (system–>model)
ii. Specification (natural language specification–>property in formal logic)
iii. Verification (algorithm to check whether a model satisfies a property).

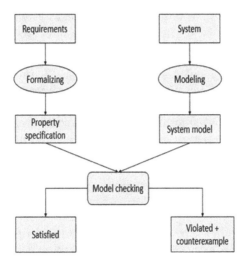

Fig. 1. Procedure of model checker [19]

Formal Verification Advantages and Drawbacks: Most formal verification tools use human-readable (or close to human-readable) languages for specifications. Thus, the results of the audit look like comprehensive documentation more than a security report. We can use mathematical methods to model and rigorously verify the correctness of smart contracts and know if the program behaves as described in the specification. Since verification is automatic, it will be performed efficiently. Formal verification could detect unknown vulnerabilities because the formal verification audit cover the whole program, with no missed cases. As for formal verification weaknesses, it is clear that formal verification detects only inconsistencies between the formal specification and the implementation. This means if there are errors or deficiencies in the specification, many errors or breaches will be left undetected. Consequently, the specifications should be prepared carefully. In addition, formal verification demands a lot of preparation from the development team.

4   Formal Verification Platforms

This section present existing platforms and approaches used for the verification of smart contracts.

4.1   VERISOL (Verifier for Solidity)

VERISOL (Verifier for Solidity) [11] it aims at prototyping a formal verification and analysis system for smart contracts developed using the Solidity programming language. It is based on translating programs written in Solidity language into programs in Boogie intermediate verification language, and then leveraging and extending the verification tool chain for Boogie programs. According to [11], the verifier "VeriSol" is built on the Boogie tool chain, because it can be used for both verification and counter-example generation. VERISOL takes as input a Solidity contract annotated with assertions, and then it yields one of the following three outcomes: fully verified, that means that the assertions in the contract are guaranteed not to fail under any usage scenario. Refuted that indicates at least one input and invocation sequence of the contract functions under which one of the assertions is guaranteed to fail. Partially verified, that is the case when VERISOL can neither verify nor refute contract correctness. It performs bounded verification to establish that the contract is safe up to k transactions. As shown in Fig. 2, VERISOL has three modules, namely (a) Boogie Translation from a Solidity program, (b) Invariant Generation to infer a contract invariant as well as loop invariants and procedure summaries, and (c) Bounded Model Checking. If VERISOL fails to verify contract correctness using monomial predicate abstraction, it employs an assertion directed bounded verifier, namely CORRAL, to look for a transaction sequence leading to an assertion violation [11]. The results of applied smart contracts in VERISOL verifier are relatively good for simple contracts. But according to the table of results in [11], the number of lines of Solidity code increases after the instrumentation (in average 159 versus 79 before the instrumentation). In addition, VERISOL finds bugs in 4 of 11 well-tested contracts and precisely pinpoints the trace leading to the violation, but the researchers did not mention the running time of VERISOL when it applied on original contracts. This leads us to conclude that VERISOL is not suitable for complex contracts.

4.2   F* Translation

In cooperation between Microsoft Research and Harvard University, a framework is done to analyze and formally verify Ethereum smart contracts using F* functional programming language [14,20]. Such contracts are generally written in Solidity [21] and compiled down to the Ethereum Virtual Machine (EVM)

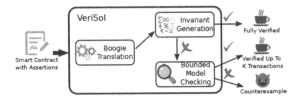

Fig. 2. Schematic workflow of VERISOL [11]

byte-code. In [14] they develop a language-based approach for verifying smart contracts. Two prototype tools based on F* are presented and a smart contract verification architecture is proposed and illustrated in Fig. 3. The contracts are translated into F* programs that call an F* runtime library for all Ethereum operations. The two tools are Solidity* and EVM*. Solidity* is a tool that compiles Solidity contracts into F* [14] in order to verify, at the source level, functional correctness specifications and safety with respect to runtime errors. EVM* is a tool that decompiles EVM bytecode into more succinct F* code hiding the details of the stack machine [14]. It allows to analyze low-level properties. Given a Solidity program and equivalent EVM bytecode, both are translated into F*. Then thier equivalence is verified using relational reasoning [22].

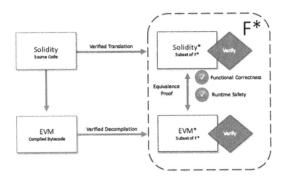

Fig. 3. F* architecture [14]

4.3   Model Checking for Smart Contracts

This work aims at establishing a generic modeling method of Ethereum application to apply a model-checking approach on smart contracts and its execution environment [23]. The proposed model is written in NuSMV input language [24] and the properties to check are formalized into temporal logic CTL (Computation Tree Logics) [25]. It has three components: the kernel layer that captures the (Ethereum) blockchain behavior, the application layer that models the smart contracts themselves (Translation rules from Solidity to NuSMV language have been provided to build the application layer), and the environment layer that determines an execution framework for the application [23]. To check whether the contracts behave as they are supposed to do, expected properties of the application have to be formalized into temporal logic. Properties include safety, fairness, reachability, real-time properties, etc. If a property does not hold, the model-checking provides a counter-example. Thus it is possible to determine the nature and the source of the defect. The method is quite generic and can be applied to various Ethereum applications. According to the case study given in [23], the model checking approach was able to verify four of the five properties. For the unsatisfied property, a counter-example was provided by the model checker.

4.4   Formal Verification of Smart Contracts Based on Users and Blockchain Behaviors Models

In [26], the authors present a new approach to model smart contract and blockchain protocol execution along with users' behaviors based on a formal model checking language. This new approach was applied to a user registry smart contract, which was then formally verified by using model checking on the contract itself by and considering the user-behavior (if it is a hacker or not). In [26], they analyzed the safety of the registry smart contract execution by introducing a hacker behavior model. The hackers purpose is to steal the identity of a user by registering with his account. Three scenarios are evaluated in order to determine the probability of the hacker to successfully register the name. In Scenario 1, the hacker finds the name after the registration of the user from the mined blocks. In Scenario 2, the hacker retrieves the name from the pending transactions data which has not been mined yet. In Scenario 3, that is the easiest, the hacker gets the name directly from the user call to the contract. Using the model checker in Behaviour Interaction Priorities (BIP) [27] and the Statistical Model Checking (SMC) to verify the probabilities, the following results were obtained: In scenario 1 the hacker has 0% success probability. In scenario 2 and 3, the hacker has an average of 12% and 25% respectively to hack the register.

4.5   ZEUS Framework

ZEUS [12] is a framework for automatic formal verification of smart contracts built by IBM India Research to verify the correctness and validate the fairness of smart contracts. ZEUS uses abstract interpretation and symbolic model checking. It is a tool-chain for smart contract verification that consists of (a) policy builder, (b) source code translator, and (c) verifier [12]. ZEUS takes as input the smart contracts written in high-level languages and leverages user assistance to help generate the correctness and/or fairness criteria in an eXtensible Access Control Markup Language (XACML) styled template [28]. It translates these contracts and the policy specification into a low-level intermediate representation (IR) by Low-Level Virtual Machine (LLVM) bitcode [29] encoding the execution semantics to correctly reason about the contract behavior. It then performs static analysis atop the IR to determine the points at which the verification predicates (as specified in the policy) must be asserted. Finally, ZEUS feeds the modified IR to a verification engine that leverages Constrained Horn Clauses (CHCs) [30,31]. CHCs provide a suitable mechanism to represent verification conditions, which can be discharged efficiently by SMT solvers (Satisfiability Modulo Theories) and quickly ascertain the safety of the smart contract.

4.6   ContractLARVA

In [32] a new concept in formal verification of smart contracts is applied by using the runtime verification tool "LARVA" [33,34]. The authors propose "ContractLARVA" to ensure that all execution paths followed at runtime satisfy the required specification [32]. In this approach, different ways to react to violations are supported. An approach based on a stake-placing strategy is also supported. In such approach, any party that can potentially violate the contract pays in a stake before running the contract, which will be given to aggrieved parties in case of a violation, but returned to the original owner if the contract terminates without violations [32]. These are automatically transformed into a safe contract which behaves just like the original one but, in addition, can identify when the specification is violated and trigger remedial behavior. All is done in a decentralized manner. This work used the subset of the DATE (Dynamic Automata with Timers and Events) without timers. The work does not show any practical application of "ContractLARVA" and all depends on the consent of the parties on the stake-placing strategy.

4.7   Formal Verification of Smart Contracts with the K-Framework

In [35], a smart contract formal verification method based on K-Framework is proposed. K-Framework is one of the most robust and powerful language definition frameworks. It allows defining the programming language and providing a set of tools for that language, including both an executable model and a program verifier. This framework provides a user-friendly, modular, and mathematically rigorous meta-language for defining programming languages, type systems, and analysis tools. Additionally, the K-Framework enables verification of smart contracts. The K-Framework is composed of 8 components listed in Fig. 4. To prove that a program always does what it should, the contract's specification is required. However, creating a formal specification through a manual process requires considerable expertise. According to [35], runtime verification of bytecode is better than this of solidity as bytecode language can be used for any high-level contract language. They applied contract specification to refine (for bytecode) manually, and then came the role of the virtual semantic machine to know what each bytecode does and the bit-level data structure it works on.

All of this is used as input to an automated theorem prover "K verification framework" with human help by adding the Hint component, and verified contract. Two messages from the prover are possible: "I created the proof that the contract is right" or "The contract is wrong."

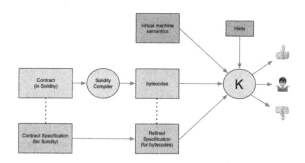

Fig. 4. Workflow of K-framework [35]

4.8 Towards Formal Verification in Isabelle/HOL

In [36], the authors used the theorem prover Isabelle/HOL and an existing EVM-formal model to verify the bytecode of smart contracts. The goal was to create a sound program logic and to use the resulting program logic for verification. This is done by splitting the contracts into basic blocks of different types. To achieve the split, they decompiled the bytecode in order to extract Control Flow Graphs (CFG). In this case, basic blocks, which consist of code sequences that are not interrupted by jumps, are the vertices of the graph. They are connected by edges, which represent the jumps [36]. In this way, each basic block is a sequential piece of code, where the first instruction is executed first, and it continues uninterrupted until the last instruction of the basic block is finished. The basic blocks are further divided into different types, depending on the last instruction of the block. The types are Terminal, Jump, Jumpi, and Next [36]. When the basic blocks are obtained, the program logic is created using Hoare logic, which has Hoare triple designed for program correctness. As a result, a framework was created for expressing the EVM bytecode using logic, which is necessary in order to use a theorem prover for verification. The entire verification procedure was successfully applied to a case study. However, the framework does not support the full syntax of Solidity. For instance, loops and the message calls to other contracts are currently not supported.

4.9 FSPVM-E

Using Hoare logic in Coq [37], which is one of the best higher-order logic theorem proving assistants, based on the Calculus of inductive construction (Cic) that supports Curry-Howard Isomorphism (CHI), the work presented in [38] provided a novel formal symbolic process virtual machine (FSPVM), called FSPVM-E [38]. FSPVM-E is used to verify the reliability, security and functional correctness properties of smart contracts. First, the authors present EVI execution-verification isomorphism, an extension of CHI that combines the advantages of model checking and theorem proving technology. EVI is the basic theory for combining Higher-Order Logic Systems (HOLS) and Symbolic Execution Technology to solve the problems in higher-order logic theorem proving. Second, FSPVM takes EVI as the fundamental theoretical framework to develop an FSPVM for Ethereum (FSPVM-E). The FSPVM-E has three main parts [38]:

- GERM: a formal memory framework that supports different formal verification specifications at the code level,
- Lolisa: an extensible formal intermediate programming language and,
- FEther: a formally verified interpreter for Lolisa. These parts work conjointly: GERM simulates the physical memory hardware structure, Lolisa is a large subset of the Solidity programming language mechanized in Coq, and finally, FEther the virtual execution engine to symbolically execute and verify the formal version of smart contracts in FSPVM-E.

5 Discussion

After investigating a set of tools related to the formal verification of the smart contracts, we summarize the different characteristics in Table 1 and then, we draw some conclusions. For F* [14], the preliminary results and the suggested approach show that it cannot handle all the Solidity syntaxes. The design of Zeus [12] is similar to VERISOL [11] in that it translates Solidity to an intermediate language and uses SMT based solvers to discharge the verification problem. As summarized in Table 1, five investigated tools are static, which means they examine the source code or bytecode of a contract without executing it. VERISOL [11] and F* [14] are the only tool that can analyze the smart contracts at solidity or bytecode level. Although the main goal of formal verification is verifying the correctness of smart contracts, some tools can also detect security issues like Zeus [12], VERISOL [11], F* [14] and K-EVM [35]. Most tools succeeded in some use-cases and their source codes have been published on Github except in [23] and [12]. As shown in Table 1, only two studied tools are based on user behavior verification. To this day, the verification is successfully done for simple smart contract and the proposed approaches do not address complex smart contracts, such as those that contain external calls or loops.

Table 1. Summary of all tools based on: type, level, code transformation and verification methods.

Tools	Verification methods	Type	Level	Behavior based	SC properties based	Code transformation
[14]	Theorem proving	Static analysis	Solidity code & Bytecode	✗	✓	F* Translation
[11]	Model checking	Static analysis	Solidity & bytecode	✗	✓	Boogie Tool-chain
[36]	Theorem proving	Static analysis	Bytecode	✗	✓	Control flow graph
[12]	Abstract interpretation & Model checking	Static analysis	Solidity code	✗	✓	AST analysis
[35]	Theorem proving	Static analysis	Bytecode	✓	✓	K langauge
[23]	Model checking	Dynamic analysis	Bytecode	✗	✓	Not applicable
[26]	Model checking	Dynamic analysis	Solidity code	✓	✗	Not applicable
[32]	Code instrumentation	Dynamic analysis	Solidity code	✓	✓	Not applicable
[38]	Theorem proving	Dynamic analysis	Solidity code	✗	✓	Not applicable

6 Conclusion

In this paper, we show an overview of the smart contracts verification methods. Due to the immutable nature of distributed ledger technology on the blockchain, a smart contract should work as intended before using it. Any bugs or errors will become permanent once published and could lead to huge economic losses. Thus, ensuring the security of smart contracts is of paramount importance to achieve trust and continuity in the Blockchain-based business process execution. To avoid such problems, verification is required to check the smart contract. The verification of smart contracts relies on two major aspects: Security assurance and Correctness of smart contracts. We focus on the verification frameworks related to the correctness of smart contracts, especially to the correctness based on Formal Verification. Some methods can ensure both, the security and correctness like Zeus and VERISOL by using the translation of code and model checking. Based on the investigated methods, one can conclude that they verify only the simple smart contracts and not the complex ones. The loops and the mutually recursive functions between two contracts are still considered as issues in verification. This motivates the need to elaborate more work on formal verification of smart contracts.

References

1. Nakamoto, S.: Bitcoin: a peer-to-peer electronic cash system, December 2008. Accessed 01 July 2015
2. Zheng, Z., Xie, S., Dai, H., Chen, X., Wang, H.: Blockchain challenges and opportunities: a survey. IJWGS **14**(4), 352–375 (2018)
3. Saberi, S., Kouhizadeh, M., Sarkis, J., Shen, L.: Blockchain technology and its relationships to sustainable supply chain management. Int. J. Prod. Res. **57**, 2117–2135 (2019)

4. Hardjono, T., Pentland, A.: Verifiable anonymous identities and access control in permissioned blockchains. CoRR abs/1903.04584 (2019)
5. Drechsler, R.: Formal System Verification. Springer, Cham (2018). https://doi.org/10.1007/978-3-319-57685-5
6. Peled, D.A.: Formal methods. In: Handbook of Software Engineering, pp. 193–222 (2019)
7. Bashir, I.: Mastering blockchain: distributed ledger technology, decentralization, and smart contracts explained. Packt Publishing Ltd. (2018)
8. Gatteschi, V., Lamberti, F., Demartini, C., Pranteda, C., Santamaria, V.: To blockchain or not to blockchain: that is the question. IT Prof. **20**(2), 62–74 (2018)
9. Almakhour, M., Sliman, L., Samhat, A.E., Gaaloul, W.: Trustless blockchain-based access control in dynamic collaboration. In: Proceedings of the 1st International Conference on Big Data and Cyber-Security Intelligence (BDCSIntell 2018), Hadath, Lebanon, 13–15 December 2018, pp. 27–33 (2018)
10. Gelvez, M.: Explaining the DAO exploit for beginners in solidity (2016)
11. Lahiri, S.K., Chen, S., Wang, Y., Dillig, I.: Formal specification and verification of smart contracts for azure blockchain. CoRR abs/1812.08829 (2018)
12. Kalra, S., Goel, S., Dhawan, M., Sharma, S.: ZEUS: analyzing safety of smart contracts. In: 25th Annual Network and Distributed System Security Symposium (NDSS 2018), San Diego, California, USA, 18–21 February 2018 (2018)
13. Rushby, J.: Theorem proving for verification. In: Cassez, F., Jard, C., Rozoy, B., Ryan, M.D. (eds.) MOVEP 2000. LNCS, vol. 2067, pp. 39–57. Springer, Heidelberg (2001). https://doi.org/10.1007/3-540-45510-8_2
14. Bhargavan, K., et al.: Formal verification of smart contracts: short paper. In: Proceedings of the 2016 ACM Workshop on Programming Languages and Analysis for Security, pp. 91–96 (2016)
15. Hildenbrandt, E., et al.: KEVM: a complete formal semantics of the ethereum virtual machine. In: 2018 IEEE 31st Computer Security Foundations Symposium (CSF), pp. 204–217. IEEE (2018)
16. Harrison, J.: Theorem proving for verification (invited tutorial). In: Gupta, A., Malik, S. (eds.) CAV 2008. LNCS, vol. 5123, pp. 11–18. Springer, Heidelberg (2008). https://doi.org/10.1007/978-3-540-70545-1_4
17. Murray, Y., Anisi, D.A.: Survey of formal verification methods for smart contracts on blockchain. In: 10th IFIP International Conference on New Technologies, Mobility and Security (NTMS 2019), Canary Islands, Spain, 24–26 June 2019, pp. 1–6 (2019)
18. Nesi, M.: A brief introduction to higher order logic and the HOL proof assistant (2011)
19. Baier, C., Katoen, J.: Principles of Model Checking. MIT Press (2008)
20. Swamy, N., et al.: Dependent types and multi-monadic effects in F. In: Proceedings of the 43rd Annual ACM SIGPLAN-SIGACT Symposium on Principles of Programming Languages (POPL 2016), St. Petersburg, FL, USA, 20–22 January 2016, pp. 256–270 (2016)
21. http://solidity.readthedocs.io
22. Barthe, G., Fournet, C., Grégoire, B., Strub, P., Swamy, N., Béguelin, S.Z.: Probabilistic relational verification for cryptographic implementations. In: The 41st Annual ACM SIGPLAN-SIGACT Symposium on Principles of Programming Languages (POPL 2014), San Diego, CA, USA, 20–21 January 2014, pp. 193–206 (2014)

23. Nehai, Z., Piriou, P., Daumas, F.F.: Model-checking of smart contracts. In: IEEE International Conference on Internet of Things (iThings) and IEEE Green Computing and Communications (GreenCom) and IEEE Cyber, Physical and Social Computing (CPSCom) and IEEE Smart Data (SmartData), iThings/GreenCom/CPSCom/SmartData 2018, Halifax, NS, Canada, 30 July–3 August 2018, pp. 980–987 (2018)

24. Cavada, R., et al.: The NUXMV symbolic model checker. In: Biere, A., Bloem, R. (eds.) CAV 2014. LNCS, vol. 8559, pp. 334–342. Springer, Cham (2014). https://doi.org/10.1007/978-3-319-08867-9_22

25. Browne, M.C., Clarke, E.M., Grumberg, O.: Characterizing finite Kripke structures in propositional temporal logic. Theor. Comput. Sci. **59**, 115–131 (1988)

26. Abdellatif, T., Brousmiche, K.: Formal verification of smart contracts based on users and blockchain behaviors models. In: 9th IFIP International Conference on New Technologies, Mobility and Security (NTMS 2018), Paris, France, 26–28 February 2018, pp. 1–5 (2018)

27. Basu, A., Bozga, M., Sifakis, J.: Modeling heterogeneous real-time components in BIP. In: Fourth IEEE International Conference on Software Engineering and Formal Methods (SEFM 2006). IEEE, pp. 3–12 (2006)

28. Sinnema, R., Wilde, E.: eXtensible access control markup language (XACML) XML media type. Internet Engineering Task Force (IETF), pp. 1–8 (2013)

29. Lattner, C., Adve, V.: LLVM: a compilation framework for lifelong program analysis & transformation. In: 2004 International Symposium on Code Generation and Optimization (CGO 2004), pp. 75–86. IEEE (2004)

30. Bjørner, N., McMillan, K.L., Rybalchenko, A.: Program verification as satisfiability modulo theories. SMT@ IJCAR **20**, 3–11 (2012)

31. Gurfinkel, A., Kahsai, T., Komuravelli, A., Navas, J.A.: The SeaHorn verification framework. In: Kroening, D., Păsăreanu, C.S. (eds.) CAV 2015. LNCS, vol. 9206, pp. 343–361. Springer, Cham (2015). https://doi.org/10.1007/978-3-319-21690-4_20

32. Ellul, J., Pace, G.J.: Runtime verification of ethereum smart contracts. In: 2018 14th European Dependable Computing Conference (EDCC), pp. 158–163. IEEE (2018)

33. Colombo, C., Pace, G.J., Schneider, G.: LARVA–safer monitoring of real-time java programs (tool paper). In: 2009 Seventh IEEE International Conference on Software Engineering and Formal Methods, pp. 33–37. IEEE (2009)

34. Colombo, C., Pace, G.J.: Runtime verification using LARVA (2017)

35. Sotnichek, M.: Formal verification of smart contracts with the k framework (2018)

36. Amani, S., Bégel, M., Bortin, M., Staples, M.: Towards verifying ethereum smart contract bytecode in Isabelle/HOL. In: Proceedings of the 7th ACM SIGPLAN International Conference on Certified Programs and Proofs, pp. 66–77 (2018)

37. Paulin-Mohring, C.: Introduction to the Coq proof-assistant for practical software verification. In: Meyer, B., Nordio, M. (eds.) LASER 2011. LNCS, vol. 7682, pp. 45–95. Springer, Heidelberg (2012). https://doi.org/10.1007/978-3-642-35746-6_3

38. Yang, Z., Lei, H.: Formal process virtual machine for smart contracts verification. arXiv preprint arXiv:1805.00808 (2018)

Understanding and Handling Blockchain Uncertainties

Xiwei Xu[1,2(✉)], H. M. N. Dilum Bandara[1,2], Qinghua Lu[1,2], Dawen Zhang[1,2], and Liming Zhu[1,2]

[1] Data61, CSIRO, Sydney, Australia
{xiwei.xu,dilum.bandara,qinghua.lu,
dawen.zhang,liming.zhu}@data61.csiro.au
[2] University of New South Wales (UNSW), Sydney, Australia

Keywords: Blockchain · Uncertainty characterisation · Pattern

1 Introduction

Blockchain is an immutable and transparent distributed ledger hosted by a Peer-to-Peer (P2P) network. Blockchain provides immutability, transparency, and data integrity to the applications built on top of it. It also provides a neutral execution infrastructure for running programs, called smart contracts. Blockchain has been integrated into software systems for purposes such as, providing decentralized and trusted data storage [15], enabling decentralized access control [2], or facilitating collaborative business processes [14].

In a large and dynamic distributed network, like blockchain, there are network-level uncertainties like lost messages, state getting out of sync, and timeouts. The design of blockchain instigates additional uncertainties, like probabilistic immutability of a Proof of Work (PoW) [8] blockchain. Moreover, transactions may get discarded due to the limited size of the transaction pool and low transaction fees. Transactions may also get reordered based on the block generation process and transaction fees. Furthermore, the blockchain node(s) that an application interacts has only a partial view of the pending transactions in the P2P network due to gossip-based transaction broadcasting [6]. Such uncertainties need to be understood and correctly handled to build reliable applications/services with desired quality of service properties on top of a blockchain.

The complex internal structure with the unique design, as well as probabilistic finality and high latency to process blockchain transactions, necessitate complex interactions between applications and the blockchain, made either directly or via a gateway. In direct interaction, the application makes API calls to the blockchain using HTTP, WebSockets, or IPC and deals with state management, message ordering, and error handling. Whereas a gateway simplifies the interaction by transparently handling state, ordering, and errors. Moreover, services such as Infura[1] and Ethercluster[2] enhance such interactions through high availability, elasticity, authentication, and data analytics.

---

[1] https://infura.io.
[2] https://www.ethercluster.com.

Z. Chen et al. (Eds.): ICBC 2020, LNCS 12404, pp. 108–124, 2020.
https://doi.org/10.1007/978-3-030-59638-5_8

The interaction with a blockchain is comprised of multiple components and asynchronous messages that are exchanged between those components. Such an interaction involving a set of well-defined roles, message semantics, and protocols in a distributed system is called a *conversation* [4]. In a large and dynamic distributed network, conversation patterns [4] are designed and applied to deal with environmental uncertainties like lost messages, state getting out of sync, and timeouts. In blockchain interactions, conversations may happen at different levels, for example, between application and blockchain, or application and gateway. When a gateway is used to interact with the blockchain indirectly, the gateway abstracts the detailed interactions with blockchain. However, the application still needs to handle uncertainties like probabilistic finality. Therefore, both direct and indirect conversations with blockchain need to tolerate the uncertainties of blockchain.

In this paper, we present uncertain state transitions in the life-cycles of transactions and smart contracts to better understand the uncertainties in blockchains. To further demonstrate the uncertainties, we present empirical data from two of the well-known blockchain platforms, namely, Ethereum and Bitcoin. We then examine a conversation pattern language for enterprise integration [3] and explore the ones that can be applied in blockchain interactions. We further propose two new patterns specific to smart contracts.

For the rest of this paper, the life-cycles of transactions and smart contract with uncertain stat transitions are discussed in Sect. 2. Section 3 presents the empirical evidence of the identified uncertainties. A collection of conversation patterns for blockchain interaction is discussed in Sect. 4. Related work is discussed in Sect. 5 before we conclude the paper in Sect. 6.

2 Blockchain Uncertainties

Transactions are the primary means of interacting with a blockchain. Smart contracts are programs that are deployed and invoked through transactions. In a blockchain with smart contracts, there are three types of transactions, namely, *cryptocurrency transfer*, *contract creation*, and *contract invocation*. A transaction is a data package with information for asset transfer, like sender, receiver, and monetary value. In the context of smart contracts, a contract creation transaction includes the (compiled) code of smart contract(s). A contract invocation transaction includes the smart contract function to call and its parameters.

Uncertainties are introduced due to the unique design of blockchain at different stages of the life-cycle of both transactions and smart contracts. We use Ethereum blockchain as an example, but most of the discussion can be generalised to Bitcoin and other PoW- based blockchain platforms with Nakamoto consensus [8]. Figure 1 illustrates a graphical representation of uncertain state transitions within the transaction and smart contract life-cycles as observed by a blockchain node. All the conversation patterns identified in Sect. 4 are annotated to show the uncertainties they can deal with. The four patterns applicable to gateways are shown separately in a dashed box on the top of Fig. 1.

2.1 Transaction and Smart Contract Life-Cycle

The life-cycle of a transaction starts when it is constructed and signed by the initiator. It is then *submitted* to the blockchain network, either directly or via a gateway. Once arrived at a miner, the miner validates the signed transaction to make sure that it is signed by the claimed account, parameters are correctly set, and the source account has sufficient funds. For example, *nonce* – a sequence number that reflects the order of transactions by an account – acts as a duplicate transaction detection and concurrency control mechanism. If invalid, the transaction is *rejected*. Otherwise, it is marked as *validated*. If the *validated* transaction is already in the transaction pool, it is *rejected*. Otherwise, it is added to the transaction pool as a *pending* transaction. A pending transaction is also *propagated* to other nodes/miners using a gossip protocol. Those miners also validate the transaction before further propagating it to the other miners.

Transactions are not treated equally, as different gas prices associated with transactions incentivise miners to sort the *pending* transactions based on their gas price. Size of the transaction pool is limited, and once reached, miners tend to *drop* transactions with lower gas prices. If a *pending* transaction is resubmitted with a higher gas price but with the same source account and *nonce*, it is added to the transaction pool and the previous transaction is *dropped*. A transaction *dropped* by all miners is *discarded* from the blockchain network.

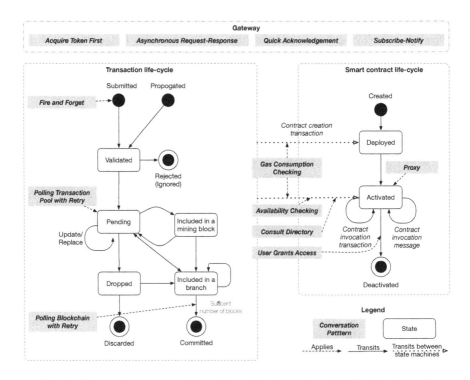

Fig. 1. Uncertain state transitions from the viewpoint of a blockchain node.

When a miner starts to mine a block, it picks a set of transactions from the transaction pool, executes them, and constructs a block ($block_{mining}$). Transactions in $block_{mining}$ are marked as *included in a mining block*. The number of transactions included in $block_{mining}$ is limited by the block gas limit, which is the maximum gas that all the transactions within a block can consume. While mining, if the miner receives a new block ($block_{new}$) from the P2P network, the miner validates it. If $block_{new}$ is valid, the miner then removes the transactions in $block_{new}$ from the transaction pool and mark those transactions as *included in a branch*. If a transaction in $block_{mining}$ is also in $block_{new}$, or if the miner already completed the mining and propagated $block_{mining}$ to the P2P network, state of those transactions is also marked as *included in a branch*. If the miner did not complete mining $block_{mining}$ before the arrival of $block_{new}$, the transactions that are in $block_{mining}$ but not in $block_{new}$ go back to the transaction pool and their state is set to *pending*. Once a transaction is *included in a branch* and when newly built blocks generate a sufficient number of confirmations, it is considered *committed* (i.e., being included into blockchain with very-high probability).

A smart contract is *created* off-chain using a suitable editor. It can then be *deployed* to the blockchain in two ways. First is to send a contract creation transaction with (complied) source code of the smart contract. The other is to send a contract invocation transaction to the factory contract [17] that already embed the code of the smart contract to be deployed. A smart contract can be deployed to a blockchain network more than once. Every deployment is a separate instance with a distinct contract address and data. As soon as a smart contract is *deployed* on the blockchain, it can be invoked using contract invocation transactions from external accounts and messages from other smart contracts as per the set access control rules. A smart contract in operation is considered to be in the *activated* state. However, while in operation, a smart contract may be *deactivated* or replaced by an updated version (an update effectively deactivates the existing contract and deploys the updated contract with its address).

2.2   Uncertainties in Transactions

Miner Rejection. Not every miner accepts and propagates valid transactions. Miners may apply additional and arbitrary rules on valid transactions to maximise their gain. For example, a miner may accept only the transactions above a specific transaction fee to maximise the transaction fee collected during block creation. A miner may also reject a transaction that is too large (in terms of its size in bytes or anticipated gas consumption) or due to rate limiting to overcome potential Denial of Service (DoS) attacks. Parameters such as the minimum transaction fee, maximum transaction size, size of the transaction pool, and rate limit are under the discretion of a miner. Thus, it is uncertain whether a valid transaction is accepted and propagated to the rest of the P2P network.

Transaction Reordering and Dropping. Pending transactions with higher gas prices are more likely to be included in the next block. However, a small number of altruistic miners may process transactions with a low gas price. This introduces another uncertainty on the global order of transactions being processed. *Nonce* in an Ethereum transaction can prevent the reordering of transactions from the same account. The design of UTXO is a similar mechanism in Bitcoin to prevent transaction reordering. However, there is no mechanism at the blockchain infrastructure-level to handle the reordering of transactions from different accounts to the same recipient account [9]. A pending transaction can be overwritten by resubmitting another transaction with the same *nonce*, and typically with a higher gas price. This mechanism provides error recovery for pending transactions where miners may drop the pending transaction in favour of the resubmitted transaction with a higher gas price. However, for this to work, the error needs to be detected while the transaction is *pending* and the transaction needs to be resubmitted without delay. Higher gas price could also increase the likeliness of including the resubmitted transaction in a block. Nevertheless, this mechanism is not guaranteed to work due to network propagation uncertainties and altruistic miners.

While a transaction could be issued into the future by setting a higher *nonce* value than the immediate one, miners add such transactions to a separate queue with limited capacity due to lack of immediate reward and potential for DoS attacks. For example, the default maximum number of non-executable transaction slots for all accounts of an Ethereum Geth node is 1024 transactions. Miners may also drop transactions that remain in the *pending* state for a too long. For example, the default timeout of an Ethereum Geth node's transaction pool is 3-h. Therefore, it is impossible to know with certainty whether all miners have dropped the transaction.

Uncommit. As immutability is probabilistic in Nakamoto consensus-based blockchains, it is uncertain whether a transaction included in a block is also permanently included in the blockchain. If the blockchain forks (i.e., the chain of blocks with the transaction becomes shorter than the longest chain), the block comprising the transaction may simply be discarded. In that case, the transactions in the block (i.e., in *included in a branch* state) go back to the transaction pool and are marked as in the *pending* state such that they can be re-included in a future block.

A commonly used strategy to ensure that a transaction is included in the blockchain with high probability is *x-confirmation* [17], which is to wait for several blocks to be added on top of the block with the transaction. This number is 12 on Ethereum with 14-s block interval and six on Bitcoin with 10-m block interval. This number is the primary factor that affects the latency between the submission of a transaction and confirmation that it has been included on the blockchain. In [13], authors show that the time between the submission of a transaction and its confirmation on Ethereum and Bitcoin could be very high depending on the set transaction fee and *x-confirmation*.

2.3   Uncertainties in Smart Contracts

As smart contracts are deployed and invoked through transactions, they inherit all uncertainties that apply to transactions. Moreover, deployment and invocation of a smart contract also introduce a specific set of uncertainties.

Out of Gas. When invoking a smart contract function, it is uncertain whether the transaction is associated with sufficient gas to execute the function. If the allocated gas limit is insufficient, the transaction fails, and all changes to assets are rolled back. However, a transaction fee is still charged for the computational effort. Hence, the same transaction cannot be resubmitted due to such failures. For example, the same *nonce* cannot be used as the transaction is recorded on the blockchain to claim the transaction fee. The gas required to execute a function can be estimated before submitting a transaction. However, it may still fail at run time, as another transaction may have altered the state of the smart contract between the gas estimation and inclusion of the transaction in $block_{mining}$.

Dead Smart Contract. A smart contract can be deactivated to prevent future invocations, e.g., using the `selfdestruct` function in Ethereum. Any assets held by the smart contract will be locked, if it is deactivated without nominating a recipient for the remaining assets. Also, assets sent to a deactivated smart contract will be locked forever. While it is possible to check whether the smart contract is alive before submitting a transaction, it may still get deactivated between the liveness checking and inclusion of the transaction in $block_{mining}$.

3   Empirical Evidence

We use empirical evidence collected from Bitcoin and Ethereum to demonstrate the impact of the uncertainties discussed in Sect. 2. We used the data from Blockchair[3], which is a blockchain search engine that covers 15 blockchain platforms. We use Blockchair API to pull pending transaction data, as such data are visible to an application/service using a blockchain. For both Ethereum and Bitcoin, we collected pending transactions for 24-h from 28/04/2020 17:30 to 29/04/2020 17:30 UTC. We made an API request every 30-s for each blockchain. To determine whether a transaction got included in a block, we considered blocks generated up to 3-days after the end of the pending transaction collection. A similar analysis was carried out in July 2019, and the observed behaviour was similar to what is presented next. Table 1 presents high-level statistics of the observed pending transactions (TXs). Next, we present a detailed explanation of Table 1.

---

[3] https://blockchair.com/.

3.1 Pending and Excluded Transactions

The number of pending transactions with time is plotted in Fig. 2a. It can be seen that both the transaction pools were busy. The upward trend in Bitcoin continued where the transaction pool increased 80K on the next two days. 0.27% of Ethereum and 0.99% of Bitcoin transactions in blocks generated within the 24-h of data collection did not appear in our collected set of pending transactions. This could be due to reasons such as, a new transaction getting included in $block_{mining}$ within the 30-s gap between our API calls, Blockchair node that collected the data not receiving all the transactions due to gossip-based transaction propagation, and parameters used by the Blockchair node's transaction pool. Nevertheless, we have been able to capture majority of the pending transactions.

Table 1. Pending transaction statistics.

Block inclusion up to	Ethereum			Bitcoin		
	24H	48H	72H	24H	48H	72H
Pending TXs	1,463,252			368,687		
Unique pending TXs	919,748			348,246		
Duplicate TXs	543,504			20,441		
% Duplicate TXs	37.14%			5.54%		
Resubmitted TXs	30,074			NA		
% Resubmitted TXs	3.27%			NA		
Pending TXs in block	874,261	874,999	876,603	335,391	336,645	344,410
Pending TXs not in a block	45,487	44,749	43,145	12,855	11,601	3,836
% Pending TXs not in a block	4.95%	4.87%	4.69%	3.69%	3.33%	1.10%

Although a transaction can be *pending* in the transaction pool as long as the miner keeps it, as shown in Fig. 2b, only 3.15% of the pending transaction in Ethereum spent more than 15-min in the transaction pool. Only 0.33% of the pending transaction spend more than 6-h in the transaction pool. Whereas 38.3% and 0.66% of Bitcoin transactions spend more than 15-min and 6-h in the transaction pool, respectively. Given the 10-min inter-block generation time in Bitcoin, transactions are expected to spend longer in the transaction pool; but, most transactions do not spend hours. However, 4.95% of the pending Ethereum transactions were not included in the blockchain after 24-h from the end of pending transaction collection. It marginally reduced to 4.69% after 72-h. Whereas 3.69% and 1.1% of the pending Bitcoin transactions were not included in the blockchain after 24-h and 72-h, respectively. This indicates that those transactions were dropped much earlier, and either may have reappeared as a different transaction or never appeared again within the data collection window. This behaviour indicates that the transaction inclusion does not improve significantly by waiting longer, as they tend to get dropped eventually from the transaction pool or continued to be overtaken by newly arriving transactions as the transaction pool remains busy.

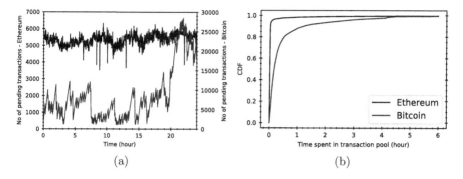

Fig. 2. Pending transactions (a) Number of pending transactions and (b) Time spent in transaction pool.

3.2 Duplicate and Resubmitted Transactions

One impact of blockchain uncertainties is the duplicate transactions where the same transaction (indicated by the same transaction hash) appears again in the transaction pool. A duplicate transaction implies that the transaction fee is not changed. In Ethereum, as shown in Table 1, more than one-third (37.14%) of the pending transactions were duplicate transactions. A busy transaction pool, as indicated in Fig. 2a, might be a reason that leads to a large portion of duplicate transactions. Among all the duplicate transactions, 539,267 were unique ones, and 58.22% of them reappeared after being *dropped* from the transaction pool. Most of the remaining duplicate transactions might come from the $block_{mining}$, where the miner was unable to mine the block before the arrival of $block_{new}$. In Bitcoin, 5.54% of the pending transactions were duplicates. Around half (51.79%) of the duplicate transactions were unique. The significant difference in the fraction of duplicate transactions between Ethereum and Bitcoin could be due to the smart contracts in Ethereum, where the decentralised applications may try to achieve faster transaction inclusion by aggressively resubmitting transactions.

Figure 3a and 3b depict the number of times a duplicate transaction reappears in Ethereum and Bitcoin transaction pools, respectively. This may happen while the previous transaction is pending in the transaction pool or after it gets dropped. For example, 58.2% of the duplicate transactions in Ethereum reappeared after they were dropped from the transaction pool. It can be seen that a small fraction of transactions reappears multiple times, and this behaviour is more prevalent in Bitcoin. Compared with Bitcoin, Ethereum has a more significant portion of duplicate transactions, which imply a more aggressive and automated way of resubmitting transactions. Figure 3a further depicts the number of appearances of resubmitted transactions in the transaction pool. This is when the transaction sender submits another transaction with the same nonce while varying other parameters like the gas price; hence, changing the transaction hash. 30,074 (2.06%) resubmitted transactions were observed during the data collection, and some of them appeared multiple times. This indicates that

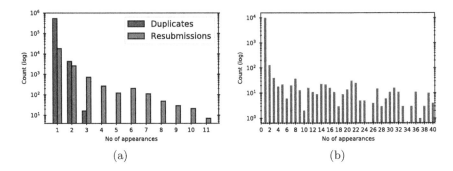

Fig. 3. Appearance of duplicate transactions in (a) Ethereum and (B) Bitcoin.

transaction senders seem to have adjusted the gas price multiple times to get those transactions included in a block. Resubmitted transactions in Bitcoin are not analysed due to the limitation of the collected data.

3.3   Reordered Transactions

Reordered transactions in Ethereum were analysed from the perspective of a smart contract. The transactions sent to three of the popular contracts were filtered, and the reorder density [12] is calculated as a metric to characterise transaction reordering. The three smart contracts were KittyCore[4] contract of CryptoKitties[5], Dice2Win[6,7], and Tether token[8]. Figure 4a to 4c plot the reorder density of the three contracts, respectively. Negative values on the x-axis indicate the transactions being accepted earlier than their arrival order to the transaction pool. Positive values indicate the transactions included later in blocks relative to their arrival order. Both Dice2Win and Cryptokitties are sensitive to transaction order and latency, as the smart contract logic include auction behaviour. Thus, low displacement can be seen on transactions related to both smart contracts. Whereas the displacement of transactions received by the Tether token was much higher, as the cryptocurrency token transfer is not very sensitive to transaction order and latency compared to auction behaviour. However, the lower displacement of transaction order and latency comes at the cost of higher transaction fees, for e.g., average gas price of Dice2Win and KittyCore transactions were 41.5 and 94.5 times higher than the Tether token, respectively.

---

[4] Address: 0x06012c8cf97bead5deae237070f9587f8e7a266d.

[5] https://www.cryptokitties.co/.

[6] https://dice2.win/.

[7] Address: 0xd1ceeeeee83f8bcf3bedad437202b6154e9f5405.

[8] Address: 0xdac17f958d2ee523a2206206994597c13d831ec7.

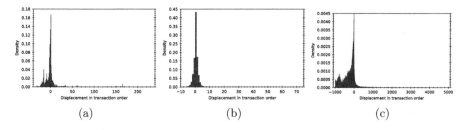

Fig. 4. Reorder density of (a) KittyCore, (b) Dice2Win, and (c) Tether token.

3.4 Failed Transactions

In Ethereum, 2.38% (21,929) of the unique pending transactions failed within 72-h. A significant portion (78.68%) failed due to errors caused during the execution of smart contracts, such as *execution reverted* and *evm:invalid jump destination*. Among all the failed transactions, 14.4% (3,159) failed due to *out of gas*. Such a relatively high fraction of *out of gas* transactions is likely to be caused due to the difficultly in estimating gas limit than carelessness of the transaction sender, as the transaction fee is charged even for a failed transaction.

Table 2 shows evidence of a transaction sequence that is affected by a paused smart contract[9]. It can be seen that though the last four transactions arrive at the transaction pool early, they were late to get into a block. In the meantime, the first transaction got included in a block and paused the smart contract (by setting a Boolean value). Consequently, the other four transactions failed. The first transaction used a gas price that was an order of magnitude higher than the other four transactions, which affected the transaction order.

Table 2. Impact of the paused smart contract.

Arrival timestamp	Arrival order	Block number	Block index	Block timestamp	Order in block	How early (sec)
1570696516	5	8713015	53	1570696512	1	
1570696506	4	8713016	71	1570696522	5	10
1570696491	3	8713016	62	1570696522	2	25
1570696463	2	8713016	70	1570696522	4	53
1570696447	1	8713016	69	1570696522	3	69

4 Conversation Patterns for Handling Blockchain Uncertainties

4.1 Applicability of Conversation Language

Four groups of fundamental conversation patterns [3] follow the life-cycle of setting up to terminating a conversation, namely: *Discovery* – patterns for one party

---

[9] Address: 0xF0155486A14539F784739Be1C02E93F28eB8e960.

to identify the conversation partners before starting interaction; *Start a conversation* – patterns to establish conversations with authentication, handshaking, and negotiating parameters; *Basic conversations* – patterns of actual conversations between two partners with a small number of messages; and *Intermediaries* – patterns of conversations involving a third party. Most of these patterns are in use, and we present examples in the following sub-sections.

The *basic conversation* group is the most applicable to the transaction interactions in blockchain, where the transaction initiator (i.e., application) and the blockchain are the two conversation partners. Although blockchain has complex internal interactions among P2P nodes, an application could treat the blockchain network as a single participant in a conversation. All four groups of patterns can be applied to smart contract interactions, which involve complex conversations among the transaction initiator and with multiple smart contracts (each smart contract could be considered as a participant in the conversation).

4.2 Transaction Conversation Patterns

Fire-and-Forget. The most basic interaction with a blockchain is the *fire-and-forget* pattern, where the transaction initiator starts the conversation by sending a transaction to the blockchain network without requesting any response from the blockchain. This pattern does not handle any blockchain-specific and environmental uncertainties, for e.g., *miner rejection* and *transaction dropping* uncertainties due to relatively low gas prices and the limited size of the transaction pool. Hence, this pattern should be applied only for less critical tasks, e.g., writing a piece of arbitrary data to the blockchain as a log record.

Polling Transaction Pool with Retry. The motivation of this pattern is to deal with *miner rejection* and *transaction reordering and dropping* uncertainties. While adopting this pattern, after submitting a transaction, the transaction initiator periodically sends inquiry messages to the blockchain (i.e., poll) to check whether the transaction is validated by a node and listed as a *pending* transaction in the transaction pool.

When a *pending* transaction is dropped from the transaction pool without advancing into the *included in a branch* state, the transaction is likely dropped due to limited transaction pool size and relatively low gas price. In this case, the transaction initiator needs to resubmit the transaction with the same *nonce*. Moreover, a higher gas price is usually needed to increase the chance to be included in a future block. With every drop, the transaction initiator needs to resubmit with the same nonce and a relatively high gas price until the transaction is eventually included in a block or maximum retry count is reached.

Polling Blockchain with Retry. This pattern deals with *uncommit uncertainty*. While this mechanism also uses polling, the target is the chain of recently produced blocks. The transaction initiator polls the blockchain to ensure that the transaction is included in a block and the desired number of child blocks are generated (i.e., *x-confirmation*). If the block with the transaction is excluded from the main chain before reaching the desired *x-confirmation* and got *dropped*, the transaction initiator needs to resubmit the transaction. Listing 1.1 is an example code snippet from Web3.js[10] that applies this pattern. Line 5 specifies a timer to keep calling *checkConfirmation* function.

```
1 var startWatching = function (existingReceipt) {
2     if (_.isFunction(this.requestManager.provider.on)) {
3         _ethereumCall.subscribe('newBlockHeaders', checkConfirmation.bind(
            null, existingReceipt, false));
4     } else {
5         intervalId = setInterval(checkConfirmation.bind(null,
            existingReceipt, true), 1000);
6     }
7 }.bind(this);
```

Listing 1.1. Polling with retry.

4.3 Smart Contract Conversation Patterns

As transactions are used to deployed smart contracts and invoke their functions, above polling patterns can also be used to overcome *miner rejection, transaction reordering and dropping, uncommit,* and *out of gas* uncertainties in smart contracts. Following are two smart-contract-specific patterns and three from other conversation pattern groups [3] that specifically apply to smart contracts.

Gas Consumption Checking (New). The motivation of this pattern is to handle *out of gas* uncertainty. eth_estimateGas function in Ethereum allows the smart contract invoker to submit a function and its arguments to a blockchain node, and get it to estimate the gas consumption by executing the function locally (invocation call or results do not propagate to the rest of the network). After submitting the estimate request, the polling pattern is required to obtain the estimated gas value. The estimated gas value is then used for the actual function invoke request. Given that a function invoke can still go out of gas at the time of execution (see Sect. 2.3), it is desirable to set a relatively higher gas value above the estimate.

Availability Checking (New). This pattern is used to deal with *dead smart contract* uncertainty. Implementation of this pattern is similar to *gas consumption checking*, where a blockchain node is consulted to check the liveness of a smart contract using Web3.js eth.getCode function before issuing the actual transaction to the blockchain. Because a smart contract can still be deactivated before the execution (see Sect. 2.3), this pattern cannot completely overcome the uncertainty. Listing 1.2 is an example code snippet that applies both of the

---

[10] https://github.com/ethereum/web3.js/blob/2a5c5cb740ee8962846ac9d5416-e6b8cc2e7d95d/packages/web3-core-method/src/index.js#L541.

patterns above before invoking a smart contract. Line 1 checks the availability of the contract. If the contract is available (i.e., *activated*), line 7 then estimates the gas consumption. The invocation transaction is sent on line 10.

Consult Directory. This pattern belongs to the *discovery* group and could be used to better deal with a dead smart contract due to upgrades. The smart contract function invoker sends a lookup transaction to a central directory implemented as another smart contract. The directory responds with the address of the active smart contract or null if deactivated. The central directory also receives messages from the smart contract to register themselves [17]. This is a widely applied pattern in the industry, for example, ENS (Ethereum Name Service)[11] is a name service built on Ethereum. However, a smart contract can still get deactivated between consulting the directory and function execution.

```
1  web3.eth.getCode(contractAddress).then(function(code) {
2      if(code == '0x') {
3          ...
4      } else {
5          let contract = new web3.eth.Contract([...], contractAddress, {});
6          contract.methods.method(para).estimateGas().then(function(gasAmount){
7              contract.methods.method(para).send({from:account, gas:gasAmount})
8              .then(function(receipt) {
9                  ...
10             });
11         }).catch(function(error) { ... });
12     }
13 }).catch(function(error){ ... });
```

Listing 1.2. Gas consumption and availability.

User Grants Access. This pattern is from the *start a conversation* group. It allows a smart contract to initiate a conversation with another smart contract on behalf of a transaction initiator. A smart contract can delegate the invoker (i.e., `msg.sender`) to invoke a function in another contract using `delegatecall`, where the function defined in the invoked contract is executed in the context of the invoking contract. The `msg.sender and msg.value`, which represent the conversation initiator, is preserved. This pattern can effectively handle dead smart contracts, as invoking smart contract can dynamically load code from another smart contract at run time. It is also more effective than the *consult directory* pattern when a large or dynamic number of contract initiators call the invoked smart contract.

Listing 1.3 is a code snippet from ConsenSys Ethereum smart contract best practices[12] using the *user grants access* pattern to implement an upgradable contract. The `fallback` function on line 9 is executed when a function identifier in the invocation transaction does not match any of the available functions in the `Relay`. `delegatecall` is used to locally execute code loaded from the functions in another contract whose address is specified dynamically by calling `changeContract` function on line 4.

---

[11] https://ens.domains/.

[12] https://consensys.github.io/smart-contract-best-practices/software_engineering/.

```
1  contract Relay {
2      address public currentVersion;
3      ...
4      function changeContract(address newVersion) public onlyOwner() {
5          require(newVersion != address(0));
6          currentVersion = newVersion;
7      }
8
9      fallback() external payable {
10         (bool success, ) = address(currentVersion).delegatecall(msg.data);
11         require(success);
12     }
13 }
```

Listing 1.3. User grants access pattern.

Proxy. This pattern overcomes a blockchain's inability to check the state of an external real-world object directly. It is not used to handle the uncertainties though. In the context of smart contracts, an *oracle* [17] is used as a proxy to reach external systems. An oracle is a contract that is deployed by a trusted third-party. Based on the requests from other contracts, the third-party proactively or reactively updates the data embedded in the oracle as per the information from external systems. There are oracle services provided for different blockchain platforms, for e.g., Provable[13] supports most of the popular blockchain platforms.

Also, a gateway can be considered as a proxy, though it is primarily used to simplify the blockchain interaction while achieving high availability and scalability. Moreover, a gateway could authenticate the application sending transactions, sign transactions on behalf of the sending accounts, and rate limit API calls.

4.4   Gateway Conversation Patterns

Quick Acknowledgment. This pattern is an enhanced version of *fire-and-forget* where the gateway sends a quick acknowledgment message after receiving a transaction from the initiator, followed by the operation results later. This way, the transaction initiator can be sure that the gateway accepted the transaction, even if processing the transaction takes a long time. The transaction could be immediately rejected if it is malformed, initiator's account does not exist, the signature is incorrect, the nonce is already used, or insufficient funds to pay the transaction fee. As such errors are common, Ethereum Web3[14] library implements this pattern to get a quick acknowledgment confirming the potential validity of a transaction.

Asynchronous Request-Response. This pattern deals with all uncertainties mentioned in Sect. 2 within a set of conversations of the same style. After

---

[13] https://provable.xyz/.
[14] https://web3js.readthedocs.io/.

sending a transaction, the initiator waits for a response message. While waiting, the initiator may engage in other tasks making the conversation asynchronous. This pattern can replace the use of multiple patterns such as *fire-and-forget* with *polling transaction pool with retry* or *polling blockchain with retry* to access details of a transaction, sign a transaction, and estimate gas consumption of a transaction. This pattern is more resource efficient than polling, especially when a suitable polling interval is difficult to estimate due to the dynamic behaviour of blockchain nodes.

Subscribe-Notify. This pattern can replace *polling transaction pool with retry* or *polling blockchain with retry* patterns by enabling the transaction initiator to get notifications from the gateway as a transaction or smart contract goes through different states during its life cycle. For example, when a transaction is submitted in Web3, the gateway first sends a *quick acknowledgement*. Then the gateway can also send a notification once the transaction is included in a block. There onwards, the block confirmations could be sent to confirm the transaction confirmation. While implementing this pattern between the application and gateway, the gateway may rely on polling both the transaction pool and blockchain to check the status of the transaction. While this pattern does not reduce the gateway's workload, it simplifies the conversation interface of the gateway service. Listing 1.4 is a code snippet from Web3 documentation[15]. When sending a transaction, the initiator may subscribe to multiple events (lines 2–5) and get notified from different stages during the life cycle of this transaction.

```
1  web3.eth.sendTransaction({from: '0x123...', data: '0x432...'})
2  .once('transactionHash', function(hash){ ... })
3  .once('receipt', function(receipt){ ... })
4  .on('confirmation', function(confNumber, receipt){ ... })
5  .on('error', function(error){ ... })
6  .then(function(receipt){ ... });
```

Listing 1.4. Subscribe-notify.

Acquire Token First. This pattern is used to ascertain the identity of a transaction initiator to the blockchain. It requires the initiator to first acquire an identification token from a token provider and include it in subsequent messages to the partner. All transactions submitted to the blockchain need to be signed by the respective address. Therefore, before sending the first transaction, the initiator needs to obtain a public-private key pair. All subsequent transactions need to be signed using the private key. The conversation of generating a key pair, uploading the public key to the blockchain (in blockchains like Hyperledger Fabric), and signing future transactions can be simplified using a gateway. Hence, a request can be made to the gateway to generate a key pair and upload the public key to the blockchain. Alternatively, it could also be generated offline and uploaded into the blockchain either directly or through the gateway. Then the digital signature on the transactions can be validated by the blockchain.

---

[15] https://web3js.readthedocs.io/en/v1.2.0/callbacks-promises-events.html.

By storing a wallet of private keys at the gateway, future transactions can be automatically signed and submitted via the gateway simplifying the application. The pattern may also include an authentication step to ensure only the authorised user can sign using the corresponding private key. For example, Web3 library provides both key generation and wallet management at the gateway. Moreover, gateways such as Infura also issue API key/token to authenticate all transactions sent via the gateway and to rate limit remote calls.

5   Related Work

Many empirical analyses are conducted to characterise blockchain transactions. Availability limitations of both Bitcoin and Ethereum are identified in [13] through the analysis of factors that affect the time behaviour of transactions. The nature and impact of the orphan Bitcoin transaction are characterised in [5]. Authors identified that the missing parents of orphan transactions usually have a larger size, lower fees, and lower transaction fee per byte. Ethereum transactions with a future *nonce* value is similar to Bitcoin orphan transaction. The empirical evidence shown in our paper focuses on the uncertain state transitions that occur during the entire life cycle of transaction and smart contracts.

An empirical study that analyzed source code and the meta-data of more than 10,000 smart contracts on Ethereum is presented in [11]. Statistics on naming policies, smart contract Ether balance, number of smart contract transactions, functions, and other quantities are used to characterise the use and purpose of smart contracts. A more comprehensive empirical study on smart contracts is conducted in [10], which is based on cross-linked data collected from multiple data sources. This analysis focuses on three characteristics, namely activity level, category, and complexity of the source code.

Patterns have become a research topic for blockchains and smart contracts. In [1], the authors categorized hundreds of smart contracts into nine categories. Other work further characterised the real-world projects and extracted architectural patterns for both smart contracts and blockchain-based applications [7,16,17]. Some of the existing architectural patterns can be applied to blockchain-based software, while other patterns are applicable only to smart contracts.

6   Conclusion

The unique design of blockchain instigates additional uncertainties other than the network-level uncertainties. Such uncertainties need to be understood and properly handled to build reliable applications on top of a blockchain. In this paper, we investigated the blockchain uncertainties with empirical evidence collected from Ethereum and Bitcoin. We then identified several conversation patterns that can help to provide robust interactions between applications/services and the blockchain to handle such uncertainties in blockchains.

References

1. Bartoletti, M., Pompianu, L.: An empirical analysis of smart contracts: platforms, applications, and design patterns. In: Brenner, M., et al. (eds.) FC 2017. LNCS, vol. 10323, pp. 494–509. Springer, Cham (2017). https://doi.org/10.1007/978-3-319-70278-0_31

2. Di Francesco, M.D., Mori, P., Ricci, L.: Blockchain based access control services. In: 2018 IEEE International Conference on Internet of Things (iThings) and IEEE Green Computing and Communications (GreenCom) and IEEE Cyber, Physical and Social Computing (CPSCom) and IEEE Smart Data (SmartData), pp. 1379–1386, July 2018

3. Hohpe, G.: Enterprise integration patterns: conversation patterns. https://www.enterpriseintegrationpatterns.com/patterns/conversation/. Accessed 11 Nov 2019

4. Hohpe, G.: Let's have a conversation. IEEE Internet Comput. **11**, 78–81 (2007)

5. Imtiaz, M.A., Starobinski, D., Trachtenberg, A.: Characterizing orphan transactions in the bitcoin network (2019)

6. Koshy, P., Koshy, D., McDaniel, P.: An analysis of anonymity in bitcoin using P2P network traffic. In: Christin, N., Safavi-Naini, R. (eds.) FC 2014. LNCS, vol. 8437, pp. 469–485. Springer, Heidelberg (2014). https://doi.org/10.1007/978-3-662-45472-5_30

7. Liu, Y., Lu, Q., Xu, X., Zhu, L., Yao, H.: Applying design patterns in smart contracts. In: Chen, S., Wang, H., Zhang, L.-J. (eds.) ICBC 2018. LNCS, vol. 10974, pp. 92–106. Springer, Cham (2018). https://doi.org/10.1007/978-3-319-94478-4_7

8. Nakamoto, S.: Bitcoin: a peer-to-peer electronic cash system (2009)

9. Natoli, C., Gramoli, V.: The blockchain anomaly. In: 2016 IEEE 15th International Symposium on Network Computing and Applications (NCA), pp. 310–317 (2016)

10. Oliva, G.A., Hassan, A.E., Jiang, Z.M.J.: An exploratory study of smart contracts in the Ethereum blockchain platform. Empirical Softw. Eng. **25**(3), 1864–1904 (2020). https://doi.org/10.1007/s10664-019-09796-5

11. Pinna, A., Ibba, S., Baralla, G., Tonelli, R., Marchesi, M.: A massive analysis of Ethereum smart contracts empirical study and code metrics. IEEE Access **7**, 78194–78213 (2019)

12. Piratla, N.M., Jayasumana, A.P.: Metrics for packet reordering-a comparative analysis. Int. J. Commun Syst **21**(1), 99–113 (2008)

13. Weber, I., et al.: On availability for blockchain-based systems. In: 2017 IEEE 36th Symposium on Reliable Distributed Systems (SRDS), pp. 64–73 (2017)

14. Weber, I., Xu, X., Riveret, R., Governatori, G., Ponomarev, A., Mendling, J.: Untrusted business process monitoring and execution using blockchain. In: La Rosa, M., Loos, P., Pastor, O. (eds.) BPM 2016. LNCS, vol. 9850, pp. 329–347. Springer, Cham (2016). https://doi.org/10.1007/978-3-319-45348-4_19

15. Wilkinson, S., Boshevski, T., Brandoff, J., Buterin, V.: Storj: a peer-to-peer cloud storage network (2009)

16. Wöhrer, M., Zdun, U.: Design patterns for smart contracts in the Ethereum ecosystem. In: 2018 IEEE International Conference on Internet of Things (iThings) and IEEE Green Computing and Communications (GreenCom) and IEEE Cyber, Physical and Social Computing (CPSCom) and IEEE Smart Data (SmartData), pp. 1513–1520 (2018)

17. Xu, X., Pautasso, C., Zhu, L., Lu, Q., Weber, I.: A pattern collection for blockchain-based applications. In: Proceedings of 23rd European Conference on Pattern Languages of Programs (EuroPLoP 2018), pp. 1–20 (2018)

Application Track

Upgradeability Concept for Collaborative Blockchain-Based Business Process Execution Framework

Philipp Klinger(✉) 🆔, Long Nguyen, and Freimut Bodendorf

University of Erlangen-Nuremberg, Lange Gasse 20, 90403 Nuremberg, Germany
{philipp.klinger,long.nguyen,freimut.bodendorf}@fau.de

Abstract. Inter-organizational business processes involve different independent participants to interact with each other to run a collaborative business process. To date, central, trusted third parties mediate between non-trusting participants adding additional process complexity as well as administrative and run costs. Recent research showed that Blockchain and Smart Contracts can replace the role of a central trusted authority in collaborative execution of processes. Smart Contracts, that represent business process logic, cannot be altered due to immutability constraints of Blockchain systems. Yet, with the help of advanced technical upgradeability concepts, upgrading contracts, therefore enabling versioning of processes on a Blockchain is possible. This paper analyzes and implements three different upgradeability concepts. The implemented patterns are evaluated with regard to an existing blockchain-based execution framework for inter-organizational business processes. Our findings suggest the Unstructured Storage Proxy pattern to be the most promising for practical use, especially regarding cost-effectiveness and minimal added complexity. The findings are derived from simulations on a real-world use case stemming from a large German electronics manufacturing company.

Keywords: Blockchain · Ethereum · Business process · Collaboration · Business process management system · Upgradeability · Proxy

1 Motivation and Problem

Recent research shows that Blockchain technology may be used to facilitate business process execution in collaborative, often cross-organizational, settings without having to rely on a mediating third party or other process participants executing parts of a collaborative process [1, 2]. Blockchain-based business process engines help to overcome the distrust in concerned parties by modeling business process logic as Smart Contracts [3, 4]. The vast majority of endeavors implementing workflow engines respectively Business Process Management Systems (BPMS) are based on Ethereum [4–10] yet other implementations exist e.g. on Bitcoin [11]. Contracts resembling process logic are stored and jointly executed on computationally capable Blockchain systems [2]. Post-execution, executed process trails can be analyzed from an event log or extracted from the data structures of the respective Blockchain implementation [12–15].

© Springer Nature Switzerland AG 2020
Z. Chen et al. (Eds.): ICBC 2020, LNCS 12404, pp. 127–141, 2020.
https://doi.org/10.1007/978-3-030-59638-5_9

A business process being executed on a Blockchain may therefore help to overcome trust issues with other related parties when jointly executing processes to reach a common goal. This is achieved through immutable process flow described by Smart Contracts. By using Smart Contracts it is possible to verify and attestate cryptographically secured, thus tamper-proof, execution history [10].

Typical cross-organizational use cases are to be found in different industries like energy markets [16], logistics [17] or the public sector [18, 19]. In the following, we will focus on a logistics use case stemming from a German electronics manufacturing company. The remainder of the paper builds upon a process execution framework on Ethereum [10] that lays the foundational premises for the upgradeability respectively versioning concept under consideration.

Executing a business process on a Blockchain, without needing to trust other business partners during execution is assumed to be solved [10]. Yet, flexibility as a key goal for process design is not at all or not addressed to a larger extent by existing frameworks. Since processes naturally need to evolve over time, e.g. due to governmental regulation, evolving business needs or changing business partners, there is a clear need for business process adaptions. Notwithstanding, this need to change processes is contradicting the principles of Smart Contracts, which are designed to be immutably written to the Ethereum Blockchain. In this paper, we address the need for upgradeable, in the sense of flexible, business processes on the Ethereum Blockchain. Updating contracts to new requirements is forbidden by design on the Ethereum Blockchain, but different strategies may be used to mitigate this deficiency introducing a process versioning concept. Challenging this basic principle of the Ethereum Blockchain, being immutable, needs to be addressed not only from a technical, but also from an organizational perspective. For this reason, we give an outlook on a voting mechanism to be used for setting a flexible and democratized contract upgrade mechanism in place. We therefore want to answer the following research question: *Which upgradeability pattern is best suited for the underlying Blockchain-based process execution framework regarding cost, organizational overhead and complexity?*

In the following, Sect. 2 gives background information on the usage of Blockchain in the context of Business Processes and introduces existing upgradeability concepts. Section 3 describes the Blockchain-based process execution framework in conjunction with the proposed upgradeability concepts for consideration. Section 4 evaluates the different concepts and Sect. 5 summarizes and deduces the most suitable concept for use with the execution framework presented.

2 Theoretical Background

2.1 Business Processes on the Ethereum Blockchain

The Blockchain's underlying protocol ensures consensus finding in the network and is also responsible for the immutability of data stored therein. As the name suggests, a Blockchain is a data structure of blocks chained to each other, containing payload such as the record of (monetary) transactions or arbitrary bytecode resembling Smart Contracts. A deployed Smart Contract may hold funds and may be invoked with its contracts address as well as call parameters to a Smart Contract's function. The caller of such Smart Contract function may be another Smart Contract. In every case, at the beginning of each contract call sequence, there must be an initiating EOA (Externally Owned Accounts), a user-owned account [20].

The basic idea of using a Blockchain to execute processes boils down to encoding a business process into a state-machine like structure, which may be encoded as Smart Contracts [10].

Using Smart Contracts to encode process flow and performable actions amongst untrusting organizations respectively parties bears the opportunity to make trusted third parties in inter-organizational process settings obsolete, thus saving expenses for the third party involved whilst maintaining trust and high process quality [2]. Trust is mainly guaranteed by the Blockchain protocol and public-key cryptography, whilst process quality is ensured by Smart Contracts on the Blockchain [21]. Process execution history may be transparently verified from the event logs [12–15].

Usually, Smart Contracts can be seen as immutable as well, since their logic performed by the EVM (Ethereum Virtual Machine) is encoded as bytecode in a tamper-proof Block once added and verified by enough other miners in the Blockchain network. One possibility to change deployed contract logic is to call a self-destruct function of a contract resulting in a rejection of all subsequent calls to the destroyed contract. Another possibility given by the low-level Solidity assembly *delegatecall* operation code (opcode), which is used to pass-through contract calls to other contracts at runtime and return the results into the context initial caller [22].

In the following, we make use of the *delegatecall* functionality to implement upgradeable contracts. As to our knowledge, none of the comparable existing process frameworks based on Ethereum do not make use of any versioning respectively upgradeability concept to date.

2.2 Smart Contract Upgradeability Concepts

In order to understand the following upgradeability concepts, we first need to introduce two basic smart contract patterns, namely the Registry and Proxy design pattern, which lay the foundations for further versioning of contracts.

The first basic concept needed for versioning contracts is the **Registry pattern** [23]. A registry maps user-defined keys to values. In our case, contract names to latest logic smart contract addresses. The invoker will then retrieve the latest smart contract version from the Registry contract. To implement the upgrade functionality, another contract pattern, the so-called "Data Segregation" [24] design pattern is needed. A decoupled contract stores contract states in a distinct contract, instead of storing business logic as well as contract storage in one contract solely. A possible solution would be to implement a mapping of key and value pairs for Data Segregation [23, 24].

Another basic concept is the **Proxy pattern**. Instead of calling a Logic contract directly, an invoker calls the Proxy contract which stores a reference to the Logic contract and the function call is forwarded ('proxied') to the assigned Logic contract [25]. In case of upgrade, the Proxy contract will update the Logic contract's address reference in the Proxy contract and refer to the latest, updated Logic contract address [25]. As a reminder, the Proxy pattern makes use of the *delegatecall* opcode to execute target bytecode stored at a contract address in the context of the calling contract. This means that the Proxy contract does not only forward requests to target Logic contract, but also represents the data storage location of the Logic contract [22]. Another important notion of the Proxy concept is the *fallback function* which is invoked when a non-available function is called in the target contract [26]. Via this *fallback function*, the Proxy contract exposes the complete interface of the linked Logic contract and forwards any requests containing any methods and parameter set to the stored Logic contract reference. This makes the forwarding mechanism more dynamic and no direct mapping of function interfaces between Proxy and Logic contract is needed.

Using the *delegatecall* opcode, the Proxy contract acts as data storage of Logic contracts [22]. However, Logic contracts do not know the presence of any Proxy contracts' states, which bears the risk of creating storage collisions. Therefore, it is up to the contract designer/programmer when using the Proxy pattern to avoid storage collisions with the Proxy contract's storage and the Logic contract's storage slots. To achieve storage collision resistance, we explore two promising Proxy patterns, which will be covered in Sect. 3.3 in more detail:

- The **'Unstructured Storage'** concept uses a random (*'non-prestructured'*) storage position slot to store states of the Proxy contract to avoid Logic contract variable storage collissions leading to unwanted sideeffects [27].
- An **'Eternal Storage'** concept defines a distinct Storage Contract, such that both Proxy and Logic contracts inherit from. In this effort a limitation is, that subsequent versions of Logic contracts cannot define new states [25]. However, our adapted design is enhanced to resolve this limitation (cf. Sect. 3.3).

Next to the previously introduced Proxy concepts, we take another promising concept under consideration:

- **'Registry with Hub Storage'** is a combination of Registry and Data Segregation pattern with a Hub-Spoke design with a shared, decoupled Data contract as a Hub-like storage set in place to store all states of Logic contracts [28].

3   Contract Design

3.1   Execution Framework Contract Structure

The remainder of this paper is based on a process execution framework initially proposed by [10]. It aims to provide a flexible contract architecture where every participant in a BPMN collaboration diagram is transformed into a separate Smart Contract. A transpiler converts BPMN process descriptions into Solidity Smart Contracts. Underlying design principles as well as differences to other existing Blockchain-based process execution frameworks are already covered in [10].

The execution framework needs to be deployed per collaboration consortium of participants that want to transact and choreograph a business process on the Ethereum Blockchain. The dBPMS framework is designed to function both in a public and a private network. It is the obligation of transacting parties to decide per collaboration or use case, whether a private or public Blockchain is the right medium to mutually transact and exchange information.

On a high level, the dBPMS framework consists of static (I) and dynamic (II) contract components per deployment (cf. Fig. 1). Like singletons, static components need to be deployed just once. They mainly provide administrative or structuring features such as commonly used libraries, abstract contracts to inherit from or a management contract to store collaborations to be executed. More in-depth description of the execution framework is given in [10].

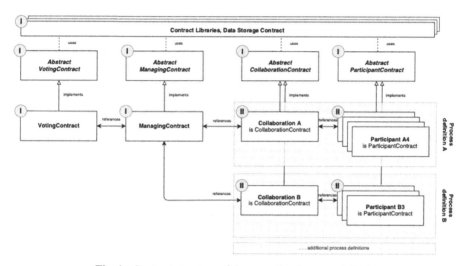

Fig. 1. Contract structure of the execution framework [10]

Also, a Voting Contract may optionally be used to ballot for deployment of new collaboration and participant contracts. Moreover, one can fairly share initial contract allocation expenses amongst the collaborating participants for deployment and setup. Currently, a slightly adapted version of the Ethereum Democracy DAO [29] contract is used. Therefore, a proposal voting period has to be defined and the Voting contract may be parametrized to the needs of the collaborating consortium, e.g. setting voting count thresholds.

Regarding this paper, the required crucial functionality is the ability to propose and vote upon execution of arbitrary bytecode through the Voting contract, once all necessary agreements are given. Moreover, it should be emphasized that a voting mechanism is highly important in the case of process upgrades. Authorized participants could potentially deploy mal-behaving contracts and, thus, trick other contributors into actions that were not intended. Therefore, every participant must be able to give his agreement to changes on process (participant) contracts, encoding the process logic and flow. If all required parties agree, execution can be triggered by the Voting contract.

3.2 Running Example

To illustrate the upgradeability concepts provided in Sect. 3.3, the concepts are applied to a real-world use case stemming from a large German electronics manufacturing company (cf. Fig. 2).

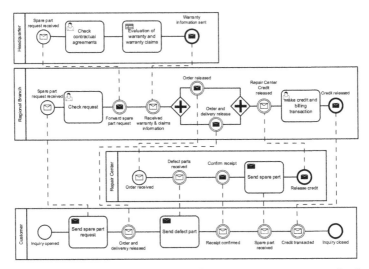

Fig. 2. Simplified BPMN collaboration diagram of a spare parts process, stemming from a large German electronics manufacturing company [10]

The collaboration consists of four participants, namely *Customer, Repair Center, Regional Branch* and *Headquarter.* The collaboration is transformed according to the dBPMS framework contract design (cf. Sect. 3.1) resulting in the static parts needed for every collaboration. Accordingly, the dynamic contracts created consist of one *Collaboration Contract* for our Spare Parts Process use case, which acts as a bracket contract for the four *Participant Contracts.*

3.3 Upgradeability Concepts

In the following, three identified upgradeability concepts (cf. Sect. 2.2) are applied to the contract structure of the collaborative process execution framework (cf. Sect. 3.1). The presented process (cf. Sect. 3.2) is used as a running example to illustrate distinct upgradeability concepts and to compare different implementations.

Unstructured Storage Proxy
It must be ensured that any Proxy contract states do not get overwritten by the proxied payload Logic contract's states. Otherwise, there will be a storage collision between the Proxy contract and the Logic contract [27], leading to unwanted results if storage slots for contract variables are allocated at the same storage position. Such a storage collision between the Proxy and Logic contract can be solved via a so-called unstructured storage

design - storing the Proxy's state at a pseudo-random slot instead of reassigning Proxy's first storage slot [30]. Using a pseudo-randomly generated storage position, e.g., by hashing a given string (cf. Code-Listing 1), the probability of getting overwritten at the same storage slot is negligible [25].

```
function setLatestLogicAddress(address newImplementation) internal {
    bytes32 position = keccak256("dbpms.proxy.implementation");
    assembly {
        sstore(position, newImplementation)
    }
}
```

Code-Listing 1. Applied logic to crate pseudo-random storage slots

Furthermore, this concept prevents the storage collision among Logic contract versions by inheriting a new version of Logic contract from the previous version to ensure that all versions have the same storage structure [25]. Also, it should be noted that a Proxy's storage cannot know about states written in a Logic contract's constructor as the constructor is run right after deployment (not being invoked by the delegatecall function of a proxy contract) and therefore may not return initialized states in the executed Logic contract constructor call to a Proxy contract [27]. To solve this problem, the code in a Logic contract's constructor may be moved to a shadowing initialize() method, that can be called by the Proxy contract during the upgrade process to initialize contract storage [27].

To implement *Unstructured Storage Proxy* concept in the context of BPMN, one Proxy contract only links to and manages exactly one Participant contract (cf. Fig. 3). For example, if the latest Customer contract is requested, the allotted CustomerProxy contract queries the latest stored Customer contract address as well as all states stored in the CustomerProxy contract.

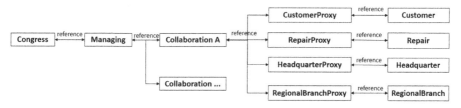

Fig. 3. Unstructured Storage Proxy concept applied to the process framework

Characteristic for this concept is the deployment of one Proxy contract per Participant. This fact can be seen as a drawback regarding contract deployment costs. Noteworthy is the relatively simple one-to-one *Proxy-to-Logic contract* mapping approach applied in this concept.

Eternal Storage Proxy

Building upon the main ideas of previously described concept, the Eternal Storage Proxy concept [31] is about creating a logically centralized Proxy managing upgrades of all Participant contracts in a corresponding Collaboration contract (cf. Fig. 4).

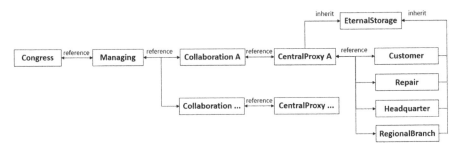

Fig. 4. Eternal Storage Proxy concept applied to the process framework

Similar to the Unstructured Storage Proxy, this concept aims at preventing storage collisions. Referring to Fig. 4, using a CentalProxy, there is a high probability of a storage collision among Participant contracts, if the same storage allocation concept would be reused as in the previously described Unstructured Storage Proxy concept, since Participant contracts are not aware of other Participant contracts writing to the same CentralProxy storage position.

To solve this problem, the previously stated *Eternal Storage Proxy* concept can be implemented by deploying a distinct EternalStorage contract [31]. It serves as a consistent storage structure, inherited by all Participant contracts.

In our EternalStorage implementation, a variable "eternalStorage" (cf. Code-Listing 2) is defined as a nested mapping (a mapping of mappings) construct, the distinct mapping layers are used to store contracts' state variables. When addressing the mapping of mappings (cf. Code-Listing 2 *"_eternalStorage"*) correctly, there is no more possibility for different contract storage slots to overlap. For example, the first key of the Generic-Storage mapping construct, a bytes32 data type, defines a unique name of a Participant contract, i.e. "FirstParticipant". On the second lookup level of the mapping, another bytes32 key refers to a value stored at that given position of the mapping as depicted in Code-Listing 3.

```
struct ValueStruct {
        bytes32 _bytes32;
        int _int;
        bytes32[] _aBytes32;
        address[] _aAddress;
... }
struct LayerStruct {
        ValueStruct _value;
        mapping(bytes32 => ValueStruct) _mapping;
}
mapping(bytes32=>mapping(bytes32=>LayerStruct)) internal _eternalStorage
```

Code-Listing 2. Shared storage structure in EternalStorage contract

```
_eternalStorage["FirstParticipant"]["state1"]._value._bytes32 =
bytes32("Receive_Credit")
```

Code-Listing 3. Example of updating a state of a Participant contract

After establishing the single shared storage structure for various contracts, both ValueStruct struct type to store simple value type and mapping of bytes32 to ValueStruct to store the mapping object type are defined (cf. Code-Listing 3). For instance, a bytes32 data type with the value "Receive_Credit" is stored in FirstParticipant contract with the state name "state1". Instead of a bytes32 value, as signified in Code-Listing 3, also other values of varying data types like address, uint, etc., may be stored and retrieved in a similiar fashion.

To complete the Eternal Storage Proxy design, getter and setter functions need to be defined as wrapper functions. All involved contracts access the shared storage mapping construct "_eternalStorage" as shown in Code-Listing 4.

```
function getArrayBytes32(bytes32 key1, bytes32 key2) public view returns
(bytes32[] memory){
    return _eternalStorage[key1][key2]._value._aBytes32;
}
function setArrayBytes32(bytes32 key1, bytes32 key2, bytes32[] memory
value) public onlyProxyOwner() {
    _eternalStorage[key1][key2]._value._aBytes32 = value;

}
```

Code-Listing 4. Getter and setter function in EternalStorage contract

The *delegatecall* opcode is again utilized to forward requests to the currently desired Logic contract. In case of our implementation, the CentralProxy handles the forwarding to the appropriate Participant contract (cf. Fig. 4). Yet, the CentralProxy does not know which Participant contract a request should be forwarded to; however, in the fallback function, the request's bytecode stored in "msg.data" variable can be retrieved and consecutively compared to each function bytecode in Participant contracts. If there is a match, the Participant contract address is successfully looked up and gets returned. Hence, this issue can be solved by creating a look-up table of arrays of function bytecodes to the latest Participant contract's addresses (cf. Table 1).

Table 1. Look-up table of participant contract's address and its function bytecodes

Exemplary function bytecodes	Latest contract address
$[0x68690...0a_1, ... 0x68690...0a_n]$	0x ... 01
$[0x68690...0b_1, ... 0x68690...0b_n]$	0x ... 02
...	...

The presented concept has certain limitations. Firstly, each function bytecode, which is the combination of function name and its parameters in a Participant contract, must be unique among the Participant contracts in a Collaboration contract. Otherwise, duplicated function bytecode exists in the lookup-table and the Logic address is returned incorrectly. Another inconvenience is the use of wrapper functions for getter and setter functions, adding complexity and thus higher execution costs.

Registry with Hub Storage

The motivation of this concept is to eliminate redundant EternalStorage contracts which are inherited by every Participant contract in the Eternal Storage Proxy concept. Only one EternalStorage contract is used in the Proxy contract to store all Participant contract's states. Moreover, when executing the look-up function to retrieve the corresponding Participant contract's address from a list of function bytecodes to make a request, the *delegatecall* opcode induces considerably high costs.

The idea of this concept is to have one distinct Registry and manage all Participant contracts differing from a central Proxy like in Eternal Storage Proxy design. A Collaboration contract retrieves the latest Participant contract's address querying the Registry contract using references in Managing contract. Hub and Spoke design is applied by storing all Participant contracts' states in a separate Storage contract. During contract execution, a Participant contract *(Spoke)* accesses its storage by calling the Storage contract *(Hub)* to retrieve and update its state (cf. Fig. 5) [28].

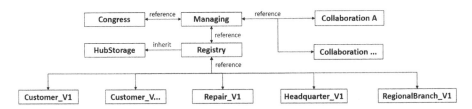

Fig. 5. Registry with Hub Storage concept applied to the process framework

All Participant contracts are managed by the unique Registry contract. The Registry identifies Participant contracts with the same contract name unequivocally using the Collaboration contract address as a discriminant. As a result, the Registry structure consists of the Participant name and Collaboration contract's address as a unique lookup key (cf. Table 2).

The Hub Storage design is similar to EternalStorage of Eternal Storage Proxy concept (cf. Code-Listing 2). The only difference is one additional layer to store the Collaboration contract's address to prevent colliding lookup entries as discussed above (cf. Fig. 5).

The HubStorage contract, which is inherited by the Registry contract, is shared among Participant contracts. Therefore, it requires an authorization mechanism to only allow the latest Participant contract to update its corresponding state in HubStorage where the look-up permission table (cf. Table 3) is defined in the Registry contract to store the permission. In Table 3, only the Participant owner's address "0x...12" is allowed to update the variable "customerState" of Customer Participant contract with Collaboration address "0x...01".

Table 2. Registry table design

Participant name	Collaboration address	Latest logic address
Customer	0x ... 99	0x ... 01
Repair	0x ... 99	0x ... 02
Headquarter	0x ... 99	0x ... 03
Customer	0x ... 98	0x ... 04
...	...	...

Table 3. Permission design to update states in HubStorage contract

Permission mapping			HubStorage mapping		
Collab. address	Particip. name	Particip. owner address	Collab. address	Particip. name	Variable name
0x ... 01	Customer	0x ... 12	0x ... 01	Customer	customerState
0x ... 01	Repair	0x ... 23	0x ... 01	Repair	repairState

4 Evaluation

The evaluation demonstrates a cost calculation of the upgradeability concepts including deployment cost, upgrade cost and running cost. First cost block comprises static components: Managing, Congress and Registry contracts are solely deployed. Secondly, dynamic components: Collaboration, Participant and Proxy contract are deployed several times depending on the number of collaboration processes defined. The following cost calculation assesses deployment and execution costs of the Spare Part Process introduced in Sect. 3.2.

The tests were performed in a local test network. Therefore, gas price is constant at 20 Gwei. At the time of writing, the price of 1 ETH is assumed to be $143,7 to give a rough cost impression.

The Eternal Storage Proxy concept is the most expensive. In Table 4 Registry has the potential to reduce costs by eliminating several Proxy contracts deployment. However, the running costs of Registry are significantly higher than for the Unstructured Storage Proxy (cf. Table 5). This is mainly caused by the requirement of the Registry concept, which includes an external call setter function to store its variables to the shared Hub storage.

As it can be seen from cost evaluation, Unstructured Storage Proxy concept is most cost-efficient. Another advantage of this approach is that Participant contracts do not have to be rewritten or restructured, which makes it easily adaptable to the dBPMS framework.

The EternalStorage contract needs to be inherited by every Participant contract in the Eternal Storage Proxy concept. This deficiency introduces surplus deployment costs,

Table 4. Deployment and upgradeability cost of three concepts under consideration

Contracts	Unstructured storage proxy		Eternal storage proxy		Registry with hub storage	
Upgrade	ETH	USD	ETH	USD	ETH	USD
Proxy/Registry[a]	0,03873	5,57	0,05113	7,35	0,04487	6,45
Static deployment						
Congress	0,06043	8,68	0,06043	8,68	0,06043	8,68
ManagingContract	0,01900	2,73	0,01900	2,73	0,02095	3,01
Registry	–	–	–	–	0,12325	17,71
Dynamic deployment						
SPPCollaboration	0,03074	4,42	0,01971	2,83	0,01971	2,83
SPPCustomer	0,05042	7,25	0,10428	14,99	0,07009	10,07
SPPHeadquarter	0,03853	5,54	0,09117	13,10	0,04885	7,02
SPPRegionalBranch	0,04757	6,84	0,10119	14,54	0,06778	9,74
SPPRepairCenter	0,03821	5,49	0,09116	13,10	0,04887	7,02
Proxy	0,11605	16,68	0,08788	12,63	–	–
Total	**0,43968**	**63,18**	**0,62594**	**89,95**	**0,50480**	**72,54**

[a]incl. method upgradeToAndCall executed

that make the concept expensive. Another drawback of this concept is the incurred cost to retrieve a Participant contract's address based on the function bytecode input in the lookup function bytecode table. Also, when inheriting the large-sized Eternal Storage contract, out-of-gas errors are likely to happen during contract deployments.

Registry with Hub Storage is advantageous from a cost perspective, since it is only deployed once in the dBPMS framework. However, the inconvenience of wrapper functions for getters and setters adds more complexity and in effect additional execution costs. As it may be seen in the breakdown of running costs, resulting execution cost surplus of the Registry with Hub Storage concept exceeds savings made during deployment phase.

The focus of this paper lies on the breakdown of execution and deployment costs of different upgradeability concepts applied to our framework. This analysis did not cover edge cases, that must be solved from an organizational, next to the technical perspective. A possible problematic scenario happens when a process needs to be upgraded that still manages running instances, yet this scenario is beyond the scope of this paper. Before upgrading, organizational and technical measures need to be put in place to cover this scenario.

Table 5. Running cost of three upgradeability concept

Contract	Method	Unstructured storage proxy		Eternal torage proxy		Registry with hub storage	
		ETH	USD	ETH	USD	ETH	USD
SPPCollaboration	createProcessInstance	0,00220	0,32	0,00220	0,32	0,00220	0,32
SPPCustomer	RECEIVE_CONF.	0,00076	0,11	0,00157	0,23	0,00107	0,15
SPPCustomer	REC._ORD_CLEAR.	0,00082	0,12	0,00162	0,23	0,00113	0,16
SPPCustomer	REC._SPARE_PART	0,00076	0,11	0,00158	0,23	0,00107	0,15
SPPCustomer	START_CP	0,00106	0,15	0,00186	0,27	0,00137	0,20
SPPCustomer	RECEIVE_CREDIT	0,00123	0,18	0,00207	0,30	0,00154	0,22
SPPHeadquarter	CHK_CON_AGREEM.	0,00082	0,12	0,00165	0,24	0,00113	0,16
SPPHeadquarter	START_HQ	0,00106	0,15	0,00188	0,27	0,00137	0,20
SPPRegion.Branch	RB_CHECK_REQ	0,00076	0,11	0,00157	0,23	0,00107	0,15
SPPRegion.Branch	REC._WARR._INFO.	0,00076	0,11	0,00157	0,23	0,00107	0,15
SPPRegion.Branch	START_RB	0,00106	0,15	0,00186	0,27	0,00137	0,20
SPPRepairCenter	RECEIVE_DEF_PARTS	0,00082	0,12	0,00165	0,24	0,00113	0,16
SPPRepairCenter	START_COM_CLEAR	0,00106	0,15	0,00188	0,27	0,00137	0,20
Total		0,01315	1,89	0,02295	3,30	0,01687	2,42

5 Summary

The paper conceptualizes and implements three upgradeability concepts in the context of a given Blockchain-based process execution framework. Starting with the Unstructured Storage Proxy, a common upgradeability concept. After initial implementation, we focus on the execution framework architecture (cf. Fig. 1) and enhance it with the Eternal Storage Proxy concept. The main idea is to reduce cost by introducing a central Proxy to manage all Participant contracts within a collaboration. We continue to improve with the goal to achieve a cost-effective central Proxy. Lastly, the Registry with Hub Storage concept is introduced. It is advantageous for deployment costs because it requires only one Registry contract to handle the upgradeability of all Participant contracts. However, the result of detailed cost calculation concerning deployment, upgrade and running cost shows that the Registry with Hub Storage concept is lacking in cost efficiency due to high running costs.

We conclude that Unstructured Storage Proxy is the most promising upgradeability concept to use in conjunction with the Blockchain-based process execution framework presented concerning cost-effectiveness as well as organizational overhead it introduced. Moreover, the Unstructured Storage Proxy concept it is practical in implementation because it is not required to follow any convention or logically restructure the original Smart Contracts.

References

1. Breu, R., et al.: Towards living inter-organizational processes. In: 2013 IEEE 15th Conference on Business Informatics, pp. 363–366. IEEE (2013)
2. Mendling, J., et al.: Blockchains for business process management - challenges and opportunities. ACM Trans. Manag. Inf. Syst. **9**, 1–16 (2018)
3. Mendling, J.: Towards blockchain support for business processes. In: Shishkov, B. (ed.) BMSD 2018. LNBIP, vol. 319, pp. 243–248. Springer, Cham (2018). https://doi.org/10.1007/978-3-319-94214-8_15
4. Weber, I., Xu, X., Riveret, R., Governatori, G., Ponomarev, A., Mendling, J.: Untrusted business process monitoring and execution using blockchain. In: La Rosa, M., Loos, P., Pastor, O. (eds.) BPM 2016. LNCS, vol. 9850, pp. 329–347. Springer, Cham (2016). https://doi.org/10.1007/978-3-319-45348-4_19
5. Madsen, M.F., Gaub, M., Høgnason, T., Kirkbro, M.E., Slaats, T., Debois, S.: Collaboration among adversaries: distributed workflow execution on a blockchain (2018)
6. Sturm, C., Szalanczi, J., Schönig, S., Jablonski, S.: A lean architecture for blockchain based decentralized process execution. In: Daniel, F., Sheng, Quan Z., Motahari, H. (eds.) BPM 2018. LNBIP, vol. 342, pp. 361–373. Springer, Cham (2019). https://doi.org/10.1007/978-3-030-11641-5_29
7. Tran, A.B., Lu, Q., Weber, I.: Lorikeet: a model-driven engineering tool for blockchain-based business process execution and asset management. In: 16th International Conference on Business Process Management, pp. 56–60 (2018)
8. López-Pintado, O., García-Bañuelos, L., Dumas, M., Weber, I.: Caterpillar: a blockchain-based business process management system. In: Clariso, R., et al. (eds.) Proceedings of the 15th International Conference on Business Process Management (BPM 2017), pp. 1–5. CEUR-WS.org, Barcelona (2017)
9. Ladleif, J., Weske, M., Weber, I.: Modeling and enforcing blockchain-based choreographies. In: Hildebrandt, T., van Dongen, B.F., Röglinger, M., Mendling, J. (eds.) BPM 2019. LNCS, vol. 11675, pp. 69–85. Springer, Cham (2019). https://doi.org/10.1007/978-3-030-26619-6_7
10. Klinger, P., Bodendorf, F.: Blockchain-based cross-organizational execution framework for dynamic integration of process collaborations. In: 15 Internationale Tagung Wirtschaftsinformatik, Potsdam, p. 15 (2020)
11. Prybila, C., Schulte, S., Hochreiner, C., Weber, I.: Runtime verification for business processes utilizing the bitcoin blockchain. Future Gener. Comput. Syst. (2020). https://www.sciencedirect.com/science/article/abs/pii/S0167739X1731837X?via%3Dihub
12. Klinkmüller, C., Ponomarev, A., Tran, A.B., Weber, I., van der Aalst, W.: Mining blockchain processes: extracting process mining data from blockchain applications. In: Di Ciccio, C., et al. (eds.) BPM 2019. LNBIP, vol. 361, pp. 71–86. Springer, Cham (2019). https://doi.org/10.1007/978-3-030-30429-4_6
13. Klinkmüller, C., Weber, I., Ponomarev, A., Tran, A.B., van der Aalst, W.: Efficient logging for blockchain applications, pp. 1–6 (2020)
14. Corradini, F., Marcantoni, F., Morichetta, A., Polini, A., Re, B., Sampaolo, M.: Enabling auditing of smart contracts through process mining. In: ter Beek, M.H., Fantechi, A., Semini, L. (eds.) From Software Engineering to Formal Methods and Tools, and Back. LNCS, vol. 11865, pp. 467–480. Springer, Cham (2019). https://doi.org/10.1007/978-3-030-30985-5_27
15. Mühlberger, R., Bachhofner, S., Di Ciccio, C., García-Bañuelos, L., López-Pintado, O.: Extracting event logs for process mining from data stored on the blockchain. In: Di Francescomarino, C., Dijkman, R., Zdun, U. (eds.) BPM 2019. LNBIP, vol. 362, pp. 690–703. Springer, Cham (2019). https://doi.org/10.1007/978-3-030-37453-2_55

16. Albrecht, S., Reichert, S., Schmid, J., Strüker, J., Neumann, D., Fridgen, G.: Dynamics of blockchain implementation - a case study from the energy sector. In: Bui, T. (ed.) 51st Hawaii International Conference on System Sciences, HICSS 2018, Hilton Waikoloa Village, Hawaii, USA, 3–6 January 2018, pp. 1–10 (2018)
17. Korpela, K., Hallikas, J., Dahlberg, T.: Digital supply chain transformation toward blockchain integration. In: Proceedings of the 50th Hawaii International Conference on System Sciences, pp. 4182–4191 (2017)
18. Guggenmos, F., Lockl, J., Rieger, A., Fridgen, G.: Blockchain in der öffentlichen Verwaltung. Inform. Spektrum **42**(3), 174–181 (2019). https://doi.org/10.1007/s00287-019-01177-y
19. Rieger, A., Guggenmos, F.: Building a blockchain application that complies with the EU general data protection regulation. MIS Q. Exec. **18**, 263–279 (2019)
20. Wood, G.: Ethereum: a secure decentralised generalised transaction ledger. https://ethereum.github.io/yellowpaper/paper.pdf. Accessed 10 Oct 2019
21. Xu, X., Weber, I., Staples, M.: Architecture for Blockchain Applications. Springer, Cham (2019). https://doi.org/10.1007/978-3-030-03035-3
22. Ethereum Foundation: Solidity Documentation - Delegtecall/Callcode and Libraries. https://solidity.readthedocs.io/en/v0.6.2/introduction-to-smart-contracts.html#delegatecall-callcode-and-libraries. Accessed 23 Jan 2020
23. Xu, X., Pautasso, C., Zhu, L., Lu, Q., Weber, I.: A pattern collection for blockchain-based applications. ACM International Conference Proceedings Series (2018)
24. Wohrer, M., Zdun, U.: Design patterns for smart contracts in the ethereum ecosystem. In: 2018 IEEE International Conference on Internet of Things (iThings) and IEEE Green Computing and Communications (GreenCom) and IEEE Cyber, Physical and Social Computing (CPSCom) and IEEE Smart Data (SmartData), pp. 1513–1520. IEEE (2018)
25. Nadolinski, E., Spagnuolo, F.: Proxy Patterns. https://blog.openzeppelin.com/proxy-patterns/. Accessed 16 Jan 2020
26. Ethereum Foundation: Solidity Documentation - Fallback Function. https://solidity.readthedocs.io/en/v0.6.2/contracts.html#fallback-function. Accessed 22 Jan 2020
27. Open Zeppelin: Proxy Upgrade Pattern - Unstructured Storage Proxies. https://docs.openzeppelin.com/upgrades/2.6/proxies#unstructured-storage-proxies. Accessed 25 Jan 2020
28. Rugendyke, D.: Upgradable Solidity Contract Design. https://medium.com/rocket-pool/upgradable-solidity-contract-design-54789205276d. Accessed 22 Jan 2020
29. Ethereum Foundation: Ethereum Frontier Guide - Democracy DAO. https://ethereum.gitbooks.io/frontier-guide/content/contract_democracy.html. Accessed 10 Jan 2020
30. OpenZeppelin: Upgradeability using Unstructured Storage. https://blog.openzeppelin.com/upgradeability-using-unstructured-storage/. Accessed 04 Feb 2020
31. Spagnuolo, F.: Smart Contract Upgradeability using Eternal Storage – OpenZeppelin blog. https://blog.openzeppelin.com/smart-contract-upgradeability-using-eternal-storage/. Accessed 04 Jan 2020

Analysis of Models for Decentralized and Collaborative AI on Blockchain

Justin D. Harris[✉]

Microsoft, Montreal/Toronto, Canada
justin.harris@microsoft.com

Abstract. Machine learning has recently enabled large advances in artificial intelligence, but these results can be highly centralized. The large datasets required are generally proprietary; predictions are often sold on a per-query basis; and published models can quickly become out of date without effort to acquire more data and maintain them. Published proposals to provide models and data for free for certain tasks include Microsoft Research's Decentralized and Collaborative AI on Blockchain. The framework allows participants to collaboratively build a dataset and use smart contracts to share a continuously updated model on a public blockchain. The initial proposal gave an overview of the framework omitting many details of the models used and the incentive mechanisms in real world scenarios. For example, the Self-Assessment incentive mechanism proposed in their work could have problems such as participants losing deposits and the model becoming inaccurate over time if the proper parameters are not set when the framework is configured. In this work, we evaluate the use of several models and configurations in order to propose best practices when using the Self-Assessment incentive mechanism so that models can remain accurate and well-intended participants that submit correct data have the chance to profit. We have analyzed simulations for each of three models: Perceptron, Naïve Bayes, and a Nearest Centroid Classifier, with three different datasets: predicting a sport with user activity from Endomondo, sentiment analysis on movie reviews from IMDB, and determining if a news article is fake. We compare several factors for each dataset when models are hosted in smart contracts on a public blockchain: their accuracy over time, balances of a good and bad user, and transaction costs (or gas) for deploying, updating, collecting refunds, and collecting rewards. A free and open source implementation for the Ethereum blockchain of these models is provided at https://github.com/microsoft/0xDeCA10B.

Keywords: Decentralized AI · Blockchain · Ethereum · Crowdsourcing · Incremental learning

1 Introduction

The advancement of popular blockchain based cryptocurrencies such as Bitcoin [1] and Ethereum [2] have inspired research in decentralized applications that

© Springer Nature Switzerland AG 2020
Z. Chen et al. (Eds.): ICBC 2020, LNCS 12404, pp. 142–153, 2020.
https://doi.org/10.1007/978-3-030-59638-5_10

leverage these publicly available resources. One application that can greatly benefit from decentralized public blockchains is the collaborative training of machine learning models to allow users to improve a model in novel ways [3]. There exists several proposals to use blockchain frameworks to enable the sharing of machine learning models. In DInEMMo, access to trained models is brokered through a marketplace allowing contributors to profit based on a model's usage, but it limits access to just those who can afford the price [4]. DanKu proposes a framework for competitions by storing already trained models in smart contracts, which do not allow for continual updating [5]. Proposals to change Proof-of-Work (PoW) to be more utilitarian by training machine learning models have also gained in popularity such as: A Proof of Useful Work for Artificial Intelligence on the Blockchain [6]. These approaches can incite more technical centralization such as harboring machine learning expertise, siloing proprietary data, and access to machine learning model predictions (e.g. charged on a per-query basis). In the crowdsourcing space, a decentralized approach called CrowdBC has been proposed to use a blockchain to facilitate crowdsourcing [7].

To address centralization in machine learning, frameworks to share machine learning models on a public blockchain while keeping the models free to use for inference have been proposed. One example is Decentralized and Collaborative AI on Blockchain from Microsoft Research [3]. That work focuses on the description of several possible incentive mechanisms to encourage participants to add data to train a model. This is the continuation of previous work in [3] by the author.

The system proposed in [3] is modular: different models or incentive mechanisms (IMs) can be used an seamlessly swapped: however, some IMs might work better for different models and vice-versa. These models can be efficiently updated with one sample at time making them useful for deployment on Proof-of-Work (PoW) blockchains [3] such as the current public Ethereum [2] blockchain. The first is a Naive Bayes classifier for its applicability to many types of problems [8]. Then, a Nearest Centroid Classifier [9]. Finally, a single layer Perceptron model [10].

We evaluated the models on three datasets that were chosen as examples of problems that would benefit from collaborative scenarios where many contributors can improve a model in order to create a shared public resource. The scenarios were: predicting a sport with user activity from Endomondo [11], sentiment analysis on movie reviews from IMDB [12], and determining if a news article is fake [13]. In all of these scenarios users benefit from having a direct impact on improving a model they frequently use and not relying on a centralized authority to host and control the model. Transaction costs (or gas) for each operation were also compared since these costs can be significant for the public Ethereum blockchain.

The Self-Assessment IM allows ongoing verification of data contributions without the need for a centralized party to evaluate data contributions. Here are the highlights of the IM as explained in [3]:

– *Deploy*: One model, h, already trained with some data is deployed.

- *Deposit*: Each data contribution with data x and label y also requires a deposit, d. Data and meta-data for each contribution is stored in a smart contract.
- *Refund*: To claim a refund on their deposit, after a time t has passed and if the current model, h, still agrees with the originally submitted classification, i.e. if $h(x) == y$, then the contributor can have their entire deposit d returned.
  - We now assume that (x, y) is "verified" data.
  - The successful return of the deposit should be recorded in a tally of points for the wallet address.
- *Take*: A contributor that has already had data verified in the *Refund* stage can locate a data point (x, y) for which $h(x) \neq y$ and request to take a portion of the deposit, d, originally given when (x, y) was submitted.

If the sample submitted, (x, y) is incorrect, then within time t, other contributors should submit (x, y') where y' is the correct or at least generally preferred label for x and $y' \neq y$. This is similar to how one generally expects bad edits to popular Wikipedia [14] articles to be corrected in a timely manner.

As proposed, the Self-Assessment IM could result in problems such as participants losing deposits and the model becoming inaccurate if the proper parameters are not set when the framework is initially deployed. In this work, we analyze the choice of several possible supervised models and configurations with the Self-Assessment IM in order to find best practices.

2   Machine Learning Models

In this section, we outline several models choices of machine learning model for use with Decentralized and Collaborative AI on Blockchain as proposed in [3]. The model architecture chosen relates closely to the incentive mechanism chosen. In this work, we will analyze models for the Self-Assessment incentive mechanism as it appeals to the decentralized nature of public blockchains in that a centralized organization should not need to maintain the IM, for example, by funding it [3].

For our experiments, we mainly consider supervised classifiers because they can be used for many applications and can be easily evaluated using test sets. In order to keep transaction costs low, we first propose to leverage the work in the Incremental Learning space [15] by using models capable of efficiently updating with one sample. Transaction costs, or "gas" as it is called in Ethereum [2], are important for most public blockchains as a way to pay for the computation cost for executing a smart contract.

2.1   Naive Bayes

The model first is a Naive Bayes classifier for its applicability to many types of problems [8]. The Naive Bayes classifier assumes each feature in the model is independent, this is what helps makes computation fast when updating and predicting. To update the model, we just need to update several counts such as the number of data points seen, the number of times each feature was seen, the number of times each feature was seen for each class, etc. When predicting, all of these counts are used for the features presented in the sparse sample to compute the most likely class for the sample using Bayes' Rule [8].

2.2 Nearest Centroid

A Nearest Centroid Classifier computes the average point (or centroid) of all points in a class and classifies new points by the label of the centroid that they are closest to [9]. They can also be easily adapted to support multiple classifications (which we do not do for this work). For this model, we keep track of the centroid for each class and update it using the cumulative moving average method [16]. Therefore we also need to record the number of samples that have been given for each class. Updating the model with one sample needs to update the centroid for the given class but not for the other classes. This model can be used with dense data representations.

2.3 Perceptron

A single layer perceptron model is useful linear model for binary classification [10]. We evaluate this model because it can be used for sparse data like text as well as dense data. The Perceptron's update algorithm only updates the weights if the model currently classifies the sample as incorrect. This is good for our system since it should help avoid overfitting. The model can be efficiently updated by just adding or subtracting, depending on the sample's label, the values for the features of the sample with the model's weights.

3 Datasets

We used three datasets were chosen as examples of problems that would benefit from collaborative scenarios where many contributors can improve a model in order to create a shared public resource. In each scenario, the users of an application that would use such a model benefit by having a direct impact on improving the model they frequently use and not relying on a centralized authority to host and control the model.

3.1 Fake News Detection

Given the text for a news article, the task is the determine if the story is reliable or not [13]. We convert each text to a sparse representation using the term-frequency of the bigrams with only the top 1000 bigrams by frequency count in the training set considered. While solving fake news detection is likely too difficult for simple models, a detector would greatly benefit from decentralization: freedom from being biased by a centralized authority.

3.2   Activity Prediction

The FitRec datasets contain information recorded from the use of participants' fitness trackers during certain activities [11]. In order to predict if someone was biking or running, we used the following features: heart rate, maximum speed, minimum speed, average speed, median speed, and gender. We did some simple feature engineering with those features such as using average heart rate divided by minimum heart rate. As usual, all of our code is public.

Fitness trackers and start-ups developing them have gained in popularity in recent years. A user considering purchasing a new tracker might not trust that the manufacturer developing it will still be able to host a centralized model in few years. The company could go bankrupt or just discontinue the service. Using a decentralized model gives users confidence that the model they need will be available for a long time, even if the company is not. This should even give them the assurance to buy the first version of a product and knowing that it should improve without them getting forced into buying a later version of the product. Even if the model does get corrupted, applications can easily revert to an earlier version on the blockchain, still giving users the service they need [3].

3.3   IMDB Movie Review Sentiment Analysis

The dataset of 25,000 IMDB movie reviews from is a dataset for sentiment analysis where the task is to predict if the English text for a movie review is positive or negative [12]. We used word-based features limited to only the most 1000 common words in the dataset. This particular sentiment analysis dataset was chosen for this work because of it's size and popularity. Even though this dataset focuses on movie reviews, in general, a collaboratively built model for sentiment analysis can be applicable in many scenarios such as a system to monitor posts on social media. Users could train a shared model when they flag posts or messages as abusive and this model can be used by several social media services to provide a more pleasant experience to their users.

4   Experiments

We conducted experiments for the three datasets with each of the three models. Experiments ran in simulations to quickly determine the outcome of different configurations. The code for our simulations is all public. The simulation iterates over the samples in the dataset submitting each sample once. For simplicity, we assumed that each scenario just has two agents representing the main two types of user groups: "good" and "bad". We refer to these as agents since they may not be real users but could be programs possibly even generating data to submit. The "good" agent almost always submits correct data with the label as provided in the dataset, as a user would normally submit correct data in a real-world use case. The "bad" agent represents those that wish to decrease the model's performance, so the "bad" agent always submits data with the opposite label that was provided in the dataset. Since the "bad" agent is trying to corrupt the model, they are willing deposit more (when required) to update the model. This allows them to update the model more quickly after the model has already been updated. The "good" agent only updates the model if the deposit required to do so is low, otherwise they will wait until later. They also check the model's recent accuracy on the test set before submitting data. In the real world, it is important for people to monitor if the model's performance and determine if it is worth trying to improve it or if it is totally corrupt. If the model's accuracy is around 85% then it can be assumed to be okay and not overfitting so ideally, it should be safe to submit new data. If incorrect data was always submitted, or submitted too often by "bad" agents, then of the model's accuracy should decrease and honest users would most likely lose their deposits because their data would not satisfy the refund criteria of the IM. We use loose terms here like "should" and "likely" because it is difficult to be general in terms of all types of models. For example, certainly a rule-based model could be used that memorizes training data. As long as no duplicate data is submitted with different labels, a rule-based model would allow each participant to get their deposits back and the analysis would be trivial. The characteristics of the agents are compared in Table 1.

Table 1. Characteristics of the agents' behaviors

Characteristic	"Good" agent	"Bad" agent
Starting balance	10,000	10,000
Average maximum deposit	50	100
Deposit standard deviation	10	3
Average time between updates	10 min	60 min
P(incorrect label)	0.01%	100%
P(submitting)	$(100 * \text{accuracy} + 15)\%$	100%

Each agent must wait 1 day before being claiming a refund for "good" data or reporting the data as "bad". This was referred to as t in our original paper. When reporting data as "bad", an agent can an amount from the initial deposit portional to the percent of "verified" contributions they have. This can be written as $r(c_r, d) = d \times \frac{n(c_r)}{\sum_{\text{all } c} n(c)}$ using the notation in our initial paper. After 9 days, either agent can claim the entire remaining deposit for a specific data sample. This was t_a in our original paper.

For each dataset, we compared:

- The change of each agent's *balance* over time. While using the IM, an agent may lose deposits to the other agent, reclaim their deposit, or profit by taking deposits that were from the other agent. We monitor balances in order to determine if it can be beneficial for an agent to participate by submitting data, whether it be correct or incorrect.

- The change of the model's *accuracy* with respect to a fixed test set over time. In a real-world scenario, it would be important for user's to monitor the accuracy as a proxy to measure if they should continue to submit data to the model. If the accuracy declines, then it could mean that "bad" agents have corrupted the model.
- The "ideal" baseline of the model's accuracy on the test set if the model were to be trained all of the simulation data. In the real-world, this would of course not be available because the data would not be known yet.

We also compared Ethereum gas costs (i.e. transaction costs) for the common actions that are done in the framework. The Update gas cost shown for each model was when the model did not agree with the provided label classification and so needed its weights to be updated. Otherwise, the Perceptron Update method would be only slightly more than prediction because a Perceptron model does not get updated if it currently predicts the same classification as the label it is given for a data sample. The gas cost of predicting is not shown because it can be done "off-chain" (without creating a transaction) which incurs no gas cost since it does not involve writing data to the blockchain. However, predicting is the most expensive operation inside of Refund and Report so the cost of doing prediction "on-chain" can be estimated using those operations. Contracts were compiled with the "solc-js" compiler using Solidity 0.6.2.

4.1   Fake News Detection

With each model, the "good" agent was able to profit and the "bad" agent lost funds. As can be seen in Fig. 1, the difference in balances was most significant with the Perceptron model. The Perceptron model has the highest accuracy yet the Naive Bayes was able to surpass its baseline accuracy.

The Perceptron model has the lowest gas cost as shown in Table 2. The deployment cost for the Naive Bayes model was much higher because each of the 1000 features effectively needs to be set twice (once for each class). The update method for the Nearest Centroid Classifier is expensive because it needs to go through most dimensions of the 1000 dimensional centroids. Prediction (which happens in Refund and Report) did not need to go through each dimension because the distance to each centroid can be calculated by storing the magnitude of each centroid and then using the sparse input data to find the difference from the magnitude just for the few features in the sparse input.

4.2   Activity Prediction

As seen in Fig. 2, with each model, all "good" agents can profit while the "bad" agent wastes lots of funds. The Naive Bayes (NB) and Nearest Centroid Classifier (NCC) models performed very well on this type of data, hardly straying from the ideal baseline. The linear Perceptron on the other hand was much more sensitive to data from the "bad" agent and it's accuracy dropped significantly several times but finally recovering.

Balances & Accuracy on Hidden Test Set

— NB accuracy when trained with all data: 81.8%
— NB Accuracy
— NB Bad Agent Balance
— NB Good Agent Balance
- - NCC accuracy when trained with all data: 67.3%
- - NCC Accuracy
- - NCC Bad Agent Balance
···· NCC Good Agent Balance
···· Perceptron accuracy when trained with all data: 90.0%
···· Perceptron Accuracy
···· Perceptron Bad Agent Balance
···· Perceptron Good Agent Balance

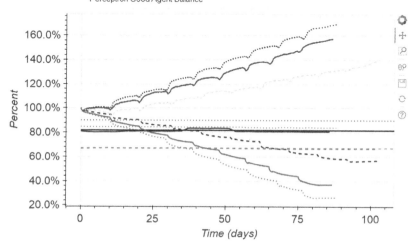

Fig. 1. Plot of simulations with the Fake News dataset.

The Perceptron model has the lowest gas cost as shown in Table 3. The gas costs were fairly close for each action amongst the models, especially compared to the other datasets. This is mostly because there are very few features (just 9) for this dataset.

4.3   IMDB Movie Review Sentiment Analysis

Figure 3 shows all "good" agents can profit while the "bad" agent loses most or all of the initial balance. All models maintained their accuracy with this type of data with the Naive Bayes model performing the best.

By only a small amount, the Naive Bayes model beats the Perceptron model for the Update method with the lowest gas cost. The gas costs for all actions are shown in Table 4. As with the Fake News dataset, the Update cost for the Nearest Centroid Classifier was high because most dimensions needs to be visited. The Naive Bayes model had a much higher deployment cost since the amount of data was effectively double since each feature needs to be set for each of the two classes.

Table 2. Ethereum gas costs for each model for the Fake News dataset. Data samples had 15 integer features representing the presence of the top bigrams from the training data. In brackets are approximate USD values from February 2020 with a modest gas price of 4gwei and ETH valued at 266 USD.

Action	Naive Bayes	Sparse nearest centroid	Sparse perceptron
Deployment	55,511,190	34,825,095	**30,719,062** (32.69 USD)
Update	281,447	6,476,417	**263,495** (0.28 USD)
Refund	172,216	152,233	**138,094** (0.15 USD)
Reward	136,800	116,689	**102,550** (0.11 USD)

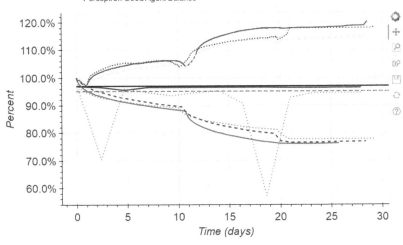

Balances & Accuracy on Hidden Test Set

— NB accuracy when trained with all data: 97.0%
— NB Accuracy
— NB Bad Agent Balance
— NB Good Agent Balance
- - NCC accuracy when trained with all data: 95.1%
- - NCC Accuracy
- - NCC Bad Agent Balance
    NCC Good Agent Balance
···· Perceptron accuracy when trained with all data: 95.1%
···· Perceptron Accuracy
···· Perceptron Bad Agent Balance
···· Perceptron Good Agent Balance

Fig. 2. Plot of simulations with the Activity Prediction dataset.

Table 3. Ethereum gas costs for each model for the Activity Prediction dataset. Data samples had 9 integer features. In brackets are approximate USD values from February 2020 with a modest gas price of 4gwei and ETH valued at 266 USD.

Action	Naive Bayes	Dense nearest centroid	Dense perceptron
Deployment	10,113,478	9,474,196	**8,977,816** (9.55 USD)
Update	**222,523** (0.24 USD)	243,164	227,047
Refund	151,070	146,768	**133,745** (0.14 USD)
Reward	115,525	111,223	**98,238** (0.10 USD)

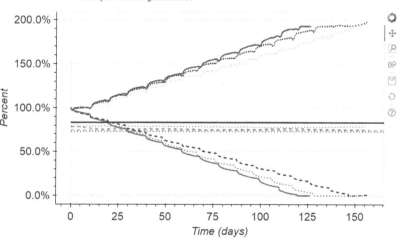

Fig. 3. Plot of simulations with the IMDB Movie Review Sentiment Analysis dataset.

Table 4. Ethereum gas costs for each model for the IMDB Movie Review Sentiment Analysis dataset. Data samples had 20 integer features representing a movie review with the presence of 20 words that were in the 1000 most common words in the training data. In brackets are approximate USD values from February 2020 with a modest gas price of 4gwei and ETH valued at 266 USD.

Action	Naive Bayes	Sparse nearest centroid	Sparse perceptron
Deployment	55,423,618	34,822,727	**30,627,174** (32.59 USD)
Update	**332,636** (0.35 USD)	6,490,180	332,905
Refund	189,954	163,593	**145,667** (0.15 USD)
Reward	154,538	128,049	**110,223** (0.12 USD)

5   Conclusion

With all experiments, the Perceptron model was consistently the cheapest to use. This was mostly because the size of the model was much less than the other two models which need to store information for each class, effectively twice the amount of information that the Perceptron needs to store. While each model was expensive to deploy, this is a one time cost to incur. This cost is far less than the comparable cost to host a web service with the model for several months.

Most models were able to maintain their accuracy except for the volatile Perceptron for the Activity Prediction dataset. Even if the model gets corrupted with incorrect data, it can be forked from an earlier time when its accuracy on a hidden test set was higher. It can also be retrained with data identified as "good" while it was deployed. It is important for users to be aware of the accuracy on the model on some hidden test set. Users can maintain their own hidden test sets or possibly use a service supplied by an organization which would publish a rating on a model based on the test sets they have.

The balance plots looked mostly similar across the experiments because the "good" agent was already careful and how we set a constant wait time of 9 days for either agent to claim the remaining deposit for a data contribution. The "good" agent honestly submitted correct data and only did so when they thought the model was reliable, this helped ensure that they can recover their deposits and earn for reporting many contributions from the "bad agent". When the "bad" agent is able to corrupt, it can successfully report a portion of the contributions from the "good" agent as bad because the model would not agree with those contributions. The "bad" agent cannot claim a majority of these deposits when reporting the contribution since they do not have as many "verified" contributions as the "good" agent. This leaves a left over amount for which either agent must wait for 9 days before taking the entire remaining deposit, hence the periodic looking patterns in the balance plots every 9 days. The pattern continues throughout the simulation because there is always data for which the deposit that cannot be claimed by either agent after just the initial refund wait time of 1 day.

Future work in analyzing more scenarios is encouraged and easy to implement with our open source tools at https://github.com/microsoft/0xDeCA10B/tree/master/simulation. For example, changing the initial balances of each agent to determine how much a "good" agent need to spend to stop a much more resourceful "bad" agent willing to corrupt a model.

References

1. Nakamoto, S., et al.: Bitcoin: a peer-to-peer electronic cash system (2008)
2. Buterin, V.: A next generation smart contract & decentralized application platform (2015)
3. Harris, J.D., Waggoner, B.: Decentralized and collaborative AI on blockchain. In: 2019 IEEE International Conference on Blockchain (Blockchain), July 2019
4. Marathe, A., Narayanan, K., Gupta, A., Pr, M.: DInEMMo: decentralized incentivization for enterprise marketplace models. In: 2018 IEEE 25th International Conference on High Performance Computing Workshops (HiPCW), pp. 95–100 (2018)
5. Kurtulmus, A.B., Daniel, K.: Trustless machine learning contracts; evaluating and exchanging machine learning models on the ethereum blockchain (2018)
6. Lihu, A., Du, J., Barjaktarevic, I., Gerzanics, P., Harvilla, M.: A proof of useful work for artificial intelligence on the blockchain (2020)
7. Li, M., et al.: CrowdBC: a blockchain-based decentralized framework for crowdsourcing. IEEE Trans. Parallel Distrib. Syst. **30**(6), 1251–1266 (2019)
8. Webb, G.I.: Naïve bayes. In: Sammut, C., Webb, G.I. (eds.) Encyclopedia of Machine Learning, pp. 713–714. Springer, Boston (2010). https://doi.org/10.1007/978-0-387-30164-8_576
9. Tibshirani, R., Hastie, T., Narasimhan, B., Chu, G.: Diagnosis of multiple cancer types by shrunken centroids of gene expression. Proc. Nat. Acad. Sci. **99**(10), 6567–6572 (2002)
10. Rosenblatt, F.: The perceptron: a probabilistic model for information storage and organization in the brain. Psychol. Rev. **65**(6), 386 (1958)
11. Ni, J., Muhlstein, L., McAuley, J.: Modeling heart rate and activity data for personalized fitness recommendation. In: The World Wide Web Conference (WWW 2019), New York, NY, USA, pp. 1343–1353. Association for Computing Machinery (2019)
12. Maas, A.L., Daly, R.E., Pham, P.T., Huang, D., Ng, A.Y., Potts, C.: Learning word vectors for sentiment analysis. In: Proceedings of the 49th Annual Meeting of the Association for Computational Linguistics: Human Language Technologies, Portland, Oregon, USA, pp. 142–150. Association for Computational Linguistics, June 2011
13. Kaggle: UTK Machine Learning Club: Fake News (2020). https://www.kaggle.com/c/fake-news/overview. Accessed 07 Jan 2020
14. Wikipedia contributors: Wikipedia – Wikipedia, the free encyclopedia (2020). https://en.wikipedia.org/w/index.php?title=Wikipedia. Accessed 08 Jan 2020
15. Schlimmer, J.C., Fisher, D.: A case study of incremental concept induction. In: Proceedings of the Fifth AAAI National Conference on Artificial Intelligence (AAAI 1986), pp. 496–501. AAAI Press (1986)
16. Wikipedia contributors: Moving average – Wikipedia, the free encyclopedia (2020). https://en.wikipedia.org/w/index.php?title=Moving_average. Accessed 3 Feb 2020

ACCTP: Cross Chain Transaction Platform for High-Value Assets

Minfeng Qi[1($\boxtimes$)], Ziyuan Wang[1], Donghai Liu[1], Yang Xiang[1], Butian Huang[2], and Feng Zhou[3]

[1] Blockchain Innovation Lab, Swinburne University of Technology, Melbourne, Australia
minfengqi@swin.edu.au
[2] Hangzhou Yunphant Network Technology Co. Ltd., Hangzhou, China
hbt@yunphant.com
[3] Vnet Foundation, Hangzhou, China
zhoufeng@vntchain.io

Abstract. Recently, with the development of blockchain technology, people not only regard blockchain as a tradable cryptocurrency but also pay attention to other areas where blockchain technology can be applied, such as high-value assets (art, diamonds, etc.). Through the study of some existing blockchain-based platforms for high-value assets, we find that the blockchain ecosystem in this emerging industry presents a state of blooming but isolated from each other. In view of the problem, we discuss some projects based on cross-chain technology and believe that using cross-chain technology is one of the best solutions. Therefore, we propose the ACCTP (Asset Cross Chain Transaction Platform) model to connect different blockchain-based transaction platforms. The model is divided into three cross-chain service layers, called C2IE, C2AE, and C2TS, which are designed to implement the functions of information exchange, asset exchange and transaction exchange respectively.

Keywords: ACCTP · Blockchain · High-value asset · Cross-chain

1 Introduction

In recent years, blockchain, as one of the most popular words, is being known by more and more people. After the halo of cryptocurrencies faded away, speculation is no longer synonymous with blockchain. Scholars and entrepreneurs are not only limited to the application of blockchain technology to the financial field but also bring the idea and technology of decentralization to art, diamond, real estate, precious metals and other high-value asset investment fields.

From the perspective of the characteristics of blockchain, as a distributed, decentralized and tamper-resistant ledger, blockchain ensures the non-tamperability and traceability of asset data, and maximizes the transparency of asset transaction records [1]. On the other hand, from the view of payment methods and consensus mechanisms of blockchain, peer-to-peer payment methods and

Z. Chen et al. (Eds.): ICBC 2020, LNCS 12404, pp. 154–168, 2020.
https://doi.org/10.1007/978-3-030-59638-5_11

existing consensus mechanisms such as PoW, PoS and DPoS provide a convenient, safe and mutually trusted trading environment for the transaction of high-value assets [2,3].

Therefore, it is a natural fit for deploying blockchain technology to the field of high-value assets due to the above sort of advantages. Currently, a variety of blockchain platforms for high-value asset transactions are emerging endlessly, such as art chains, diamond chains, gold chains, etc. However, due to the difference in the underlying technology, the majority of platforms exist in the form of an independent chain which has its own user group. Users need to repeatedly register the same assets and personal information on different platforms, which leads to waste of resources and hinders the industry to play the scale benefit and network effect.

In order to overcome the obstacles of information sharing and asset exchange between different blockchain platforms, we propose an ACCTP model based on cross-chain technology. The platform provides three functions: information exchange, asset exchange and trading exchange. Data and tokens on different chains can be shared, exchanged and synchronized in real-time so that the connected platforms are no longer isolated from each other.

In summary, the contributions of our work are:

- We discuss the advantages of combining blockchain with the field of high value assets and point out the existing problems and challenges in the industry.
- We provide a thorough overview of on-going blockchain platforms of high value assets, as well as the projects applying cross-chain techniques.
- We propose an innovative blockchain hub, through the application of a variety of cross-chain techniques, connecting different blockchain platforms to achieve information sharing and asset exchanges between chains.

2   Related Work

In this section, we first provide a comprehensive overview of blockchain-enabled platforms for high-value assets. Then, we discuss some popular cross-chain projects which applied various cross-chain technologies. In the end, we highlight the novelty of our ACCTP solutions by comparing with those related works.

2.1   High Value Asset Platforms

Due to the problems of unknown source, inconvenient circulation, difficult management and large number of counterfeits in the art industry [4], the combination of blockchain and art has become a new direction for the development of the art market. Blockchain enabled art platform serves as an alternative type of internet archive tool for digital arts [5,6]. Recently, many scholars and entrepreneurs have proposed the idea and practice of blockchain-enabled art platform. Monograph [7] adopts a combination of digital media and artwork information to encrypt, and permanently records the copyright of digital artwork on the Bitcoin blockchain. R.A.R.E. [8] realizes three functions of discovering, collecting and displaying digital artwork. Wang et al. [9] proposed an ArtChain platform which enables commercial-grade transactions around art assets. Oxowns.art [10] enables buyers to purchase and resale ownership of the artwork.

The rise of the diamond trading platform supported by blockchain technology is to solve the problems such as unknown-origin, blood or fake diamonds, etc. [11]. Everledger [12–14] combines blockchain technology with AI, IoT and nanotechnology, creating a digital twin for every diamond. Gem Communication Platform (GCP) ensures the authenticity of diamonds by using the characteristics of the blockchain [15]. GlitKoin platform [16] facilitates the decentralized global diamond trading by maintaining a record of origin, certification, trading history for each diamond. Pure Diamond Blockchain [17] collects and digitizes the information of each diamond on its blockchain, including cultivation, refinement and appraisal. In addition, there are other blockchain-based platforms that trade gold [18,19], real estate [20], and other high-value assets [21,22].

2.2 Cross Chain Techniques

The cross-chain technique empowers chains to communicate and operate with each other [23]. In 2015, Blockstream team [24] proposed the liquid Network prototype using the method of side-chain technique to realize the value transfer between chains. Lightning Network [25] constructs RSMC (recoverable sequence maturity contract) and HTLC (hashed time lock contract), which ensures the pre-deposited fund allocation and transfer time limitation respectively. BTC Relay [26] enables smart contracts and applications based on Ethereum to interact with Bitcoin by using relay technique. Cosmos [27] and Polkadot [28] projects are committed to the interoperability of blockchain. Cosmos builds a Cosmos hub-centric network architecture. Each blockchain is considered as a zone and connected to the hub in the way of Peg Zone. While in Polkadot network, Relay Chain and Parachain replace Cosmos hub and Zone. Although they have similar model architecture, there are many difference, such as designs of proof-of-stake, consensus protocols, security, and governance.

2.3 ACCTP Solutions

Overall, based on our analysis of current blockchain-based platforms for high-value asset, shown in Table 1, we believe the field of combining blockchain technology with high-value assets is still in the infancy. At this stage, a relatively complete blockchain platform ecosystem has not yet been formed, that is, the building of each platform is based on different underlying technologies, and the programming languages used are also different. Furthermore, most platforms implement their own tokens to attract their own user base, which has lead to the isolation of user base and the formation of bad competition in the industry. Users need to repeatedly register the same user and asset information on different platforms, which greatly reduces the user's experience of the blockchain platform, and also hinders the wide-ranging promotion and application of the platform.

Table 1. A summary to current blockchain-enabled high-value asset platforms.

Platform	Blockchain Ecosystem	ICO-Tokens	Field
Monograph	Bitcoin	-	Digital art
R.A.R.E.	Ethereum	Ether	Digital art
ArtChain	Ethereum	ACG&ACGT	Art
Oxowns.art	Ethereum	Ether	Digital art
Everledger	Hyperledger Fabric	-	Diamond
GCP	Hyperledger Fabric	GCC	Diamond & Gem
GlitKoin	Hyperledger Fabric	GTN	Diamond
Pure	Ethereum	ERC-20	Lab-growth Diamond
DGX	Hyperledger Fabric	DGX	Gold & Precious Metals
Emergent	Hyperledger Fabric	G-Coin	Gold
ShelterZoom	Hyperledger Fabric	-	Real-estate
V-Chain	Ethereum	-	Car
Deposit-P	Consortium	-	Used-car

Compared to those isolated blockchain-based high-value asset platforms, our proposed ACCTP model provides a novel solution to the problems mentioned above. It can be highlighted in three aspects as follows.

- ACCTP proposes a novel cross-chain solution (will be described in detail in Sect. 3), which is not covered by other related work. It draws on the advantages of multiple cross-chain mechanisms and applies these mechanisms to different cross-chain layers. In this way, each cross-chain layer has different functions, while as a whole, these cross-chain layers can communicate with each other, which greatly improves the efficiency of cross-chain.
- ACCTP will have its own independent development environment and language, which means that it can form its own network, instead of developing in the Ethernet or Hyperledger ecosystem. There are pros and cons to doing so. The good thing is that the future development space of ACCTP will be huge because the construction of future platforms can be based on the underlying technology and languages of ACCTP. While the bad aspect is that it requires a large amount of up-front investment because the development of the ecosystem is not easy.
- ACCTP will not develop tokens, which means that the development of ACCTP will not be financed by tokens. The purpose of this is that ACCTP only wants to be a "seaport" connecting various platforms. By creating aisles connecting various platforms, users on all connected platforms become a whole. Therefore, essentially it does not have its own user base, and there are reasons to believe that it does not need to attract users with tokens.

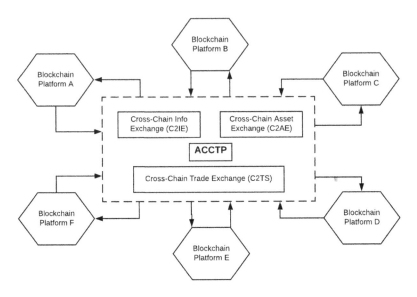

Fig. 1. ACCTP model

3   System Design and Architecture

In this section, we demonstrate our ACCTP (Asset Cross Chain Transaction Platform) model which uses cross-chain technology to realize the transfer of asset and product information among multiple blockchain platform networks with different architectures. As shown in Fig. 1, we have designed the cross-chain services of ACCTP in three layers, including cross-chain information exchange (C2IE), cross-chain asset exchange (C2AE) and cross-chain trading service (C2TS). Different blockchain platforms are connected with ACCTP through peg technique (explained in the section five). ACCTP enables them to communicate and operate with each other. The asset and product information registered on different blockchains can be shared in real-time, and different tokens can be freely exchanged.

3.1   Consensus Mechanism

ACCTP adopts a consensus mechanism based on PBFT. In Sect. 4, we introduced the participants of the model. One of the types of participants is Relayer. Relayer is responsible for verifying and submitting new block headers to each block header chain maintained by the ACCTP system. In order to ensure that a malicious relayer does not undermine the consistency and security of ACCTP data, we adopt a PBFT-based consensus mechanism, that is, each block is generated by a unique master node (referred to here as the Relayer). When the master Relayer receives $2f + 1$ (f refers to the number of tolerable malicious nodes) the similar verification result (the hash digest of the new block calculated by the other relayers based on the transaction result), then it can officially submit a new Block header and update database.

3.2   Scalability

Different from the traditional single-chain scheme in which the entire network nodes share a blockchain, the ACCTP model adopts a multi-chain design idea, that is, there are multiple independent sub-chains corresponding to the connected blockchain platform in the ACCTP system. Each sub-chain updates the information and status of the corresponding blockchain platform in real time. In this way, ACCTP can realize the processing of multiple concurrent requests at the same time, breaking through the limitation of the processing capacity of a single node, thereby improving the overall performance of the system.

3.3   Privacy

Although ACCTP aims to share asset information on various blockchain platforms, when it comes to privacy-related information such as transaction data, ACCTP uses a multi-channel approach to avoid the leakage of privacy. At the C2AE and C2TS layers, ACCTP establishes a special channel for both parties to a transaction to record the data generated by the transaction. Only users on the channel have access to the data, which protects the user's privacy to a certain extent.

3.4   Data Security

In terms of data security, while providing real-time data sharing and exchange for multiple blockchain platforms, ACCTP does not store data in the middle process, effectively avoiding illegal access and tampering of data. In addition, in order to prevent malicious blockchain from connecting to the platform, ACCTP has standard processes and requirements for the verification of platform qualification and identity, such as the number of active users on the blockchain, the type and number of assets, the amount and number of transactions, etc.

4   Cross-chain Enablement

As the core part of the whole article, this section mainly introduces the specific technical implementation process of ACCTP for cross-chain service. In the above section, it is mentioned that ACCTP is divided into three different cross-chain service layers, namely C2IE, C2AE and C2TS. According to this logic, we divide the section into three parts, and will explain the technical implementation of these service layers, respectively.

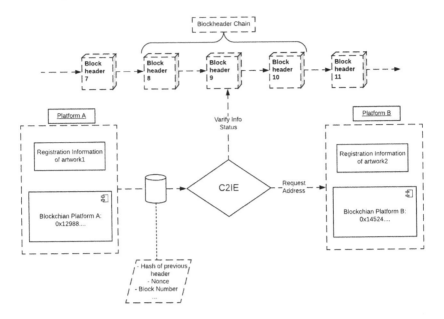

Fig. 2. C2IE-Layer schematic

4.1   Cross-chain Information Exchange (C2IE)

C2IE is a cross-chain information exchange layer, which is used to verify and exchange products information on blockchain platforms connecting to the system. This information refers to the product data registered by the user on the blockchain. Take the art platform as an example. The information includes registration information, exhibition information, artist information, gallery information, collector's information, etc.

C2IE mainly uses Relay cross-chain mechanism [29]. The specific implementation method of Relay mechanism is that after obtaining the block head information of the side chain, the Relay chain uses the same consensus verification method as the side chain, and then proves the operation and data of the side chain through the proving Merkle branch.

Figure 2 briefly illustrates the components and workflow of C2IE. As shown in the figure, C2IE is mainly composed of a block header chain, also known as Relay chain. The system supports real-time sharing of multiple blockchain information, but as a simple example, the figure only shows the communication between two blockchain platforms. Platform B requests registration information about artwork1 from C2IE system. After receiving this request, C2IE immediately sends a request to each platform (platform A here), asking each blockchain platform to provide the block header information of the latest block. After platform A transmits block header information to C2IE, the system verifies the information status of artwork1 in platform A according to the information. If the verification

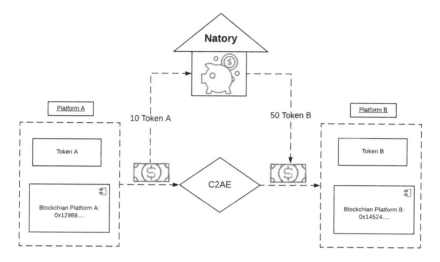

Fig. 3. C2AE-Layer schematic

passes, the system grants the temporary access right and address of data about artwork1 to platform B.

As an intermediary for multi-party information exchange, C2IE maintains multiple block header chains corresponding to the connected blockchain platforms within the system. These block header chains are the keys to verifying the status of transactions and information on the blockchain as shown in the figure.

4.2 Cross-chain Asset Exchange (C2AE)

C2AE is a system to exchange or transfer cryptocurrencies or assets of among different blockchain platform. At present, most blockchain platforms have their own tokens, just like most countries in the world have their own legal currencies. The biggest problem is that these tokens are difficult to exchange because of the different underlying technologies of the blockchain, which is not conducive to the transactions between the blockchain.

In order to overcome this problem, we adopt the Notaries cross-chain mechanism to achieve assets exchange. The notary mechanism refers to that when the two sides of the transaction exchange different tokens, a third party with mutual trust acts as the notary to verify and confirm the transaction [29]. We treat C2AE as a single centralized institution here with fast transaction processing and strong compatibility. As shown in Fig. 3, a user of blockchain platform A wants to convert 10 tokens A into token B on platform B. When the user submits a currency exchange request to C2AE, C2AE will send 50 tokens B to the collection address on blockchain B according to the current currency exchange rate of the market.

To some extent, this centralized notarial mechanism relies on the reputation of its own institutions to replace the trust mechanism created by technology. The

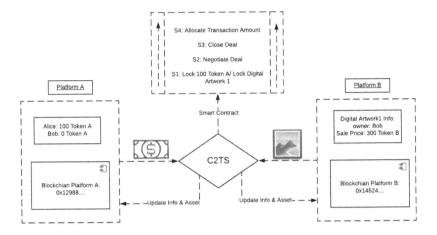

Fig. 4. C2TS-Layer schematic

premise of using this system is that the ACCTP platform needs to be accepted and trusted by a wide range of users. At the same time, the platform itself needs to have strong financial strength. Because when more and more blockchains are connected to the platform, ACCTP needs a variety of tokens as reserves to ensure the reputation of currency exchange.

4.3 Cross-chain Trading Exchanges (C2TS)

C2TS is a transaction matching system for high-value assets on two blockchain platforms. It can use tokens on one platform to directly purchase assets on another platform, such as artwork.

We propose a trading model based on Hash locking cross-chain mechanism to realize the real-time exchange of money and goods on different blockchains. Hash locking [29] refers to that when the two sides of the transaction exchange different tokens, they lock their tokens in a special address in advance, requiring both sides to provide the unlocking key of tokens for asset withdrawal within a specified time.

C2TS realizes two functions. One is matchmaking, the other is updating blockchain status. We use the following figure to illustrate how the system works. Alice, a user on platform A, wants to trade with Bob on platform B because she is interested in a digital artwork1 of Bob. As a result, they sent a request to C2TS for a transaction. C2TS executes the smart contract of the transaction after receiving the request. Alice and Bob respectively invested 100 token A and the digital artwork1 as a pledge. After negotiation and agreement between the two parties in a limited time, the transaction is concluded (Alice buys Bob's artwork1 with 80 token A). C2TS automatically allocates the final transaction amount to both parties, and updates the account status of both parties on both platforms in real-time.

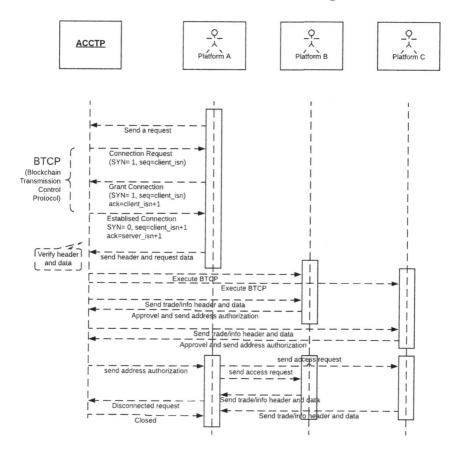

Fig. 5. Multi-chain communication sequence diagram

In the above trading mechanism, the pledge of tokens and artworks provides the basis of mutual trust for both parties, while the ingenious time limit and key transfer logic ensure the atomicity of the transaction, that is, if the transaction is not successful, the assets and artworks will be rolled back to the state before the transaction.

5 Model Improvements

In this section, we make some specific supplementary explanations on the ACCTP model, in terms of multi-chain interaction processes, platform connection approaches, and event participants. Furthermore, we discuss the practical use-cases that our model can be applied in.

5.1   Multi-chain Communication Processes

In order to support the interaction between different blockchain platforms, we propose a cross-chain interaction protocol called Blockchain Transaction Control Protocol (BTCP). This protocol provides a universal cross-chain standard within the ACCTP ecosystem, enabling secure data transmission, secure routing and forwarding between platforms. We explain how this protocol works by simulating the interaction between multiple platforms and ACCTP (shown in Fig. 5).

When ACCTP receives the request from platform A, ACCTP starts performing BTCP. It sends a request to establish a connection to platform A, then platform A authorizes the connection, and ACCTP sends a message that the connection is established to platform A. At this point, the BTCP of the entire connection process has ended. After completing the connection, platform A continues to send to ACCTP a request carrying a request line, a request header, and a request data. After ACCTP verifies that the request is valid, it executes BTCP to platform B and platform C (by parsing the request address carried in the request header). Finally, after a series of interactive requests, platform A obtains temporary access rights to the addresses of platform B and platform C, and completes the request. In addition, it is worth noting that after the end of the entire request, ACCTP also needs to perform disconnected BTCP with the platforms that established the connection, which has avoided being in a long-connected connection state.

5.2   Platform-Pegging Technique

Due to the differences in the underlying architecture technologies of various blockchain platforms, such as different packaging technologies adopted by network layers and consensus layers, it is difficult to communicate between different blockchain platforms. The emergence of ACCTP has solved this problem to a great extent. By establishing a Pegging Aisle inside ACCTP, blockchain platforms based on different architectures can be connected to ACCTP in a two-way pegging approach, and then use the BTCP protocol to interact with different layers of ACCTP to realize cross-chain functions.

As shown in Fig. 6, some blockchain platforms (such as platform C and D in the figure) based on the underlying technology and ecosystem of Ethereum and Bitcoin cannot directly interact with ACCTP. We propose that the indirect connection between the existing blockchain platforms and ACCTP can be realized by establishing a direct connection between Ethereum, Bitcoin and other public chains and ACCTP (the aisle built on the ACCTP language). When more and more blockchain platforms based on the ACCTP development language (such as platform A and B in the figure), by following the BTCP protocol, information sharing and asset conversion between platforms will become simpler and faster.

5.3   Participants of ACCTP

For the blockchain, the type, number, and level of activity of the participants are critical [30], and ACCTP is no exception. In the design of the ACCTP model,

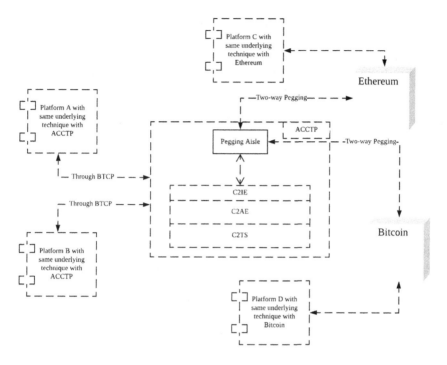

Fig. 6. Pegging Aisle - A Aisle connected to blockchain platforms

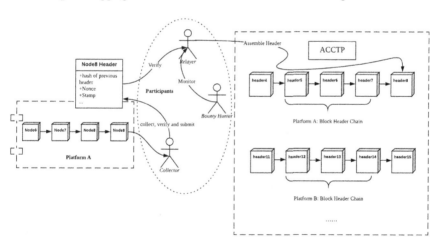

Fig. 7. Roles of participants in ACCTP

the participants supporting the effective work of the platform and maintaining the security of the blockchain can be divided into the following three categories: collector, relayer, and bounty hunter.

In Fig. 7, the collector is responsible for collecting and verifying the each round block generated by blockchain platform, and submitting the block header to the relayer. Every time the collector submits a block header, it will get some submission bonuses. Relayer will verify the block header information submitted by the collector. When the verification is passed, the block header will be assembled on the corresponding blockchain in ACCTP by relayer. The existence of Relayer ensures that the state and information of the blockchain maintained by ACCTP and the externally connected blockchain platform are consistent. Bounty hunter oversees the work of relayers and collectors and relies on reporting illegal blocks and nodes for rewards.

5.4 Practical Applications

The biggest difference between ACCTP and other high-value asset blockchain platforms is its functionality. Its purpose is not just to apply blockchain technology (distributed storage of data, tamper-proofing and traceability), but to achieve the exchange of assets and information between different chains, avoiding users to repeatedly register the same on different chains Asset information. This is also the reason why we think this model has wide application prospects. At present, all high-value asset blockchain-based platforms can connect and request each other through this model. If it is an platform developed based on the existing public chain ecosystem, we can indirectly connect the platform by creating a pegging aisle between ACCTP and the public chain. If it is a platform developed based on the ACCTP ecosystem in the future, it can be directly connected.

In addition, from the perspective of applications, ACCTP is not limited to a single type of high-value assets. Its compatibility is another feature of this model. In theory, ACCTP can connect high-value asset platforms in any field, such as art, diamonds, gold, real estate, automobiles, and even options. In general, ACCTP based on cross-chain technology has greatly improved the applicable fields of the blockchain platform and formed a network effect in these areas.

6   Conclusion and Future Work

In this paper, we have discussed the advantages of combining blockchain technology in the field of high-value assets (such as art, diamond and etc.), and pointed out the current challenges for the ecosystem of blockchain enabled high-value asset platforms. In order to solve the problems that platforms cannot communicate and operate with each other, we propose an ACCTP model based on cross-chain technology. ACCTP has multiple cross-chain service layers which use different cross-chain technologies to meet the needs of information sharing, token exchange, asset transaction among blockchain platforms, respectively.

The attempt of applying cross-chain into blockchain-based high-value asset platforms is undoubtedly a landing experiment of cross-chain technology, and we believe it will inspire more landings of cross-chain projects in the field of high-value assets. However, we have to point out that the design of ACCTP is not consummate enough. There are still some problems that are not fully considered, such as the way of communicate between cross-chain service layers; And when more and more blockchain platforms are connected to ACCTP, how can ACCTP solve network congestion and token reserve? In future, we plan to work on perfecting and implementing our design by addressing these issues.

References

1. Tam Vo, T., Wang, Z., Karunamoorthy, D., Wagner, J., Abebe E., Mohania, M.: Internet of blockchains: techniques and challenges ahead. In: IEEE International Conference on Internet of Things (iThings) and IEEE Green Computing and Communications (GreenCom) and IEEE Cyber, Physical and Social Computing (CPSCom) and IEEE Smart Data (SmartData), Halifax, NS, Canada, pp. 1574–1581 (2018)
2. Nofer, M., Gomber, P., Hinz, O., Schiereck, D.: Blockchain. Bus. Inf. Syst. Eng. **59**(3), 183–187 (2017)
3. Pereira, J., Tavalaei, M.M., Ozalp, H.: Blockchain-based platforms: decentralized infrastructures and its boundary conditions. Tech. Forecast. Soc. Change **146**, 94–102 (2019)
4. Shaw, A.: Art business blockchain. Apollo **188**(667), 104–105 (2018)
5. Scherling, L.: Blockchain Technologies In Community-based Arts (Working Paper). Columbia University (2017)
6. Mcconaghy, M., Mcmullen, G., Parry, G., Mcconaghy, T., Holtzman, D.: Visibility and digital art: blockchain as an ownership layer on the Internet. Strategic Change **26**(5), 461–470 (2017)
7. Martin, Z.: Digital art as 'Monetised Graphics': enforcing intellectual property on the blockchain. Philos. Technol. **3**, 15–41 (2016)
8. R.A.R.E Homepage: R.A.R.E Digital Art Market. https://www.rareart.io/. Accessed 2017
9. Wang, Z., Yang, L., Wang, Q., Liu, D., Xu, Z., Liu, S.: ArtChain: blockchain-enabled platform for art marketplace. In: IEEE International Conference on Blockchain (Blockchain), Atlanta, GA, USA, pp. 447–454 (2019)
10. Anon: 0xowns.art presents a blockchain platform that's turning ownership into art. M2 Presswire. Accessed 5 Apr 2019
11. Researchers from Hong Kong Polytechnic University: Describe Findings in Blockchain Technology: Blockchain-technology-supported Platforms for Diamond Authentication and Certification in Luxury Supply Chains. J. Eng. (2019)
12. Everleger Homepage. https://www.everledger.io/industry-solutions/diamonds/. Accessed 2019
13. Lomas, N.: Everledger Is Using Blockchain To Combat Fraud. Starting With Diamonds, TechCrunch (2015)
14. Choi, T.M.: Blockchain-technology-supported platforms for diamond authentication and certification in luxury supply chains. Transp. Res. Part E Logist. Transp. Rev. **128**(1), 17–29 (2019)
15. Gem Correspondent: Gem Correspondent Company Unveils Blockchain-based Diamond Trading Platform. Wireless News (2019)
16. GlitKoin: The Token Sale Is Live. GlitKoin Blockchain Diamond Trading Platform, M2 Presswire (2018)

17. Anon: Pure diamond blockchain technology - jewellery industry's new ground-breaking innovation. J. Eng. 714 (2018)
18. Eha, B.: U.K. mint testing blockchain trading platform for digital gold. American Banker, 182(71) (2017)
19. Anon: Emergent Technology Announces Gold Blockchain Platform. PR Newswire. Accessed 5 Feb 2018
20. Anon: ShelterZoom's Blockchain Real Estate Platform Launches in the U.S. Wireless News. Accessed 31 Dec 2017
21. Obour, A., Kwame, O., et al.: V-chain: a blockchain-based car lease platform. In: IEEE International Conference on Internet of Things (iThings) and IEEE Green Computing and Communications (GreenCom) and IEEE Cyber, Physical and Social Computing (CPSCom) and IEEE Smart Data (SmartData), pp. 1317–1325 (2018)
22. Zhang, J., et al.: Towards transparency and trustworthy: a used-car deposit platform based on blockchain. In: IEEE 19th International Conference on Software Quality, Reliability and Security Companion (QRS-C), pp. 46–50 (2019)
23. Wang, H., Cen Y., Li, X.: Blockchain router: a cross-chain communication protocol. In: IEEA 2017 (2017)
24. Anon: Blockstream Launches the Liquid Network. ICT Monitor Worldwide. Accessed 11 Oct 2018
25. Lee, S., Kim, H.: On the robustness of lightning network in bitcoin. Pervasive Mobile Comput. **61**, 101108 (2020)
26. BTC-Relay: Welcome to BTC-Relay's documentation. BTC-Relay Documentation (2016). https://btc-relay.readthedocs.io/en/latest/
27. Anon: Welcome to the hub of all hubs: Cosmos has launched. TechCrunch. Accessed 17 Mar 2019
28. Palkadot Homepage (2017). https://polkadot.network/
29. Buterin, V.: Chain Interoperability. https://allquantor.at/blockchainbib/pdf/. Accessed 2016
30. Hardjono, T., Lipton, A., Pentland, A.: Toward an interoperability architecture for blockchain autonomous systems. IEEE Trans. Eng. Manag. **5**(99), 1–12 (2019)

Lekana - Blockchain Based Archive Storage for Large-Scale Cloud Systems

Eranga Bandara[1]([✉]), Xueping Liang[2], Sachin Shetty[3], Wee Keong Ng[4],
Peter Foytik[3], Nalin Ranasinghe[5], Kasun De Zoysa[5], Bård Langöy[1],
and David Larsson[1]

[1] Pagero AB, Gothenburg, Sweden
{eranga.herath,bard.langoy,david.larsson}@pagero.com
[2] Virginia State University, St. Petersburg, VA, USA
xliang@vsu.edu
[3] Old Dominion University, Norfolk, VA, USA
{sshetty,pfoytik}@odu.edu
[4] School of Computer Science and Engineering, Nanyang Technological University,
Singapore, Singapore
awkng@ntu.edu.sg
[5] University of Colombo School of Computing, Colombo, Sri Lanka
{dnr,kasun}@ucsc.cmb.ac.lk

Abstract. Blockchain is a form of a distributed storage system that stores a chronological sequence of transactions in a tamper-evident manner. Due to the decentralized trust ecosystem in blockchain, various industries have adopted blockchain to build their applications. This paper presents a novel approach to building a blockchain-based document archive storage platform, "Lekana". The Lekana platform can be adopted by service providers that require frequent document operations, such as "Pageroonline", a cloud-based e-invoicing provider in Europe. With Lekana we introduce a novel approach to store an immutable hash chain of archived data which are owned by the customers in the blockchain. The proposed Lekana platform is built on top of Mystiko which is a highly scalable blockchain storage platform targeted for big data. We have integrated real-time data analytics and machine learning techniques into the Lekana platform by using the Mystiko-Ml machine learning service on Mystiko blockchain. By integrating the Lekana platform with blockchain technology, we have addressed major issues in most cloud-based, centralized storage platforms (e.g. lack of data privacy, lack of data immutability, lack of traceability and lack of data provenance). As a case study in the paper, we present how "Pageroonline" cloud-based e-invoicing provider stores their archived document data and archived document hash chain in the blockchain-based Lekana platform.

© Springer Nature Switzerland AG 2020
Z. Chen et al. (Eds.): ICBC 2020, LNCS 12404, pp. 169–184, 2020.
https://doi.org/10.1007/978-3-030-59638-5_12

1   Introduction

1.1   Cloud Storage

There are various types of cloud-based storage platforms available, such as Amazon S3 [1], Google cloud platform [2] and Azure cloud archive [3]. Most of these storage services are governed by a central authority. Centrally controlled services tend to lack privacy, traceability, immutability, or data provenance features. Due to these reasons, data fraud and attacks are easier to accomplish and can happen more frequently. Unauthorized third parties such as hackers or employees of the cloud service company may access the data and alter them. Once data fraud happens, it's hard to trace and identify the attackers. To address these issues on centralized cloud storage systems, system designers have integrated decentralized blockchain platform due to its decentralized and immutable ecosystem.

1.2   Blockchain

Blockchain provides a tamper-evident, shared digital ledger that records data in a public or private peer-to-peer network in the form of a distributed peer-to-peer storage. Each node in the blockchain has the same order of data, which is immutable. Since blockchain is a distributed storage, it needs a consensus algorithm to order and maintain consistency of data among the nodes. Currently, there are various blockchain platforms in the market. Bitcoin [4], Ethereum [5], Bigchaindb [6], Hyperledger [7], Mystiko [8] are some examples. Some of these blockchains are mostly used for electronic currencies such as Bitcoin. Ethereum and Hyperledger blockchains go beyond crypto-currency to support different types of asset storage models that relate to other forms of business or e-commerce activities. Mytiko, Bigchaindb blockchains are targeted for big data applications.

Novel blockchain platforms introduce a programming interface referred to as "smart contracts" to interact with the blockchain ledger. The smart contracts interpose additional software layers between the clients and the blockchain storage. Client requests are directed to scripts called smart contracts that perform the logic needed to provide a complex service such as managing state, enforcing governance, or checking credentials. With smart contracts, developers do not need to execute queries to save or retrieve data from blockchain storage. Instead, smart contracts provide a programming interface to interact with the underlying blockchain storage models. The existing blockchain systems come with different smart contract platforms. For example, Ethereum has the Solidity platform [9], and Hyperledger Fabric has the Chaincode platform [7]. Kadena has Pact [10], and RChain has Rholang [11]. Mystiko comes with a concurrency enabled Aplos smart contract platform [8,12], which is adopted in this paper.

1.3   Lekana

This paper introduces a novel approach to build the blockchain-based document archive platform, Lekana, with the ability to address the previously mentioned issues on cloud storage systems and support data provenance in the cloud.

As a case study, this platform is built on Pageroonline which is a cloud-based e-invoicing platform [13]. Pageroonilne is one of the largest e-invoicing providers in the world. It accumulates over one millions electronic documents per day. Pageroonline keeps documents for at most two years. After two years, the document data is archived. Lekana platform is built to store Pagerooinline's archive documents information and their payloads (pdf, xml, image byte streams). All two-year-old documents, and their payloads are saved in the Lekana archive storage and its integrity is protected in the off-chain storage of the blockchain.

The Lekana platform is built on top of Mystiko blockchain, which is highly scalable in terms of storage capability. Mytiko blockchain maintains a hash chain of the archived documents. Actual archived document information and payloads (pdf, xml, image byte streams) are stored in an Apache Cassandra [14] off-chain storage platform. When the document is archived, the payloads are saved in off-chain storage, and the hash chain will be updated on Mystiko providing an immutable record ensuring the integrity of the payload. Archive document hash chain creation, retrieval and validation functionalities are implemented with Aplos smart contracts on Mystiko blockchain. Mytiko blockchain comes with the Mystiko-Ml machine learning service, which is integrated with Apache Spark [15]. Lekana platform is integrated with the Mystiko-Ml service to do real-time data analytics, machine learning, and visualization with the data on the blockchain.

In this paper, a performance evaluation of the underlying blockchain storage in Lekana platform is presented. The evaluation shows the scalability and transaction throughput features in Lekana platform when using different blockchain systems. Following are the main contributions from Lekana.

1. Blockchain based document archive storage platform, with the ability to address the common issues in cloud based data storage (lack of data privacy, lack of data immutability, lack of traceability, lack of data provenance).
2. Blockchain has been used to store an immutable hash chain of archiving documents which are owned by the customers.
3. To address the privacy concerns in the blockchain, off-chain storage has been integrated to the blockchain.
4. As a case study, discussion about integrating Lekana platform to build production grade archive storage service in Pageroonline [13], one of the largest cloud-based e-invoicing platform in the world.
5. Introduced a mechanism to build machine learning models (e.g. isolation forest [16] unsupervised machine learning algorithm based anomaly detection model) with the data on blockchain and off-chain storage in the Lekana platform.

1.4   Outline

The paper is organized as follows. Section 2 introduces the architecture of Lekana platform. Section 3 illustrates the Lekana platform implementation and functionality. Section 4 presents the performance evaluation of the Lekana platform. Section 5 introduces the related work. Section 6 is the conclusion and some future work of the Lekana platform.

2   Lekana Architecture

2.1   Overview

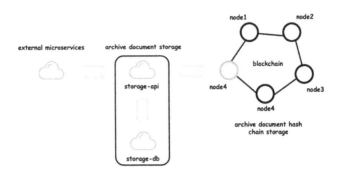

Fig. 1. Lekana architecture. Archive document information stored in storage-db. Archive document hash chain data stored in blockchain.

Lekana is a blockchain-based document archive service. All the archive document information, document payloads, and document hash chain information are maintained in Lekana, which provides APIs to create archive documents, search archive documents and validate hash chain functions. Figure 1 shows the architecture of the Lekana platform. There are two main components in the Lekana platform.

1. Archive document storage (off-chain storage which stored all archive document information and document payloads)
2. Document hash chain (Blockchain storage which stored hash chain of the archive documents)

2.2   Archive Document Storage

All archive document information and document payloads will be stored in archive document storage. Archive document storage comes with two main components "storage-api" and "storage-db". The archive document information and payloads will be stored in the storage-db (off-chain storage of blockchain) in Lekana platform. It is an off-chain storage built on top of a distributed database. Archive document storage-api exposes API's to create, search and validate the hash chain of the archive documents. External services interact with the API to create, search and validate archive documents. To create archive document, it will send an archive document and create request to storage-api with archive document meta data information and payloads. When the archive document create request is received, it will save the archive document information and payloads in the storage-db (distributed database). Then it will interact with blockchain (e.g. blockchain smart contract) to create the hash chain record for the archive document. All archived document hash chain records are stored in the blockchain.

2.3   Document Hash Chain

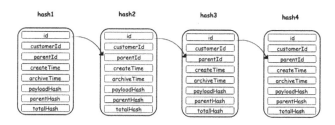

Fig. 2. Lekana archive document hash chain of the customer which stored in blockchain. One hash record refers to its parent hash record.

Lekana platform uses the blockchain to keep the archive document hash records. It gives a decentralized mechanism to check immutability of archive documents. After archiving, the record should be immutable, changes to the recorded documents should not be made, only new records added. By saving archive document hashes in blockchain, it gives a way to track the updates to the document. Blockchain keeps the document hash as a blockchain asset. Figure 4 shows the structure of the asset. The document hash record keeps a reference to its parent document hash, Fig. 2. These hashes are stored per user in the blockchain. When a new hash record is created, it searches for the last hash record which corresponds to a given user. Then it adds that hash record id as the **parentHash**. Finally it calculates the total hash based on **parentHash**, **createTime**, **archiveTime** and **payloadHash**. To calculate the total hash, it concatenates **parentHash**, **createTime**, **archiveTime**, **payloadHash** and gets the **SHA256** hash of it. In this way, we build customers' archive document hash chain on top of the blockchain. Each hash record refers to its parent hash record.

The hash chain based archive is designed for integrity such that it is not possible to remove a single document from the archive without breaking a cryptographic chain. The integrity check on the archive hash chain will reveal such an action. The hash chain data in the blockchain can be exposed to outside parties (e.g. customers in "Pageroonline") to verify the integrity of the documents. For example, "Pageroonline" customers can fetc.h their archive document data from storage-api and hash chain data from the blockchain. Then they can validate the hash chain with the actual archive document data and check the integrity of the archive documents. By storing document data in the archive-storage (off-chain storage) and hash chain data on the blockchain Lekana has addressed the common issues in cloud based data storage, lack of data privacy, lack of data immutability, lack of traceability, lack of data provenance.

3   Lekana Functionality

3.1   Overview

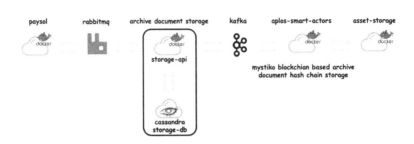

Fig. 3. Lekana architecture in Pageroonline cloud platform. Apache cassandra based storage-db used as the off-chain storage. Mystiko blockchian used to build the document hash chain.

As a use case demonstration, Lekana platform is built on Pageroonline which is a cloud-based e-invoicing platform [13]. Pageroonilne accumulates over one million electronic documents per day. Pageroonline keeps these documents for at most two years. After two years, the document data is archived. Lekana platform is built to store Pagerooninline's archive document information and their payloads (pdf, xml, image byte streams). All two-year-old documents and their payloads saved in the Lekana archive storage are protected in the off-chain storage of the blockchain. The architecture of the Lekana platform implementation of Pageroonline is shown in Fig. 3.

We have used Apache Cassandra based distributed database as the storage-db in Pageroonlines' Lekana platform. All archive document information is stored in Cassandra database tables. External microservices (e.g. "Paysol") interacts with storage-api service to create, search, and validate the archive documents. Pageroonline uses Rabbitmq [17] as the microservice message broker. The service communication protocols is defined with Google Protobuf messages [18]. Protobuf API is exposed with storage-api to create, search, and validate the hash chain of the archive documents. External microservices in pageroonline interact with the API through Rabbitmq to create, search, and validate archive documents. For example, the microservice named "Paysol" sends an archive document create Protobuf message (with archive document information, payloads) to storage-api. Then it will save archive document information and payloads in the Apache Cassandra based storage-api (off-chain storage). After that it interacts with Mystiko's blockchain smart contract and create the hash chain record for the archive document. Mystiko blockchain exposes Apache Kafka [19] based asynchronous API to communicate with smart contracts.

The Lekana platform document hash chain is built on top of Mystiko blockchain, which is highly scalable in terms of storage capability. Mystiko blockchain is built with microservice based distributed system architecture [20]. All services are dockerized [21] and available for deployment using Kubernetes [22]. Since Pageroonlines services are also built as a microservice architecture, by deploying with docker/kubernetes we are able to easily integrate Mystiko blockchain with Pageroonline platform. In Lekana, Mytiko blockchain maintains the hash chain of the archived documents. This hash chain is exposed to customers in Pageroonline to verify the integrity of the documents and guarantee the data provenance without revealing actual document payloads or metadata information in the archive storage.

3.2   Hash Chain Functions

```
{
  "id": "<hash id>",
  "customerId": "<document owner customer id>",
  "parentId": "<last archive document id of the customer>",
  "createTime": "<document create time>",
  "archiveTime": "<document archive time>",
  "payloadHash": "<document payload hash>",
  "parentHash": "<parent document hash>",
  "totalHash": "<total hash>"
}
```

```
{
  "id": "<transaction id>",
  "execer": "<transaction executing user>",
  "messageType": "create",
  "customerId": "<document owner customer id>",
  "documentId": "<document id>",
  "parentId": "<last archive document id of the customer>",
  "createTime": "<document create time>",
  "archiveTime": "<document archive time>",
  "docHash": "<document payload hash>",
  "digsig": "<digital signature of the message>"
}
```

Fig. 4. Lekana Hash assert structure in Mystiko blockchain.

Fig. 5. Lekana CreateHash message in Mystiko blockchain.

Hash chain create, validate and search functions are implemented as Smart contracts. Smart contracts are built using the Scala functional programming language [23–25] based Akka actors [26–28] in Mystiko blockchain. Aplos Smart Actors in Mystiko blockchain consume transaction messages via Kafka message broker [19] with a reactive streams approach [29,30]. There is a smart

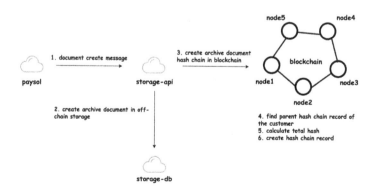

Fig. 6. Lekana create archive document flow. First create archive document in off-chain storage. Then add hash chain record in the blockchain.

actor named `HashChainActor` which manages the hash chain functions. This actor defines three smart contract functions, `CreateHash`, `ValidateHashChain`, `SearchHashChain`. These functions are invoked through the transaction messages which come to the `HashChainActor` via Apache Kafka.

`CreateHash` corresponds to the creating of a new hash chain record for the customer and document. Transaction messages correspond with `CreateHash` described in Fig. 5. When this function is invoked, it first finds the last hash chain record corresponding to the given customer (parent hash), then calculates the total hash with parent hash to create a new hash record in the Mystiko storage (ledger), Fig. 6. `ValidateHashChain` to do the hash chain validation of a given customer. It retrieves the hash chain of a given customer with `fromDate` to `toDate` and validates against the actual document payloads stored in document storage service. If any alteration is made to the document payload, it can be detected in `ValidateHashChain` function, Fig. 7. `SearchHashChain` facilitates the Hash chain search function. It searches the hash chain records of the given customer with `fromDate` to `toDate`. `SearchHashChain` and `ValidateHashChain` functions are exposed to third party customers via HTTP REST API. By using this API any customer can verify their archive documents status and hash chain, such as whether hash chain and documents have been altered or not.

3.3   Analytics and Machine Learning

Mystiko blockchain keeps all transactions, blocks, asset information on Apache Cassandra based Elassandra Storage [31]. It exposes Apache Lucene index [32] based Elasticsearch APIs [33] for transactions, blocks and assets on the blockchain. We have integrated Kibana analytic dashboards [34] with Elasticsearch API to visualize real-time and historical data on Mystiko blockchain. Mentioned above, Mystiko blockchain comes with Mystiko-Ml, an Apache Spark-based machine learning and analytics service. It establishes supervised or unsupervised machine learning models with the existing data on Mystiko Cassandra

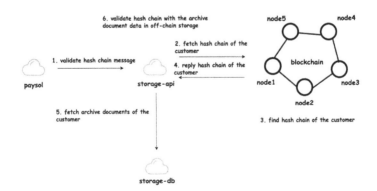

Fig. 7. Lekana validate customer hash chain flow. First fetch hash chain of the customer from the blockchain. Then fetch archive document data from the off-chain storage. Finally validate hash chain with the archive document data in off-chain storage.

storage (both on-chain and off-chain). These models can be used to do predictions of real-time data. We have integrated Mystiko-Ml service into the Lekana platform to build an isolation forest unsupervised [16] model with the off-chain storage data.

4   Performance Evaluation

Performance is evaluated for the underlying blockchain storage in Lekana platform. The evaluation shows the scalability and transaction throughput features in Lekana platform when using different blockchain storages. To obtain the results, we have deployed Lekana blockchain on multi-node Mystiko cluster (4 nodes) and multi-node Hypeledger fabric cluster. Hyperledger fabric runs with a Kafka based consensus with 3 Orderer nodes, 4 Kafka nodes, 3 Zookeeper nodes and LevelDB [7] as the state database. Mystiko blockchain runs with 4 Kafka nodes, 3 Zookeeper nodes and Apache Cassandra [14] as the state database. We use Apache Cassandra [14] as the storage-db (off-chain storage) in the archive document storage service. The evaluation results are obtained based on the following five metrics.

1. Invoke Transaction throughput
2. Query Transaction throughput
3. Transaction scalability
4. Transaction latency
5. Search performance

4.1   Invoke Transaction Throughput

For this evaluation, we recorded the number of invoke transactions that can be executed in the underlying blockchain ledger. Invoke transaction creates a record

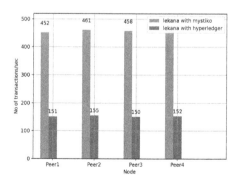 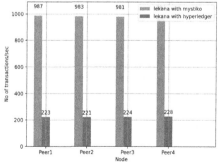

Fig. 8. Invoke transaction throughput of Lekana platform in different blockchain ledgers.

Fig. 9. Queary transaction throughput of Lekana platform in different blockchain ledgers.

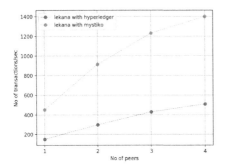

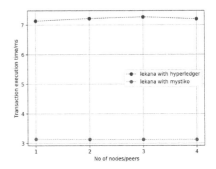

Fig. 10. Transaction scalability of Lekana platform in different blockchain ledgers.

Fig. 11. Transaction latency of Lekana platform in different blockchain ledgers.

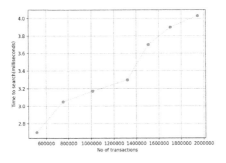

Fig. 12. Search performance of Lekana storage.

in the ledger and updates the status of the assets. We flood invoke transactions for each blockchain peer and recorded the number of executed transactions. As shown in Fig. 8, we have obtained consistent transaction throughput in different blockchain peers in Lekana platform.

4.2 Query Transaction Throughput

For this evaluation, we recorded the number of query transactions that can be executed in the underlying blockchain ledger of the Lekana platform. Query transactions just query the status from the ledger. They neither create a transaction in the ledger nor update the asset status. We flooded query transactions for each blockchain peer and recorded the number of completed transactions. As shown in Fig. 9, we compare the query transaction throughput of Lekana platform in different blockchain environments. Since query transactions are not updating the ledger status, it has higher throughput compared to invoke transactions. For example, search transaction throughput of Mystiko ledger-based Lekana platform is 2 times higher than invoke transaction throughput, and search transaction throughput of Hyperledger Fabric ledger-based Lekana platform is 1.5 times higher than invoke throughput.

4.3   Transaction Scalability

For this evaluation, we record the number of invoke transactions (per second) over the number of blockchain peers in the Lekana platform. We flood concurrent transactions in each blockchain peer and record the number of executed transactions. Figure 10 shows transaction scalability results for the Lekana platform. When adding blockchain nodes to the cluster it linearly increase the transaction throughput.

4.4   Transaction Latency

Next, we evaluate the transaction latency of the underlying blockchain ledger in the Lekana platform. We flood concurrent transactions in each blockchain peer and calculate the average transaction latency. Figure 11 shows the transaction latency results of Lekana platform in different blockchain environments. When adding nodes to the cluster a consistent latency is maintained in Lekana platform.

4.5   Search Performance

Finally, we evaluate the search performance of the Lekana storage service. Lekana platform provides ability to search data in its storage using Elasticsearch [33]. For this evaluation, we issue concurrent search queries to the Lekana platform and compute the search time. As shown in Fig. 12, to search 2 million records, it takes only 4 ms. The Apache Lucene index-based Elasticsearch storage is the main reason yielding a fast search in the Lekana platform.

5   Related Work

Existing research has been conducted to build decentralized storage systems on top of the blockchain. In this section, we outline the main features and architecture of these research projects.

Archain. [35] is a blockchain-based document archive system, developed for the state archive-keeping committee of the Republic of Tatarstan (Russia). It keeps document information in blockchain transactions. Each accepted document corresponds to one transaction record in the blockchain. The system can be described as an interaction of participants of three roles: Administrator, Expert, and User. Roles are selected and assigned to members through the Certification Authority. Users create and upload documents to the network. Administrators select an expert for each of the created documents and add them to the archive after the expert's approval. Experts make decisions on documents – if the document is improperly formalized, has some metadata missing, or doesn't comply with local legislation, then it should be denied from transferring to the archive.

Archangel. [36] is a blockchain-based decentralized platform for ensuring the long-term integrity of digital documents stored within public archives. It uses

Table 1. Blockchain based storage platform comparison

Platform	Implemented Blockchain	Implemented architecture	Consensus	Scalability	Smart contract support	Deduplication support	Off-chain support	Full-text search support
Lekana	Mystiko	Microservices	Paxos	High	Yes	No	Yes	Yes
Archain	Archain	Monolith	PoW	Low	No	No	Yes	No
Archangel	Ethereum	Monolith	PoS	Low	Yes	No	Yes	No
Yugala	Mystiko	Microservices	Paxos	High	Yes	Yes	Yes	Yes
Sia	Sia	Monolith	PoW	Low	Yes	No	Yes	No
Filecoin	IPFS/Filecoin	Monolith	PoS/PoR	Mid	Yes	Yes	No	No
Storj	Ethereum	Monolith	PoS	Low	Yes	Yes	No	No
Swarm	Ethereum	Monolith	PoS	Low	Yes	No	No	No

blockchain as a basis for ensuring the provenance and integrity of documents during the process of preserving the records (curation) and upon release (presentation). Archangel uses the Ethereum blockchain to record digital signatures (derived from either scanned digital or born-digital archival images) of the documents. The process works by creating a hash of the original digital document, recording that on the blockchain, preserving that document in the archives, and then subsequently checking that the document has not been altered by comparing the hash of the preserved document with the hash originally recorded on the blockchain.

Yugala. [37] Yugala is encrypted cloud storage for IoT data/Big data. It proposes a blockchain-based lightweight, encrypted cloud storage architecture, which maintains file confidentiality. Yugala removes the traditional centralized data deduplication and increases file integrity by using a decentralized blockchain. In particular, it discusses two approaches for file confidentiality with data deduplication: one uses double hashing and the other symmetric encryption. Yugala storage is built on top Mystiko blockchain. All data deduplication handling functions (with double hashing and symmetric encryption) have been implemented with Aplos smart contract on Mystiko blockchain.

Sia. [38] is a decentralized cloud storage platform that intends to compete with existing storage solutions, at both the P2P and enterprise level. Instead of renting storage from a centralized provider, peers on Sia rent storage from each other. Sia itself stores only the storage contracts formed between parties, defining the terms of their arrangement. These smart contracts are stored in their public blockchain systems like bitcoin. They have a preference for the Proof-of-Work (PoW) consensus and use ASIC chips for Siacoin mining. Their Proof of Storage algorithm is utilized to further protect and validate proofs and file contracts on the network.

Filecoin. [39] is an open-source project designed to create a permanent, decentralized method of data storage and sharing. It is an advanced IPFS [40] version with a blockchain incentive mechanism and even the off-chain trading market for file storage. The network provides a decentralized hub on which people who have excess storage capacity can offer it to those in need of capacity. Individuals and businesses pay to store data on the storage provider's hardware. Filecoin utilizes a proof of storage concept (similar to PoW) to determine if a miner has conducted his storing/retrieving duties. The concept has two elements: Proof-of-replication and Proof-of-spacetime. Proof-of-replication is used by storage providers to show that they have stored a unique set of data to the space it owns. Proof-of-spacetime enables storage providers to show that data has been stored over a specific period. This is done by requiring a storage provider to show sequential instances of Proof-of-replication.

Storj. [41] is an open-source platform that leverages Ethereum blockchain to provide end-to-end encrypted cloud storage services. Instead of maintaining its own data centers, the Storj platform relies on a peer-to-peer network of individuals or entities sharing their storage space. Their technology revolves file sharing, similarly to how torrents work and separate parts of the files to users in the network. When a user requests the file, Storj uses a distributed hash table to locate all the shards and pieces them together. These files are also encrypted before sharing and the person uploading it has their private key to validate ownership. Storj uses private verification, which means the data owner is supposed to do the auditing job here with pre-generated nonces/salts and the classic Hash (block, nonce/salt). Unlike Filecoin and Sia, Storej does not support smart contracts on the blockchain that set the rules and requirements for storage. Instead, Storj users pay for what they use.

Swarm. [42] is a distributed storage platform and content distribution service on the Ethereum web3 stack. The primary objective of Swarm is to provide a decentralized and redundant store for dapp code and data as well as blockchain and state data. Swarm is also set out to provide various base layer services for web3, including node-to-node messaging, media streaming, decentralized database services and scalable state-channel infrastructure for decentralized service economies. It splits the data into blocks called chunks, which have a maximum size limit of 4K bytes and distribute among the nodes. It provides ENS (Ethereum Name System), which is implemented as a smart contract on the Ethereum network. It can be considered as the equivalent of the domain name service (DNS) that facilitates content naming in traditional internet services.

The comparison summary of these storage platforms and the Lekana platform is presented in Table 1. It compares Running blockchain platform, Implementation architecture, Consensus, Scalability, Smart contract support, Deduplication support, Off-chain storage support, Full-text search support details.

6   Conclusions and Future Works

With Lekana we have introduced a blockchain-based, scalable, decentralized document archive storage platform. Lekana has addressed the common issues in centralized cloud-based storage platforms (e.g. lack of data privacy, lack of data immutability, lack of traceability) while supporting data provenance in the cloud. By using Mystiko blockchain to build the Lekana platform we were able to align the Lekana platform with high transaction load in Pageroonline. We have presented the scalability and transaction throughput features of the platform with empirical evaluations.

We also introduced a blockchain-based novel approach to keeping an immutable hash chain of archiving data for customers. This chain can be accessed by outside parties (e.g. customers in Pageroonline) to verify the integrity of the documents without revealing actual document payloads or metadata information. Most recently we have integrated Lekana version 1.0 with pagerooinline cloud platform, following the agile continuous delivery approach when building and releasing the product every month.

Acknowledgements. This work was funded by the Department of Energy (DOE) Office of Fossil Energy (FE) (Federal Grant #DE-FE0031744).

References

1. Amzon s3. https://aws.amazon.com/s3/
2. Krishnan, S.P.T., Gonzalez, J.L.U.: Building Your Next Big Thing with Google Cloud Platform. Apress, Berkeley, CA (2015). https://doi.org/10.1007/978-1-4842-1004-8
3. Jennings, R.: Cloud Computing With the Windows Azure Platform. Wiley, New York (2010)
4. Nakamoto, S.: Bitcoin: A Peer-to-peer Electronic Cash System (2008)
5. Buterin, V., et al.: A next-generation smart contract and decentralized application platform, white paper (2014)
6. McConaghy, T., et al.: Bigchaindb: a scalable blockchain database, white paper, BigChainDB (2016)
7. Androulaki, E., et al.: Hyperledger fabric: a distributed operating system for permissioned blockchains. In: Proceedings of the Thirteenth EuroSys Conference, p. 30. ACM (2018)
8. Bandara, E., et al.: Mystiko-blockchain meets big data. In: IEEE International Conference on Big Data (Big Data), pp. 3024–3032. IEEE (2018)
9. Solidity. https://solidity.readthedocs.io/en/develop/
10. Popejoy, S.: The pact smart contract language, June 2017 (2016). http://kadena.io/docs/Kadena-PactWhitepaper.pdf
11. Eykholt, E., Meredith, L.G., Denman, J.: RChain architecture documentation (2017)
12. Bandara, E., Ng, W.K., Ranasinghe, N., De Zoysa, K.: Aplos: smart contracts made smart. In: Zheng, Z., Dai, H.-N., Tang, M., Chen, X. (eds.) BlockSys 2019. CCIS, vol. 1156, pp. 431–445. Springer, Singapore (2020). https://doi.org/10.1007/978-981-15-2777-7_35
13. Pageroonline. https://www.pagero.com/about-pagero/
14. Lakshman, A., Malik, P.: Cassandra: a decentralized structured storage system. ACM SIGOPS Oper. Syst. Rev. **44**(2), 35–40 (2010)
15. Meng, X., et al.: MLlib: machine learning in Apache Spark. J. Mach. Learn. Res. **17**(1), 1235–1241 (2016)
16. Liu, F.T., Ting, K.M., Zhou, Z.-H.: Isolation forest. In: 2008 Eighth IEEE International Conference on Data Mining, pp. 413–422. IEEE (2008)
17. Videla, A., Williams, J.J.: RabbitMQ in Action: Distributed Messaging for Everyone. Manning, New York (2012)
18. Varda, K.: Protocol buffers: Google's data interchange format. Google Open Source Blog, Available at least as early as July, vol. 72 (2008)
19. Kreps, J., Narkhede, N., Rao, J., et al.: Kafka: a distributed messaging system for log processing. In: Proceedings of the NetDB, pp. 1–7 (2011)
20. Schwartz, A.: Microservices. Informatik-Spektrum **40**(6), 590–594 (2017). https://doi.org/10.1007/s00287-017-1078-6
21. Docker documentation, August 2018. https://docs.docker.com/
22. Kubernetes documentation. https://kubernetes.io/docs/home/?path=users&persona=app-developer&level=foundational
23. Odersky, M., et al.: An overview of the Scala programming language. Technical report (2004)
24. The scala programming language. https://www.scala-lang.org/
25. Hughes, J.: Why functional programming matters. Comput. J. **32**(2), 98–107 (1989)

26. Akka documentation. https://doc.akka.io/docs/akka/2.5/actors.html
27. Hewitt, C.: Actor model of computation: scalable robust information systems (2010). arXiv preprint arXiv:1008.1459
28. Hoare, C.A.R.: Communicating sequential processes. Commun. ACM **21**(8), 666–677 (1978)
29. Akka documentation. https://doc.akka.io/docs/akka/2.5/stream/
30. Destounis, A., Paschos, G.S., Koutsopoulos, I.: Streaming big data meets back-pressure in distributed network computation. In: IEEE INFOCOM 2016-The 35th Annual IEEE International Conference on Computer Communications, pp. 1–9. IEEE (2016)
31. Middelkamp, A.: Online. Praktische Huisartsgeneeskunde **3**(4), 3 (2017). https://doi.org/10.1007/s41045-017-0040-y
32. Welcome to Apache Lucene. http://lucene.apache.org/
33. Elastic stack and product documentation — elastic. https://www.elastic.co/guide/index.html
34. Kibana product documentation. https://www.elastic.co/products/kibana
35. Galiev, A., Prokopyev, N., Ishmukhametov, S., Stolov, E., Latypov, R., Vlasov, I.: Archain: a novel blockchain based archival system. In: 2018 Second World Conference on Smart Trends in Systems, Security and Sustainability (WorldS4), pp. 84–89. IEEE (2018)
36. Collomosse, J., et al.: Archangel: trusted archives of digital public documents. In: Proceedings of the ACM Symposium on Document Engineering 2018, p. 31. ACM (2018)
37. Sarada Prasad Gochhayat, S.S.P.F., Herath, E.: Yugala: blockchain based encrypted cloud storage for IoT data. IEEE Blockchain (2019)
38. Vorick, D., Champine, L.: Sia: Simple decentralized storage. Nebulous Inc. (2014)
39. Benet, J., Greco, N.: Filecoin: A decentralized storage network. Protoc, Labs (2018)
40. Benet, J.: IPFS-content addressed, versioned, P2P file system (2014). arXiv preprint arXiv:1407.3561
41. Wilkinson, S., Lowry, J., Boshevski, T.: Metadisk a blockchain-based decentralized file storage application. Technical report (2014)
42. Hartman, J.H., Murdock, I., Spalink, T.: The swarm scalable storage system. In: Proceedings of the 19th IEEE International Conference on Distributed Computing Systems (Cat. No. 99CB37003), pp. 74–81. IEEE (1999)

Dynamic Role-Based Access Control for Decentralized Applications

Arnab Chatterjee[1][✉], Yash Pitroda[1][✉], and Manojkumar Parmar[1,2][✉]

[1] Robert Bosch Engineering and Business Solutions Pvt. Ltd., Bangalore, India
{arnab.chatterjee,yash.pitroda,manojkumar.parmar}@bosch.com
[2] HEC Paris, Jouy-en-Josas Cedex, France

Abstract. Access control management is an integral part of maintaining the security of an application. For access control management on the *Distributed Ledger Technology (DLT)*, available traditional access control frameworks are inadequate. Existing access control management mechanisms are tightly coupled with the business logic, resulting in an adverse impact on the overall software quality for DLT based *Decentralized Applications (dApps)*. In this paper, we propose a novel framework to implement dynamic role-based access control for dApps. The framework completely decouples the access control logic from the business logic and provides seamless integration with any dApp. The smart contract architecture allows for the independent management of business logic and execution of access control policies. The framework also facilitates secure, low cost, and a high degree of flexibility of access control management. Additionally, it promotes decentralized governance of access control policies and efficient smart contract upgrades. In this paper, we evaluate the framework on relevant various software quality attributes to understand its more profound implications on access control techniques. The framework can be implemented in any smart contract programming language exhibiting *Turing* completeness. We use the *Solidity* programming language to implement the framework and discuss the results.

Keywords: DLT · Blockchain · Access control · Authorization · Security · Confidentiality · RBAC · Dynamic RBAC

1 Introduction

Distributed Ledger Technology (DLT) and decentralized applications (dApps) have revolutionized how businesses are imagined. The proliferation of enterprise systems brings sophistication into modern day to day transactions. Transactions today range across multiple system boundaries. Conventional information security practices are challenging to adhere to while building and maintaining such complex systems. DLT promises to simplify some of these sophistications.

DLT acts as a shared, immutable ledger between these systems, offering a single source of truth for exchanged data. However, concerns around information security, especially data confidentiality laws and regulations with based

© Springer Nature Switzerland AG 2020
Z. Chen et al. (Eds.): ICBC 2020, LNCS 12404, pp. 185–197, 2020.
https://doi.org/10.1007/978-3-030-59638-5_13

DLT systems, have become one of the disinclinations towards enterprise DLT adoption [1,2]. Two of the core defining characteristics of information security triad, i.e., Confidentiality, Integrity, and Availability (CIA) are Confidentiality and Integrity [3]; access control is critical to preserve these characteristics.

Access control defines and constrains what a user can do in a system. In other words, it authorizes the user for certain activities that the user wishes to perform. Access Control mechanisms are often more complicated [3] than just defining users' permissions. For example, it can define when and how the resources might be used, like allow access during defined periods, allow a user a limited number of accesses, or conduct votes before granting access to specific resources.

Computation, whether a particular user has certain rights to access resources, usually happens in a siloed and insecure computational context in current non-DLT solutions. Secure computation is now possible in smart contracts on DLT, backed by consensus on the outcome of the computation. Access control to shared business logic on the smart contract is crucial for data integrity and information security. Two of the widely accepted and used Blockchain platforms, namely Hyperledger Fabric [4] and Ethereum[5], supports access control mechanisms in smart contracts. However, they fall short in the following areas:

1. **Lacks Modifiability**
   Upgrading roles, granting and revoking permissions for a role is often cumbersome, leading to source code change and smart contract redeployment. This is because role-based or attribute-based access control is often performed inside the target function. This approach leads to tight coupling of business logic and access control logic. For example, *modifiers* in *Solidity* [6] are applied at the target source code site, i.e., along with the function definition [7–9].

2. **Governance Chaos**
   Governance mechanisms, for example, collection of approvals of stakeholders as signatures for altering access permission, need to be re-executed every time on the deployment of the updated contract. A change in either of roles, permissions, or policy requires the entire business logic smart contract to be redeployed. Hence, also, it must be preceded by re-audits, consent from stakeholders. These unnecessary changes result in chaos in governing the change management process [10].

3. **Cost**
   The tight coupling problem and the need for change in business logic as well as access control logic lead to multiple contract upgrades and redeployments. Redeployment of contracts ensues expenditure of gas (in some cases) and expensive security audits [11].

4. **Security**
   Smart contracts, if upgraded, necessitate backward compatibility. Security vulnerabilities may arise in executing the new contract on old data with new permissions [12,13]. This becomes a major concern for other members of the network.

5. **Integration with Identity Management Suite**
   Integration and interoperability with cloud Identity Management Solutions (IdMs) become complicated as each cloud provider has non-standard IdM suites with different role definitions and attributes [14]. An ideal network might contain actors on heterogeneous infrastructure, viz. different cloud vendors, on-premise, or hybrid. Each can have its own IdM suites. Defining the roles and access control policies in a non-standard way or midway changes of smart contracts can engender IdM integration issues.

6. **Performance Issues**
   Performance of existing solutions are slow and expensive in nature (in gas measurements) [7] as they involve nested calls back and forth with policy execution contracts (discussed in Sect. 6).

7. **Compromised Usability**
   Development and reusability of the contract are compromised due to the tight coupling problem. The developer often has to worry about defining the correct roles (which might be vague during smart contract definition) in the function definition [13].

This paper consists of the following sections. Section 2 describes the problem statement formally. Section 3 introduces the contribution of this paper. Section 4 talks about the solution *Dynamic Role-Based Access Control*, and introduces the mathematical primitives of the problem domain and describes the policy execution for access control. Section 5 discusses the solution architecture using Unified Modelling Language (UML) notation and evaluates the framework against standard *Software Quality Metrics* [15]. Section 6 discusses, interprets, and describes the significance of the findings and explores a few use-cases of the framework. Section 7 closes the paper with the possible future directions to enhance the solution. Finally, Sect. 8 summarises the problem and the solution.

2 Problem Statement

One of the significant challenges of implementing access control mechanisms is continual shifts in the business process landscape [16,17]. Different use-cases require specific access control mechanisms based on the roles of users and business workflows. Implementing access control in a cross-organizational shared ledger requires dynamics to accommodate these rapidly changing needs. Since smart contract is the executable logic that resides on the immutable ledger, one needs to implement access control in the contracts.

However, the smart contract logic is often meant to focus on operations and core business logic on the shared data. The semantics of today's smart contract languages does not allow access control to be decoupled from the business logic itself. Change in access control rules requires touching business logic code because access control logic is often coded alongside the business logic. For example, *modifiers* in *Solidity* [18] are applied to the function definition. *Hyperledger Fabric* uses attributes (i.e., role) from the *client certificate* to perform an access control check within the function [19] containing the business logic. In a nutshell, the Identity Management of the ledger innately lacks a dedicated access control mechanism module. The access control logic, coupled with the business logic, allows for limited flexibility to change either independently.

This kind of tightly coupled code leads to the violation of the *Single Responsibility Principle* [20]. As a consequence, several problems arise - increased cost of redeployments and audits, governance and voting chaos, performance, and compromised usability (as described in Sect. 1).

3   Our Contribution

This solution framework described in this paper (henceforth referred to as *solution*) aims to tackle the problems described in Sect. 1). The solution undertakes the problem of high coupling [20] by using a *Permission Manager* (deployed as a contract). *Permission Manager* acts as a gatekeeper to check the user details, the roles or attributes the user possesses, and the contract function the user is trying to access. It then evaluates access based on the set of configured access control rules. On successful evaluation, it delegates the function call to the target function, or blocks otherwise. In this approach, the business logic is decoupled from the access control code.

This sort of loosely coupled [20] design allows for dynamic upgrade [21] and configuration of smart contracts and roles without the additional cost, governance problems, performance, and usability issues.

4   Dynamic Role-Based Access Control

Dynamic Role-Based Access Control is inspired by PERM Modelling Language [22]. It provides a generic solution framework to define permissions in a smart contract. The mathematical primitives of the entity sets like *roles, users, policies* and *functions*, are first defined in a ledger agnostic manner. Next, the management of these entity sets i.e., creation, retrieval, update and deletion, are described. Finally, how these entity sets are used to execute a policy at runtime is elaborated.

4.1   Primitives

The following section defines the primitives used to define role-based access control through the rest of the paper.

1. A **User** is an entity and the set $U = \{u_1, u_2, \ldots, u_n\}$ is a finite set of n users
2. A **Role** is an entity and the set $R = \{r_1, r_2, \ldots, r_p\}$ is a finite set of p roles that a *User* can possess.
3. A **Function** is an entity and the set $F = \{f_1, f_2, \ldots, f_q\}$ is a finite set of q functions that can be executed in a smart contract by *Users*

4. The relation between F and R is defined by $F_R : R \rightarrow F$, a many-to-many mapping consisting of the *Functions* that can be accessed by *Users* possessing a set of *Roles* and is called the **Function-Role mapping**
5. The relation between U and R is defined by $U_R : U \rightarrow R$ a many-to-many mapping consisting of the *Roles* that *Users* possess and is called the **User-Role mapping**
6. A **Request** *Req* consists of a tuple $Req = (u_i, f_j)$ where $u_i \in U, \forall i = \{1, 2, ..., n\}$ and $f_j \in F, \forall j = \{1, 2, ..., q\}$

4.2   Policy Execution

The policy is executed whenever a *User* tries to access a *Function*. The *Request Req* arrives at the system; the target contract accepts the *Request* and delegates it to the *Permission Manager* which breaks down the request tuple attributes into u_i and f_j.

If $u_i \in U$, find the range/co-domain of u_i from U_R. Let the range be $r_i \subseteq R$.

If $f_j \in F$, find the range/co-domain of f_j from F_R. Let the range be $r_j \subseteq R$.

For an authorized request check $r_i \cap r_j \neq \phi$.

5   Solution Architecture

5.1   Management of Entities

The mathematical concepts demonstrated previously are implemented using UML.

The block diagram of the solution is represented in Fig. 1. It shows a layered diagram of the different management components forming the architecture of the system. The description of each of these manager components are described below.

1. **Role Manager**: Manages roles in the system, i.e., R.
2. **Function Manager**: Manages functions in the system, i.e., F
3. **User Manager**: Manages user details (discretionary to implementation to cater for data privacy) and roles possessed by the users (using the *User's* unique identifier) i.e., U and U_R
4. **Policy Manager**: Manages roles that are eligible to access a function, i.e., F_R
5. **Permission Manager**: Orchestrates the flow among the Role, Function, User and Policy Manager, validate the flow and output a boolean response.

The entities and the Application Programming Interfaces (APIs) for the described management components are depicted in Object-Oriented Programming (OOP) paradigm using a UML class diagram in Fig. 2.

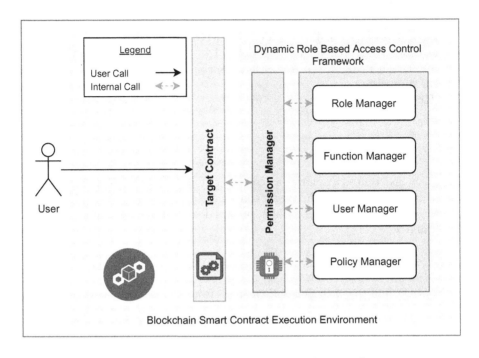

Fig. 1. Block diagram of the solution framework

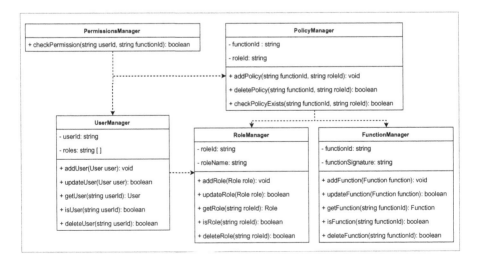

Fig. 2. UML Class Diagram of the solution framework

5.2   Policy Execution Sequence

The sequence of events that follow the policy execution described in Sect. 4.2 is depicted in the sequence diagram in Fig. 3.

1. The user invokes a function f_j with arguments. The user identity u_i also flows along and lands in the target smart contract. Since smart contract functions (i.e., *Solidity* or *Chaincode* functions) are directly callable by the user, the call requires interception at the target function site for authorization check. This is a reference to a function *modifier* invoking the *Permission Manager* contract in *Solidity*. In *Hyperledger Fabric Chaincode*, this is a call to *Permission Manager Chaincode* from the root level *invoke* function. This need for the interception at the target function site can be obviated if similar interception mechanisms are available from the Blockchain platform level.
2. The target contract delegates these arguments to the *Permission Manager*.
3. The *Permission Manager* gets the role (say r_i) of the user u_i. With f_j and r_i it invokes *Policy Manager*.
4. The *Policy Manager* checks for policy mapping function f_j with r_i. It returns an *Authorization Success* response if a mapping was found.
5. The decision is propagated back to the target contract, where it resumes execution in case of a *Authorization Success* response or throws an *Authorization Error* otherwise.

For the sake of brevity, the following checks from the request *Req* are omitted from the sequence diagram:

1. Existence of user $u_i \in U$
2. Existence of function $f_j \in F$
3. Existence of role $r_p \in R$
4. Complex scenarios for checking access control as discussed in 5.3(1b)

5.3   Evaluation of Solution Using Software Quality Metrics

The current approach supports implementation in Generation 2 Blockchain solutions like Ethereum and Hyperledger Fabric. It is implemented in *Solidity* (version 0.5.11) for Ethereum Virtual Machine. Below is the evaluation against Software Quality Metrics [15], viz., *Maintainability, Governance, Security*, and *Performance*.

1. **Maintainability and Extensibility**
   (a) Decoupling of business logic and data - This facilitates backward compatibility of data with a newer version of business logic. For example, in case of a change in role management logic, only the role component can be replaced, with the data of roles intact. This type of decoupling can be achieved using the *Eternal Storage Design Pattern* [23] in Solidity programming language.

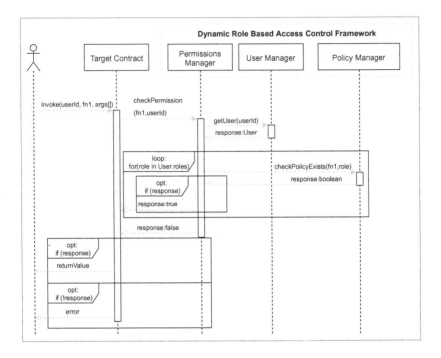

Fig. 3. UML sequence diagram of the solution framework

(b) Provision for Complex Policies - The solution allows for capturing complex policies on the Role, Function, and User. For example, it is possible to configure the Policy Manager to mandate the *User* to have m out of p roles to grant access to a function.

(c) Data Consistency - During creation, retrieval, update, and deletion, the solution also checks linkages of entities in the system, viz. roles, functions, users, and policies. These checks prevents accidental deletions and preserve data consistency.

(d) Integration with IdM suites - Usage of pre-established pseudonymous identifiers for roles and users facilitates easy integration with Identity Management solutions. A one-to-one mapping between ledger identifiers (via smart contract identifiers like smart contract address, name, version) and IdM identifiers enable management of Users and Roles directly from the IdM itself. Since the contract identifiers do not change due the decoupled approach of this solution, the aforementioned one-to-one mapping need not be modified.

2. **Governance** - The solution supports centralized/decentralized management of access control policies. On-chain mechanisms for decision making could be implemented in a centralized (single person/organization responsible for change of access control policies) or decentralized/democratic way (a cohort voting for change in access control policies). Such complex decision making

and on-chain governance are arduous and challenging using conventional coupled access control techniques.

3. **Security (Privacy)** - The solution is flexible to store pseudonymous role identifiers against pseudonymous user identifiers and obliges confidentiality of personal data. The mechanism of storing and mapping roles to users is discretionary to the implementation. Personal data can be avoided on the ledger. Since the solution is entirely hinged on smart contracts, it is suitable to use private transactions to store and manage contract data, compounding the flexibility of confidentiality of the solution.

4. **Performance (Resource Utilization)**

   As a performance metric, resource utilization [15] of the solution (implemented in *Solidity*) is compared against OpenZeppelin's implementation for Access Control [7]. *Gas* [5] metric is used for the comparison. Below are two important observations:

   (a) One time Deployment costs for this solution are higher than OpenZeppelin's solution. When one compares the number of upgrades (say N_{UG}) in the overall lifecycle of a contract, due to changes in business logic, access control, users, and policies in an enterprise context, this solution is deployed once and hence economical. However, the solution from Open-Zeppelin requires re-deployment for every change in role or policies. These redeployments ensue high long-term costs. Also, OpenZeppelin requires a new contract to be deployed every time a new role is added into the system, making the contracts, even more, costlier for multiple roles. Table 1 summarises the approximate costs of deploying the same contract for one role and N_R roles. It also compares the cost of upgrading the contract N_{UG} times.

   The costs for this solution is constant if one extrapolates it for N_R roles and N_{UG} upgrades, whereas it increases linearly for Open Zeppelin's solution.

   (b) Our solution fares better for long term transaction cost efficiency. One time transaction Costs (Gas Used) for this solution are approximately 40% higher than OpenZeppelin's solution. However, the cost for Open-Zeppelin's solution increases linearly when more roles are added, and complex computation needs to be executed when checking role access to a function. The lack of dynamism in OpenZeppelin's solution as discussed in Sect. 1, is chiefly responsible for this linear increase in transaction cost. The transaction costs for authorization checks in our solution remains constant even when scaled for multiple roles.

6 Discussion

The solution approaches the well-known problem of role-based access control from a decentralized perspective. It takes into consideration that multiple parties involved in the ledger are unknown, and each function has a set of access-control rules called policies. The solution becomes significant when access control policies are ambivalent during smart contract definition and development, but may

Table 1. Deployment cost comparison for this solution vs. OpenZeppelin's solution

	This solution	OpenZeppelin's solution
One time deployment cost for one role and zero upgrades (Gas used)	~9536190	~359268
Deployment costs for N_R roles with N_{UG} upgrades (Gas used)	~9536190	~359268 $\times N_R \times N_{UG}$

grow or change over time, as new policies and business logic emerge progressively. It offers a dynamic perspective, considering the need for flexibility and control over authorization [1]. It also looks at the need for having a mechanism to add or modify the access control metadata nimbly without encumbrances. The framework considers the dynamic landscape of businesses, and costly audits of smart contracts, accounting for the lack of mature and automated formal smart contract verification techniques [24].

Additionally, the approach described aids in implementing a decentralized change management process [10]. The approach also leads to better usability of the core business logic contracts allowing them to change independently, without the developer having to worry about the roles and permissions allowed for the given smart contract function. The solution can be applied to a wide variety of use cases. Some are mentioned below:

1. Supply chain applications require critical flexibility [25] in the operations done by actors. The path taken by an asset (downstream or upstream) is not fixed and it is imperative to keep the network and operations open to any participant—this solution aids in managing access control for different actors who may come and go over time.
2. Any Decentralized Autonomous Organization (DAO) [26] or Decentralized Autonomous Corporation (DAC) requires decisions to be democratic. This solution enables the democratization of access control management for various business functions.
3. Decentralized Finance (DeFi) [27] dApps like the ones that enable crowdfunding require to be flexible with Access Control Permission. For example, business logic to determine the credit score, funds settlements on behalf of a lender, and the likes are dynamic and require the intervention of multiple stakeholders. Access control management of these operations requires flexible permissions at the smart contract level – the solution is imperative in such a situation.

7   Future Work

Some of the means how the described solution is extensible in the future are as follows:

1. The policy manager is extensible to evaluate sophisticated policies as discussed in Sect. 5.3(1b).
2. The change mechanism for access control policies can be extended to include voting to enable decentralized decision making for change management of access control policies, as discussed in Sect. 5.3(2) [10].
3. The current approach requires the manual management of functions and users in the *Function Manager* and *User Manager*, respectively. This approach can be automated. Automatic synchronization with IdM provider eliminates the need for manual user and role synchronization. Likewise, after a smart contract's deployment, the source of the contract can be parsed to extract the function details and register them with the *Function Manager*.
4. Ethereum smart contract implementations can be optimized for Gas Costs. The current implementation does not focus on gas optimization best practices.

8   Summary

In this paper, we have demonstrated an approach to solve the problem of decentralized role-based access control. The demonstrated mechanism is loosely coupled [20] with the business logic, allowing both the access control policies and the business logic to change independently. This segregation of concerns allows for the following benefits: natural and independent auditing of smart contracts and its deployment, dynamic governance, reduced costs of change management, and easier integration with IdMs. This paper also demonstrated the architecture, its evaluation, comparison against available frameworks, and use cases for dynamic access control. The presented solution framework is suited for use in both enterprise and public dApp context. We expect this framework to enable flexible access control management in dApps and address specific challenges for enterprise DLT adoption.

Acknowledgment. We want to thank Sri Krishnan V, Presanna Venkadesh Sundararajan, and Mohan B V from Robert Bosch Engineering and Business Solutions Private Limited, India, for their valuable comments, contributions and continued support to the project. We are grateful to all expert for providing us with their valuable insights and informed opinions ensuring completeness of our analysis and study.

References

1. Chatterjee, A., Parmar, M.S., Pitroda, Y.: Production challenges of distributed ledger technology (DLT) based enterprise applications. In: International Symposium on Systems Engineering (ISSE), IEEE ISSE 2019, Edinburgh, United Kingdom (Great Britain), September 2019

2. Haig, S.: Blockchain enters "Trough of Disillusionment" according to Gartner
3. Ferraiolo, D., Kuhn, D.R., Chandramouli, R.: Role Based Access Control. Artech House, Norwood (2007)
4. Androulaki, E., et al.: Hyperledger fabric: a distributed operating system for permissioned blockchains. CoRR abs/1801.10228 (2018)
5. Wood, G., et al.: Ethereum: A secure decentralised generalised transaction ledger. Ethereum project yellow paper, vol. 151, no. 2014, pp. 1–32 (2014)
6. Dannen, C.: Introducing Ethereum and Solidity. Apress, Berkeley, CA (2017). https://doi.org/10.1007/978-1-4842-2535-6
7. OpenZeppelin: Access control. https://docs.openzeppelin.com/contracts/2.x/access-control. Accessed 06 Sept 2020
8. Cruz, J.P., Kaji, Y., Yanai, N.: RBAC-SC: role-based access control using smart contract. IEEE Access **6**, 12240–12251 (2018)
9. Yuan, E., Tong, J.: Attributed based access control (ABAC) for web services. In: IEEE International Conference on Web Services, ICWS 2005, p. 569, July 2005
10. Chohan, U.W.:The decentralized autonomous organization and governance issues. Available at SSRN 3082055 (2017)
11. Destefanis, G., Marchesi, M., Ortu, M., Tonelli, R., Bracciali, A., Hierons, R.: Smart contracts vulnerabilities: a call for blockchain software engineering? In: International Workshop on Blockchain Oriented Software Engineering (IWBOSE), pp. 19–25. IEEE (2018)
12. Luu, L., Chu, D.H., Olickel, H., Saxena, P., Hobor, A.: Making smart contracts smarter. In: Proceedings of the 2016 ACM SIGSAC Conference on Computer and Communications Security, pp. 254–269. ACM (2016)
13. Parizi, R.M., Amritraj, D.A.: Smart contract programming languages on blockchains: an empirical evaluation of usability and security. In: Chen, S., Wang, H., Zhang, L.J. (eds.) ICBC 2018. Lecture Notes in Computer Science, vol. 10974, pp. 75–91. Springer, Cham (2018)
14. Yasin, A., Liu, L.: An online identity and smart contract management system. In: IEEE 40th Annual Computer Software and Applications Conference (COMPSAC), vol. 2., pp. 192–198. IEEE (2016)
15. ISO Central Secretary: Systems and software engineering – Systems and software Quality Requirements and Evaluation (SQuaRE) – System and software quality models. Standard ISO/IEC 25010:2011, International Organization for Standardization, Geneva, CH (2011)
16. Bauer, L., Cranor, L.F., Reeder, R.W., Reiter, M.K., Vaniea, K.: Real life challenges in access-control management. In: Proceedings of the SIGCHI Conference on Human Factors in Computing Systems, pp. 899–908. ACM (2009)
17. Wikibooks: Fundamentals of information systems security/access control systems
18. Dannen, C.: Introducing Ethereum and Solidity. Apress, Berkeley (2017). https://doi.org/10.1007/978-1-4842-2535-6
19. Gaur, N., Desrosiers, L., Ramakrishna, V., Petr, N., Baset, S.A., ODowd, A.: Hands-on blockchain with Hyperledger: building decentralized applications with Hyperledger Fabric and composer. Packt Publishing, Birmingham (2018)
20. Martin, R.C.: Agile Software Development: Principles, Patterns, and Practices. Prentice Hall, Upper Saddle River (2002)
21. Lin, I.C., Liao, T.C.: A survey of blockchain security issues and challenges. IJ Netw. Secur. **19**(5), 653–659 (2017)
22. Luo, Y., Shen, Q., Wu, Z.: PML: An interpreter-based access control policy language for web services (2019)

23. Volland, F.: Eternal storage. https://fravoll.github.io/solidity-patterns/eternal_storage.html. Accessed 06 Sept 2020
24. Bhargavan, K., et al.: Formal verification of smart contracts: short paper. In: Proceedings of the 2016 ACM Workshop on Programming Languages and Analysis for Security, pp. 91–96. ACM (2016)
25. De Souza, R., Zice, S., Chaoyang, L.: Supply chain dynamics and optimization. Integrated Manufacturing Systems (2000)
26. Jentzsch, C.: Decentralized autonomous organization to automate governance. White paper, November 2016
27. Schär, F.: Decentralized finance: On blockchain- and smart contract-based financial markets, March 2020

Blockchain Applications in Healthcare – A Review and Future Perspective

Naga Ramya Sravanthi Narikimilli[1], Anup Kumar[1(✉)], Antara Debnath Antu[1], and Bin Xie[2]

[1] Department of Computer Science and Engineering, University of Louisville, Louisville, KY, USA
ak@louisville.edu

[2] InfoBeyond Technology LLC, Louisville, KY, USA

Abstract. A digital transformation in health care is the positive impact of technology in health care. Wearable fitness technology, telemedicine, and AI-enabled medical devices are concrete examples of digital transformation in health care. And these are supposed to revolutionize the health care industry by improving patient care, streamline operations, and reducing costs but instead, it is facing significant challenges on cybersecurity and privacy of patient data, invoicing and payment processing, medical supply chain, drug integrity. Blockchain technology can absolve the healthcare industry from facing these challenges; it can establish a blockchain of medical records. Blockchain is considered to be a highly secure, transparent, and immune to hackers due to its digital encryption, it also plays a prominent role in reducing the intermediate fees as it is entirely decentralized. This review paper scrutinized the potential of blockchain technology to refine the security, privacy, and interoperability of healthcare data and after the detailed analysis of the current significant challenges in the healthcare sector, we proposed few advanced uses of blockchain in health care domain like Blockchain consortium, Smart contract-based health care intelligent claim processing and prior authorization and Wearable fitness device integration and monitoring health.

Keywords: Blockchain · Healthcare · Patient care · Cybersecurity · Patient privacy

1 Introduction

The Healthcare industry is one of many industries that exploit the advantages of digital transformation. It acts as a catalyst for improving patient care and building efficient, streamlined operational processes that meet the needs of patients, healthcare organizations, and caregivers alike. The healthcare industry is in its transition from fee for service to value-based care with the adoption of breakthrough technologies like Artificial Intelligence, Big data Analytics; Cloud computing, Consumerism, Customer relationship management, and Internet of things (IoT). Digital transformation is not only assisting the health care industry to deliver high quality and secured patient care but also in driving greater business efficiency to reap significant benefits.

© Springer Nature Switzerland AG 2020
Z. Chen et al. (Eds.): ICBC 2020, LNCS 12404, pp. 198–218, 2020.
https://doi.org/10.1007/978-3-030-59638-5_14

Due to these advancements, Health care providers have more access to the vast amount of patient data than ever before. This data can be private information concerning individuals or organizations. A major challenge in the healthcare industry is cybersecurity. Health care organizations should be vigilant against cyber threats [1]. For example, In 2018, the healthcare sector undergone 15 million patient records compromised in 503 breaches, which is three times the amount seen in 2017. In just halfway through 2019 these numbers are escalated to more than 25 million patient records. And another major breach happened in early May of 2019; 8-K filing with the Securities and Exchange Commission revealed that the vendor, The American Medical Collection Agency (AMCA) was hacked for 8 months which resulted in the breach of 25 million patients [1]. Third-party vendors and phishing attackers were behind most of these security incidents.

Because the health care industry is highly data-driven, it should be massively regulated for both privacy and transparency issues and they should also employ exemplary data governance systems in place since highly sensitive and regulated information (like medical records, insurance claims, or personal payment information) flows through healthcare provider systems. The increased complexity of IT networks that power today's healthcare organizations, as well as the sheer volume of data traversing these, has added the challenge of ensuring network and data security [2].

Patient's medical data when dispersing through various medical institutions that have different data standards results not only in the low level of interoperability but also overload patient medical expenses. The government's big push toward electronic health information exchange (HIE) 2009 helped in digitizing all patient records. This portion of the legislation called the Health Information Technology for Economic and Clinical Health (HITECH) [3] Act has provided more than $35 billion in incentives to promote and expand the adoption and use of EHRs by eligible hospitals and health care professionals. However, even after adopting 96% of EHR programs healthcare sector is far from achieving interoperability across all settings of care. By 2015, only 6% of health care providers could share patient data with other clinicians who use an EHR system different from their own [4]. This lack of interoperability is not helping the healthcare industry to reduce its administrative complexity and pushing towards patient-centered care is still far from realization. Between 2017–2022, global health care spending is expected to rise 5.4% annually to just over $10 trillion [5]. Health care providers are stressing rigorous financial management, efficient operational performance, outcomes-based care, and innovative solutions to help address this rise in spending.

Blockchain could help the healthcare care industry to move from volume to value-based care by building a robust decentralized data platform providing inherent transparency, traceability, and security. According to the World Economic Forum survey report, 10% of the worldwide gross domestic product will be stored in Blockchain by 2027 [6]. Considering the prospects of the Healthcare ecosystem, blockchain technology can offer a seamless decentralized platform where information about medical records, credential evaluation records, provider directories, drug supply chain information, insurance, and claim information can be securely recorded, tracked and managed. The ensured integrity of ledger, accuracy, and immutability is essential for enforcing strict medical practices and for rendering error-free medical services and efficiently managing the drug supply chain. Traditionally healthcare industry treated data as commodity and competition instead of care. Decentralization of data along with security and transparency improves interoperability and collaboration in the healthcare industry thus reducing overall administrative cost.

Even though there are multiple numbers of survey papers on blockchain for specific applications, the scope of this paper is to identify the significant challenges faced by Healthcare industry in each of its stakeholders and then evaluating the key capabilities of blockchain in such a way that it can mitigate or completely eradicate the identified challenges in a productive manner. Detailed information on blockchain irrespective of its application in a specific industry is presented in [7–10]. To add this here are few potential sources of instances that demonstrate the use of blockchain to solve specific healthcare challenges. First is a detailed version of a prototype providing a proof-of-concept system by substantiating the principles of blockchain to secure interoperable EHR systems is proposed in [11]. To add to the list of blockchain applications the usage of cryptographic functions to attain privacy in a patient-centric health care data management system is explained in [12]. Another example blockchain-based smart contracts in addressing security concerns of remote patient monitoring systems and the data transactions in an IoT healthcare system is demonstrated in [13]. The evaluation metrics to assess blockchain-based applications in terms of their capability, compliance, and feasibility in the healthcare domain is provided in [14]. Finally, the authors in [15] presented the study of blockchain to protect the healthcare data which is hosted in the cloud and the challenges associated with it.

The rest of the paper is organized as follows. Section 2 provides the baseline information about blockchain along with its fundamental features and functionalities that empower in Healthcare industrial applications. Section 3 summarizes the significant challenges that are currently faced by the healthcare industry and evaluating the need for blockchain in solving such issues. Section 4 proposes the advanced blockchain applications in the healthcare industry to solve challenges like double-spending problems [16, 17] in health insurance, smart contract-based claim processing with prior authorization, etc. Section 5 shows future work ideas related to blockchain and Sect. 6 concludes the paper.

2 Blockchain Overview

Traditionally network applications follow client-server architecture where all the operations are controlled and authorized by a central server. This centralized control limits the ability to share data and lacks transparency. Blockchain works on a peer-to-peer distributed system where all the nodes get a copy of the same data and act upon the same rules. Blockchain is a distributed ledger in which data gets added as a chain of blocks. This chain grows as new data get appended to it continuously. Asymmetric cryptography and distributed consensus algorithms protect user security and ledger consistency [18]. The inherent nature of blockchain design provides multiple benefits which are depicted in Fig. 1 and a brief description of the functionality of key elements of blockchain is outlined in Table 1.

Table 1. Key characteristics of blockchain architecture

Key elements	Functionality
Cryptography	Cryptography is a complex mathematical algorithm that acts as a firewall for attacks. All information on the blockchain is hashed cryptographically ensuring enhanced security
Immutability	Records made in blockchain cannot be changed or deleted
Provenance	With blockchain, it is possible to track the origin of every transaction inside the blockchain ledger
Decentralization	It has open access control to anyone connected to the network. The data can be stored, accessed, monitored, and updated on multiple systems
Anonymity	For every node in the blockchain network has a generated address despite user identity. Thus, making the system more reliable and secure
Transparency	The information stored in each node of blockchain is transparent to the potential users. Users can verify and track transactions in the public, decentralized ledger

2.1 Decentralization and No Single Point of Failure

In Blockchain data gets stored in all the participating nodes in the network. Each node validates block and adds to the chain as data grows. At any given point of time, all the participants have the same chain of blocks and thus the same data. It adds redundancy however avoids central authority and provides the ability to query data in real-time and allows working on a shared schema of data thus attaining standardization.

This nature of the distribution of data across all participating nodes helps to achieve network fault-tolerance and high availability. In contrast, cloud-centric applications are prone to Denial of Service (Dos) Attacks, one compromised node could bring down the entire network and the possibility of a rogue node to update or corrupt data. Whereas in the blockchain network, because of decentralization along with computational consensus algorithms helps to reject any updates from malicious node [19, 20].

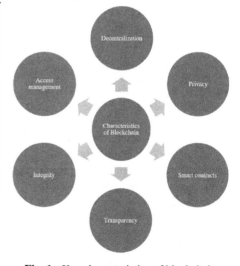

Fig. 1. Key characteristics of blockchain

2.2 Transparency and Integrity

Data recorded once in blockchain cannot be altered. Blockchain uses hashing and consensus (proof of work) [18] to add a block of data to the chain. When a transaction is initiated it is going to pool of transactions that need to be verified. These transactions are broadcasted to all the nodes in the blockchain. Miner nodes pick up pending transactions from the pool of transactions and validated transactions are placed in the block which consists of data (collection of transactions), a hash of the current state of the chain and previous hash to form a link in the chain. This block is then validated by the rest of the node and adds to their chain if it is valid and continues to work on the pending transactions. Transactions are validated as per the rules established as part of the network and proof of work is going to help solve the Byzantine General problem [21] to reach consensus among nodes. If any node attempts to alter any transaction committed, it will regenerate a new hash and breaks the link.

2.3 Privacy and Access Management

Traditionally privacy and access management are controlled by a central authority (sharing institute) for the cloud-based repositories. Such kind of system is vulnerable to attacks and has been breached over times [22]. Fundamentally this system has few problems such as Users cannot control their data beyond sharing institution and the risk of re-identification of users remain when dealing with anonymized data sets. Traditional methods such as k-anonymity [23], l-diversity [24], and t-closeness [25] are not enough.

Existing data sharing mechanisms have one of two challenges: the first capable of sharing but poor control over data. As a result, sharing institutions or users cannot control data after sharing. This raises privacy concerns as there is no technical barrier to stop re-identification even after anonymizing data sets. The second remains strong control over data but not capable of efficient sharing, which defeats the purpose.

Blockchain provides privacy and access management using advanced cryptographical methods such as hashing. In blockchain users can general self-identities by public and private cryptography keys [26]. These keys could be used to identify, authenticate, and contrive access control in a scalable, distributed, and secure manner. A Public key is used as an identifier of the user and a private key is used for encryption of the data. The public key can also be treated as pseudo-identity as it may or may not directly related to the actual identity of the user, this behavior of the blockchain helps to achieve privacy-preserving identity in public ledgers and the same system can be used to map public keys to real identity in permissioned blockchain or private blockchain.

Decentralization of privacy has been discussed in the paper Decentralizing Privacy: Using Blockchain to Protect Personal Data [27]. In this paper approach of controlling access to data by user granted permission has been discussed in the context of mobile application, where a user sets access control and data as transactions in the block of chain on distributed nodes. Users can create any number of compounded identities by combining public key of the user (identity owner) and the public key of mobile service (delegated identity) and each compounded identity can have a set of access rules set as access transactions. Compounded identity also embeds the symmetric key for encryption of data. This system solves the problem of access control and privacy.

2.4 Identity Management

A need for decentralized identity management is very evident as there is a need for data sharing is increasing and for establishing a single source of truth. There are multiple identity systems exists today such as central identity management scheme in which central authority controls identity, Federated identity management scheme in which identity is established in one system and can be trusted used in another system such as single sign-on systems and User-central network anonymity scheme in which user owns and controls identity [28].

By combining the decentralized blockchain principle with identity management, a digital ID can be generated and committed to the network of blockchain. This digitalID is a combination of the public key and private key. The public key establishes identity and private key controls security by encryption of data [29]. Once digitalID committed to the blockchain it cannot be tampered or altered it acts as a digital fingerprint that can be used for verification of identity. In the context of blockchain, this unique behavior of digitalID can help identify accurate patient information, which is imperative to provide better care.

Some of the major projects or startups such as ShoCard [30], uPort [31] are discussed in Blockchain for Identity management paper [32].

2.5 Smart Contracts

Nick Szabo introduced the concept of smart contracts in 1994 and defined a smart contract as "a computerized transaction protocol the executes the terms of the contract" [33]. In the context of Blockchain, smart contracts are self-executable scripts that reside on the blockchain and allow processing of distributed, heavy automated workflows. Every smart contract has a unique address, it can be executed by initiating a transaction on this address. A smart contract executes independently and automatically based on already established constructs. Smart contracts enable a multi-step transactional process in a trustless network among non-trusting stakeholders. A smart contract could effectively remove the role of the middle player and thereby reducing the timeline and improving efficiency with a less transactional cost. This nature of smart contracts opens a new opportunity in which not only data could be distributed and shared across non-trusting stakeholders in a secure, verifiable manner but also provides an ability to act on the data at runtime. The use of smart contracts in IoT has been discussed in the paper Blockchains and Smart Contracts for the Internet of Things [34], in which sharing of services and resources leading to the creation of a marketplace of services in a cryptographically verifiable manner.

A smart contract could enable creating healthcare marketplace services ranging from claim processing to medical billing in a secure transparent manner. This avoids administrative overhead on the healthcare industry and effectively combat fraud in billing and insurance-related administration. One study estimated that the aggregate value of challenged claims in health insurance ranges from $11 billion to $54 billion annually [35].

Table 2. Challenges faced by the primary stakeholders of the healthcare industry

Stakeholder	Current challenges
Pharmaceutical industry	• Counterfeit drugs and global quality control [36, 37] • Tracking and regulating the drug supply chain [38] • Overprescription • Clinical trials • Challenges related to payments and negotiations between pharmacies, whole salaries, hospitals
Health insurance	• Healthcare fraud which involves the filing of dishonest health care claims to turn a profit • Increasing costs [39] • Administrative burdens to maintain provider directories. • Minimizing the expensive errors on healthcare claims like record-keeping mistakes
Hospital health care professionals	• Implementing value-based care • Improving patient quality and experience • Addressing rising pharmacy costs
Credentialing and licensing of health care workforce	• Lack of transparency and avoidable costs [40, 41] • Time intensive and cost inflated credentialing and degree verification [42, 43]
Electronic health record management and research	• Possibility of single-point failure in a centralized system [44] • Lack of immutable logs for the learning process • In research areas, lack of privacy-preserving methodologies while performing data mining
Genomics	• Increase in the cost of human genome sequencing [45] • Nontransparent consent management for data sharing [46] • Facing privacy issues while performing identity verification [47] • Lack of novel incentive mechanisms to drive genomic data generation and data sharing
Clinical trials	• Accessing and managing clinical trial data [48] • Data integrity and provenance for the clinical trial process [49] • Updating and maintaining patient consent [50] • Patient recruitment and lack of data access [51]

Typical blockchain architecture is depicted in Fig. 2 When a new transaction has initiated a block that represents the transaction is created and is validated via hashing (crypto hashing), this block is transmitted over the network for validation. All the validated blocks are then added to the existing blockchain.

3   Evaluating Need of Blockchain in Healthcare Industry

This section contributes to providing an extensive identification of major stakeholders in the healthcare industry and the current significant challenges faced by their stakeholders. Followed by investigating a conducive way to mitigate these challenges while utilizing the potential upsides of blockchain features that are mentioned in Sect. 2. Finally, a flow chart is presented in Fig. 4 to help an individual in analyzing different scenarios that occur before navigating to the blockchain as a solution and it also guides in choosing the right type of blockchain-based on their existing problem.

The stakeholders are identified as those entities that are integrally involved in the healthcare system and substantially affected by reforms to the system. The major stakeholders in the health care system are Patients, hospitals, Pharmaceutical companies insurance companies, Health care professionals, Policymakers [52], etc. which in turn has another level of stakeholders. For example, as illustrated in Fig. 3 Pharmaceutical company is one of the major stakeholders of the healthcare industry which in turn Biotechnologists and these industries, in turn, has their stakeholders, representing each stakeholder as a node in the network. Every node in this network creates, modifies, and transfers the data from one form to other forms. For example, the data entered by the patient in Kiosk of a doctor's office to the advancements in Genomics. The wealth generated from the data together with data is transferred through all these nodes of the network via different layers, irrespective of the fact that the underlying market can be either public or private. The term data is used to refer to anyone of the intangible assets in the healthcare industry. For example, provider service agreements, licensing agreements, EHRs, patents, trade names, Medicare certifications, etc.

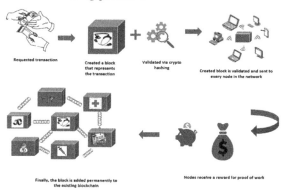

Fig. 2. Typical blockchain process flow in a healthcare domain

Each stakeholder is facing different types of challenges based on the asset (intangible) they are trying to access. Major threats faced by the primary stakeholders in the healthcare industry are summarized in Table 2. Although the ease of data is helpful, it is posing dangerous risks of security and privacy issues to the end-users. To safeguard this health information government passed the Health Insurance Portability and Accountability Act (HIPAA) to safeguard this data and set proper access rights to the people who can access the data. However, with the widespread use of technology in healthcare, the cyber-attacks and data breaches are also booming parallelly. It is when the need for encrypting the data came to light. Encrypting the data not only protects the integrity of the data but also assure compliance with HIPAA rules. The current state of cybersecurity in the healthcare industry is illustrated in [53].

Another serious challenge is identified to be soaring healthcare costs. A survey that is conducted by the Bureau of labor statistics on consumer expenditures, shows that the amount spends on healthcare by an average American is raised by 101% in the last 34 years [54]. One of the salient reasons behind this is identified as administrative costs. After examining the current state of the healthcare industry where every stakeholder is battling to reduce administrative cost by eliminating waste, improving the interoperability, and streamlining the process. In every healthcare transaction, there will be movement of data across different het-

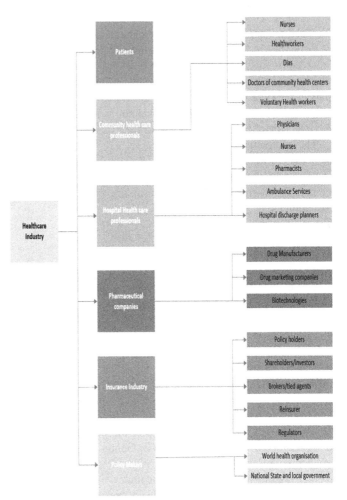

Fig. 3. Major stakeholders in the healthcare industry

erogeneous systems this movement between incompatible systems adding a lot of administrative costs which in turn does not lead to making informed decisions. Drug costs, malpractice costs, defensive medicine, etc. add to the list of other reasons for the increase in health care costs.

The potential applications of blockchain to advance the health care industry [55] are listed in Table 3. Blockchain technology provides exclusive opportunities which include Smart contracts, identity verification, fraud detection, immutable audit trails, and decentralized management to enhance the medical insurance claim process, improved medical record management, and accelerated clinical trials. Many researchers exploited the use of blockchain as a ledger of patient care data and also proposed several projects to store various healthcare data like provider directories, care plans data, clinical trial data, precision medicine data, Pharmaceutical supply chain data, biomarker data in [56–62].

After carefully examining the challenges of all the stakeholders they are categorized into two key logical areas:

1. Data accessibility, integrity, and interoperability
2. Traceability and Operations management

Before proceeding with the discussion on these logical areas, general enlightenment for deciding in which scenario we can adopt blockchain and what type of block to be used in a particular scenario is illustrated in Fig. 4 and the in-depth knowledge on different types of blockchain are discussed in [63]. And detailed steps and scenarios involved in the adoption of blockchain in [64].

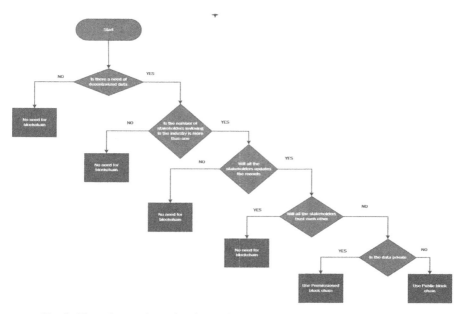

Fig. 4. Flow chart to determine the need for blockchain in the healthcare industry

3.1 Data Accessibility, Integrity, and Interoperability

A decentralized and shared set of reference data between all the stakeholders is needed. Today, all the different stakeholders keep their copy of data and update it according to some procedures established as part of their process, maybe email or fax when an information update happens. As recently as 2012, an estimated 63% of physicians are still using a fax machine or email as a primary means of communication. Deep massive effort and investment in health information systems and technology, and many years of widespread availability, the full promised benefits of EHRs are far from fruition. And the reality is that most physicians still must fax, and mail patient records the way they did a decade ago. This is because of incompatible integration between stakeholders. For example, patient records are now dispersed between hospitals and providers. This lack of interoperability adding overhead in collecting data and providing care. This lack of patient records is not helping to take preventive measures thus failing to provide better care. Since insurance companies don't have this data to track patient health information, we are not able to provide value-based care instead we are providing volume-based care payers are crediting providers based on visits and services rather incentivizing based on improvement in patient health.

There is a need for a distributed record system that must be used and shared across all the stakeholders. In this way, all the participants in the network can have their copy of data. Examples of this data could patient medical records, claim information, provider directories, credential evaluations of providers.

Table 3. Functionalities of blockchain-based applications in the healthcare industry

Blockchain-based applications in health industry	Functionality
Smart contracts	These are certain computer protocols that are created to verify and accomplish or negotiate a contract without third parties [68]
Fraud detection	Blockchain uses a transparent ledger to continuously track payments, prescriptions, and medical documentation. This transparent nature of blockchains could certainly prevent data from being altered/stolen [69]
Identity verification	Blockchain is developed in such a way that it provides open-source access to everyone connected to the network. Thereby providing very easy access to verify identities [70]
Drug traceability/drug ledger	Blockchain can keep track of the entire lifecycle of manufacturing a drug. Each of its transaction is added to an immutable timestamped block. Companies implementing blockchain have a distributed ledger shared among the parties involved in the manufacturing and distribution of a drug [71]
Immutable audit trail	Blockchain ledger could remain permanent and maintain an unalterable history of transactions. It is because of this immutable feature blockchain transformed the auditing process not only to the quick, efficient cost-effective procedure but also inculcated trust and integrity to the data [72]

By putting this information in distributed ledger helps to attain interoperability by eliminating information blockage. The benefits imply accurately identifying patient information imply reduced errors in rendering medical services and in helping customers to make informed decisions, improving real-time access to critical data. All these by avoiding high transaction costs and by reducing waste.

Considering the nature of the data in healthcare it could be placed in permissioned blockchain in such a way data access and management could be controlled based on a set of established authorization principles along with immutability and integrity. When introducing blockchain, privacy services control who can see what across the network of participants and helps to maintain immutability.

3.2 Traceability and Operations Management

Traceability and verifying authenticity are a major issue in the pharmaceutical industry. By 2023, every company in the US pharmaceutical supply chain is required to meet regulations outlined in the Drug supply security act. These regulations required that every unit of a prescription drug in the supply chain has a unique serial number that can be tracked through an electronic, interoperable system. This created a need to share data across stakeholders such as drug distributors and drug manufacturers and regulators. One such project aimed at developing a distributed drug ledger is MediLedger [65].

Traditionally tracking in the supply chain system has been using RFID technology by the advent of blockchain along with smart contracts traceability has been taken to step further. Blockchain creates a distributed ledger of reference data to be used across different steps in the supply chain. Using smart contracts blockchain networks could be integrated with cross-domain services to perform a certain action when given policies are met. In the case of drug supply, smart contracts could monitor and track given drug inventory across cross markets. For example, regulators can monitor the supply and consumption of the drug at any given instance using smart contracts. In case of supply and consumption added is not equivalent to inventory smart contract trigger an alarm along with audit trail information in the supply chain [66, 67].

4   Advanced Use Cases

4.1   Blockchain Consortium – Managing Provider Directories

Healthcare insurance providers are double-spending millions of dollars to manage provider directories. Managing provider directories involves validation and verification of details of every in-network provider. Traditionally this process involves collecting and verification of data manually and the nature of data is prone to changes more frequently, forcing insurance players to do repetitive and redundant work.

Blockchain technology can help solve this problem by building permissioned blockchain of provider data, in which all the non-trusted parties can make updates and retrieve shared data in a secured without double-spending all with transparency and low transaction cost.

4.2   Wearable Fitness Device Integration and Monitoring Health

The growing use of fitness devices provides an opportunity to shift the healthcare industry towards the wellness industry to build a healthy society. However, sharing of personal vital information poses privacy and security concerns which are limiting the potential of the healthcare market to shift left. Using blockchain this data could be distributed and secured. A user can share health information with any healthcare service application by controlling access rights. Data along with access restrictions could be submitted as a transaction to the blockchain network. Cryptographic hash keys (public key and private key) controls identity and security. This model could be a simulation of sharing privacy data to any mobile application in a controlled blockchain network and this approach has been discussed in the paper Decentralizing Privacy: Using Blockchain to Protect Personal Data.

Using smart contracts takes this approach a step further and creates a marketplace for smart healthcare applications that could revolutionize the wellness industry.

4.3   Smart Contract-Based Health Care Intelligent Claim Processing and Prior Authorization

Using smart contracts in the blockchain network provides an ability to execute and take a decision on an already established contractual basis. This contract could be before patient authorization or referral from a primary care physician or insurance policy contract. This setup helps to process claims automatically without any middle layer or manual intervention. For instance, a patient can seek service from a specialist in that process upon sharing the public key of the patient, a provider can determine insurance eligibility, prior medical history, and any authorization policy patient might have already set up. Upon rendering the service provider can update the transaction which could trigger a smart contract aimed at processing claims. Based on the data submitted smart contracts can settle or deny a claim. This process eliminates a lot of administrative burdens and avoids excessive billing and insurance-related cost.

4.4   Tracking Counterfeit Drugs Using Blockchain

Pharmaceutical companies and the drug supply chain can exploit the decentralized ledger to track and authenticate drugs movement on the immutable record trail. Blockchain can record the transactional details of a drug, creating a chain of information assisting the companies and manufacturers in disclosing the corrupted/contaminated drugs before they reach end-users. Only those users with a specific key can update or modify the details in the block. It is because of the key features of blockchain which include decentralization, encryption method, and immutability large amounts of potential data can be distributed, and it utilized to track the secured goods at each stage in its supply chain process. The concept of Gcoin blockchain to create transparent drug transaction data is demonstrated in [73].

5   Further Recommendations

Despite all the cutting-edge features of Blockchain technology and its adaptability in the Healthcare industry, SWOT analysis affirmed that there some drawbacks and threats associated with implementing and developing blockchain.

5.1   Less Scalable

One of the key threats associated with the adoption of blockchain is its ability to scale. With the swift increase in the data volume in the healthcare industry which is due to the advancements in data analytic tools and medical imaging, availability of real-time medical data RPM devices, wearables, EHRs, insurance companies and more. Whenever new data is processed, every node adds information to its ledger, with this rapid increase in the data, it possesses limitations on hardware, an increase in the risk of bulking the overall system and leads to higher response time (for validation purposes) [76]. Several alternative solutions are appearing to fix this issue like Hard forks, soft forks (Segwit) or Segregated witness, Lightening networks, Plasma cash. Detailed information on these methodologies is presented in [77, 78]. A real-time example of solving this scalability issue with an alternative is depicted in [79] in this paper they implemented a tree-based data processing and batching method to handle a large volume of medical data.

5.2   Energy Consumption in Blockchain

Blockchain validates the digitized transactions, this validation procedure comprises processing a complex algorithm that authenticates the transactions resulting in a block of data added to the blockchain. As this is a decentralized technology myriad of computers operating simultaneously compete with each other to validate a transaction that involves the consumption of vast amounts of energy which is mostly generated from fossil fuels. Increase energy consumption might contribute to the scarcity of this energy supply which leads to the global environmental issue. There are several ways proposed to solve this problem like moving away from the proof of work validation method and focusing sustainable ways to mine bitcoin and more ways were presented in [80]. And another alternative to enable peer to peer transactions via microgrid architectures is illustrated in [81]. Another alternative is to find ways of utilizing solar and wind energy for mining. However, a significant amount of research is taking place to reduce the energy consumption in bitcoin mining and a practical example is Cryptoclastic which is the largest bitcoin miner is Spain is in its way to construct a solar firm to ensure a sustainable crypto mining in [82].

5.3   Less Number of People Trained in the Blockchain Technology

The demand for blockchain developers was initially occurred due to the lack of understanding about technology and the availability of minimum resources. For every instance of a cutting-edge technology, technical community requires initial transition time to adopt the technology. After it is sustained in the market for certain period of time, educational institutions introduce the relevant course work for not only creating the awareness among people but also to improve the number of skilled professionals in certain technology at an impressive rate.

5.4 Lack of Standardization

Blockchain can be used in the healthcare industry for many transactional purposes like logging events (patient data at Kiosk), insurance details. Lack of standardization makes it difficult for the stakeholders or vendors to trust and adopt blockchain. Recently IBM Watson together with FDA are performing collaborative research to define secure, efficient and scalable health data exchange [83, 84]. To enhance the power of blockchain technology, private agreements and community principles are enforced at a global scale to shift the cost of trust and coordination to network.

5.5 Regulation and Governance [85]

To keep up the advancements in any technology, it is very important to set proper regulation and governance in place. To handle the inefficiencies of the conventional system, blockchain technology occasionally diverts from the existing regulations. In order to constraint this issue, Recently US government not only supported the development of blockchain but also provided the governance in terms of technologies growth and expansion like "Resolution Supporting Digital Currencies and Blockchain Technology" bill, "Blockchain Regulatory Certainty Act" and more [86, 87]. For instance, A demonstration of governance of blockchain in financial networks is available in [88].

5.6 Interoperability Issues

Interoperability is the key characteristic of blockchain that plays a vital role in both the pros and cons. It is one of the main reasons for exhibiting low enterprise adoption of blockchain. For example, in the Pharmaceutical drug supply chain industry, consider the transaction of a single drug from manufacturer to the patient, one should have a strong belief in several intermediate systems/parties that involve in transaction. To attain complete interoperability of the system, it is essential to define and follow Standards internationally, such that one can have access control for authentication and authorization of the transactions. A successful implementation of blockchain in a Privacy-preserving framework for access control and interoperability of electronic health records using blockchain technology using a framework named Ancile is shown in [89]. Besides the standards, to achieve interoperability in a blockchain implementation of different functionalities like notary scheme, relay scheme, Hash locking and more were discussed in [90]. Organizations or Stakeholders utilizing blockchain platforms are potentially in need to invest in building protocols and standards to control the quality and authenticity of transactional data.

5.7   Initial Costs for the Adoption of Blockchain

Blockchain technology is still in its developing phase. Estimating initial costs depends on many factors like finding the right professionals that can deliver end products in time, how to build and sell the cryptocurrencies and more. In further cost estimation solely depends on the project requirements.

5.8   Security and Attacks in Blockchain [91]

Records stored in blockchain are immutable in nature. This theoretical immutability of blockchain is amplified as the size of the network increases. But not every blockchain application needs to be an extensive blockchain network, thus increasing the chance for 51% attack and other forms of manipulation. It is the situation where a group of nodes that control 51% of the hashing power of a blockchain possesses the capacity to alter the records of blockchain that is when two miners calculating the hash at the same time and got the same results then the blockchain might split and result in two chains for the users. In a positive 51%, attack situation Blockchain could have catastrophic consequences. An analysis of real-time if this attack and the advanced protected techniques to control the attacks are discussed in [92, 93]. To mitigate 51% attack, alternative techniques proposed here are pirl Guard, Chainlocks, Merged mining and many more. Another case study of detecting 51%attack and the detailed analysis of security is described in [94]. In addition to 51% attack there exists other threats associated with PoW and PoS protocols namely Sybils attack, DDos's attack, etc. A detailed analysis of attacks and their relationship between each other is described in [95].

5.9   Smart Contracts

Smart Contracts can be erroneous, as their code is available in public and they become autonomous entries once they are created thereby increasing the scope of hackers [96]. Since Blockchain is immutable, to remove the code bugs developers should create new contracts and then duplicate all the data from the old one. For instance, a smart contract-based attack happened on Ethereum in June 2016 where $60 million dollars has been stolen [97]. Taking into account both difficulty in updating the contracts and high exploit risk, Smart contract developers should be very cautious and apply defensive programming techniques in such a way they can mitigate vulnerabilities. Some examples of ideas of these techniques are shown in [98, 99].

6   Conclusion

To understand the applicability of a cutting-edge blockchain technology in the healthcare industry a structured review has been performed in this paper where the salient features of blockchain are identified and significant challenges faced by the healthcare-related stakeholders are listed and addressed challenges and their scope of solving them using blockchain technology. Technological platform setup using blockchain to transition from data as a commodity or competition attitude to value-based service in the healthcare industry has been discussed in detail. Opportunity to reduce excessive administrative costs and increasing transparency in healthcare services and the opportunity to revolutionize the smart healthcare marketplace also has been discussed in detail.

References

1. Davis, J.: HealthITSecurity, 23 July 2019. https://healthitsecurity.com/news/the-10-biggest-healthcare-data-breaches-of-2019-so-far
2. Haggerty, N.E.: Healthcare and digital transformation. Netw. Secur. **2017**(8), 7–11 (2017)
3. https://www.hipaajournal.com/what-is-the-hitech-act/
4. https://www.modernhealthcare.com/article/20160531/NEWS/160539990/hospitals-achieve-96-ehr-adoption-rate-data-exchange-still-needs-work
5. https://www2.deloitte.com/global/en/pages/life-sciences-and-healthcare/articles/global-health-care-sector-outlook.html
6. http://www3.weforum.org/docs/WEF_GAC15_Technological_Tipping_Points_report_2015.pdf
7. Christidis, K., Devetsikiotis, M.: Blockchains and smart contracts for the internet of things. IEEE Access **4**, 2292–2303 (2016)
8. Zheng, Z., Xie, S., Dai, H., Chen, X., Wang, H.: An overview of blockchain technology: architecture, consensus, and future trends, pp. 557–564. IEEE (2017)
9. Karafiloski, E.: Blockchain solutions for big data challenges: a literature review. IEEE (2017)
10. Swan, M.: Blockchain: Blueprint for a New Economy, 1st edn. O'Reilly Media, Sebastopol (2015)
11. Ekblaw, A., Azaria, A., Halamka, J.D., Lippman, A.: A case study for blockchain in healthcare: "MedRec" prototype for electronic health records and medical research data (2016)
12. Al Omar, A., Rahman, M.S., Basu, A., Kiyomoto, S.: MediBchain: a blockchain based privacy preserving platform for healthcare data. In: Wang, G., Atiquzzaman, M., Yan, Z., Choo, K.-K.R. (eds.) SpaCCS 2017. LNCS, vol. 10658, pp. 534–543. Springer, Cham (2017). https://doi.org/10.1007/978-3-319-72395-2_49
13. Griggs, K.N., Ossipova, O., Kohlios, C.P., Baccarini, A.N., Howson, E.A., Hayajneh, T.: Healthcare blockchain system using smart contracts for secure automated remote patient monitoring. J. Med. Syst. **42**(7), 130 (2018)
14. Zhang, P., Walker, M.A., White, J., Schmidt, D.C., Lenz, G.: Metrics for assessing blockchain-based healthcare decentralized apps (2017)
15. Esposito, C., De Santis, A., Tortora, G., Chang, H., Choo, K.K.R.: Blockchain: a panacea for healthcare cloud-based data security and privacy? IEEE Cloud Comput. **5**(1), 31–37 (2018)
16. Mingxiao, D., Xiaofeng, M., Zhe, Z., Xiangwei, W., Qijun, C.: A review on consensus algorithm of blockchain. In: IEEE International Conference on Systems, Man, and Cybernetics (SMC) (2017)
17. Lin, I.-C., Liao, T.-C.: A survey of blockchain security issues and challanges. Int. J. Netw. Secur. **19**, 653–659 (2017)
18. https://www.researchgate.net/publication/318131748_An_Overview_of_Blockchain_Technology_Architecture_Consensus_and_Future_Trends
19. Zyskind, G., Nathan, O., Pentland, A.S.: Decentralizing privacy: using blockchain to protect personal data (2015)
20. Piscini, E., Dalton, D., Kehoe, L.: Blockchain & Cyber Security. Deloitte (2017)
21. https://www.mail-archive.com/cryptography@metzdowd.com/msg09997.html
22. Anonymous: Data breaches cost the healthcare industry an estimated $6.5 billion. Micrographics **29**, 3–5 (2011)

23. Sweeney, L.: K-anonymity: a model for protecting privacy. Int. J. Uncertain. **10**, 557–570 (2002)
24. Machanavajjhala, A., Kifer, D., Gehrke, J., Venkitasubramaniam, M.: L-diversity: privacy beyond k-anonymity. In: Proceedings of the International Conference on Data Engineering, Atlanta, GA, USA, 3–7, vol. 2006, p. 24 (2006)
25. Li, N., Li, T., Venkatasubramanian, S.: T-closeness: privacy beyond k-anonymity and l-diversity. In: Proceedings of the International Conference on Data Engineering, Istanbul, Turkey, vol. April 2007, pp. 106–115 (2007)
26. https://www.w3.org/2016/04/blockchain-workshop/interest/hardjono-pentland.html
27. Zyskind, G., Nathan, O., Pentland, A.S.: Decentralizing privacy: using blockchain to protect personal data. In: 2015 IEEE Security and Privacy Workshops (2015)
28. https://www.nec.com/en/global/solutions/blockchain/blockchain-for-digital-identity.html
29. Shrier, D., Wu, W., Pentland, A.: Blockchain & infrastructure (identity, data security). Connection Science & Engineering Massachusetts Institute of Technology, May 2016
30. ShoCard: Blockchain revolutionizing identity management (2016). https://shocard.com/cpt_news/blockchain-revolutionizingidentity-management
31. Torstensson, J., Mitton, Z., Sena, M., Lundkvist, C., Heck, R.: Uport: a platform for self-sovereign identity (2016). https://uport.me/library/pdf/whitepaper.pdf
32. https://www.cs.bgu.ac.il/~frankel/TechnicalReports/2016/16-02.pdf
33. Szabo, N.: Smart Contracts (1994). http://szabo.best.vwh.net/smart.contracts.html
34. Smart contracts in IoT. https://ieeexplore.ieee.org/abstract/document/7467408
35. https://www.americanprogress.org/issues/healthcare/reports/2019/04/08/468302/excess-administrative-costs-burden-u-s-health-care-system/
36. Mackey, T.K., Liang, B.A.: Improving global health governance to combat counterfeit medicines: a proposal for a UNODC-WHO-Interpol trilateral mechanism. BMC Med. **11**(1), 233 (2013)
37. Vruddhula, S.: Application of on-dose identification and blockchain to prevent drug counterfeiting. Pathog. Glob. Health **112**(4), 161 (2018)
38. Mackey, T.K., Nayyar, G.: A review of existing and emerging digital technologies to combat the global trade in fake medicines. Expert Opin. Drug Saf. **16**(5), 587–602 (2017). https://doi.org/10.1080/14740338.2017.1313227
39. Sweeney, L.: Simple demographics often identify people uniquely. Health **671**(2000), 1–34 (2000)
40. Blankenship, J.C., Rosenfield, K., Jennings, H.S.: Privileging and credentialing for interventional cardiology procedures. Catheter. Cardiovasc. Interv. **86**(4), 655–663 (2015)
41. Van Amerongen, D.: Physician credentialing in a consumer-centric world. Health Aff. **21**(5), 152–156 (2002)
42. Credentialing and privileging of pharmacists: a resource paper from the Council on Credentialing in Pharmacy. J. Am. Pharm. Assoc. **54**(6), e354–e364 (2014)
43. Salzman, S., Vetting Physician: Credentials: Tech to the Rescue? – Blockchain touted as ensuring that docs are who they say they are. MedPage Today (2018). https://www.medpagetoday.com/practicemanagement/
44. Furlonger, D., Valdes, R., Kandaswamy, R.: Hype Cycle for Blockchain Business, 3 December 2018. https://www.gartner.com/doc/3884146/hype-cycle-blockchain-business
45. Khan, R., Mittelman, D.: Consumer genomics will change your life, whether you get tested or not. Genome Biol. **19**(1), 120 (2018)
46. Lindor, N.M., Thibodeau, S.N., Burke, W.: Whole-genome sequencing in healthy people. In: Mayo Clinic Proceedings, vol. 92, pp. 159–172 (2017)
47. Laestadius, L.I., Rich, J.R., Auer, P.L.: All your data (effectively) belong to us: data practices among direct-to-consumer genetic testing firms. Genet. Med. **19**(5), 513–520 (2017)

48. Kuo, T.T., Zavaleta Rojas, H., Ohno-Machado, L.: Comparison of blockchain platforms: a systematic review and healthcare examples. JAMIA **26**(5), 462–478 (2019)
49. GDPR Resources & Information. https://www.gdpr.org. Accessed 18 Feb
50. Office for Human Research Protections. U.S. Department of Health & Human Services, 18 February 2019. https://www.hhs.gov/ohrp/regulations-and-policy/regulations
51. How Blockchain can Transform the Pharmaceutical and Healthcare Industries. PhUSE Emerging Trends & Technology, 18 February 2019. https://www.phuse.eu/documents//working-gro ups/deliverables/phuse-blockchain-white-paperfinal-version-1-18843.pdf
52. Current operations of heath care systems. http://samples.jbpub.com/9781284108163/Cha pter2.pdf
53. Le Bris, A., El Asri, W.: State of Cybersecurity & Cyber Threats in Healthcare Organizations. ESSEC Business School (2016)
54. Leonhardt, M.: (2019). https://www.cnbc.com/2019/10/09/americans-spend-twice-as-much-on-health-care-today-as-in-the-1980s.html
55. Engelhardt, M.A.: Hitching healthcare to the chain: an introduction to blockchain technology in the healthcare sector. Technol. Innov. Manag. Rev. **7**(10) (2017)
56. Baxendale, G.: Can blockchain revolutionise EPRs? ITNow **58**(1), 38–39 (2016)
57. Mettler, M.: Blockchain technology in healthcare: the revolution starts here. In: IEEE 18th International Conference on e-Health Networking, Applications and Services (Healthcom), vol. 2016, pp. 1–3 (2016)
58. Yue, X., Wang, H., Jin, D., Li, M., Jiang, W.: Healthcare data gateways: found healthcare intelligence on blockchain with novel privacy risk control. J. Med. Syst. **40**, 218 (2016)
59. Blough, D., Ahamad, M., Liu, L., Chopra, P.: MedVault: ensuring security and privacy for electronic medical records. NSF CyberTrust Principal Investigators Meeting (2008)
60. Sarwal, A., Insom, P.: BitHealth (2016). https://devpost.com/software/bithealth
61. Gem. Gem Health Network (2016). https://gem.co/health/
62. Ivan, D.: Moving toward a blockchain-based method for the secure storage of patient records. In: ONC/NIST Use of Blockchain for Healthcare and Research Workshop, Gaithersburg (2016)
63. Zheng, Z., Xie, S., Dai, H., Chen, X.: An overview of blockchain technology: architecture, consensus, and future trends. In: 6th IEEE International Congress on Big Data (2017). https:// doi.org/10.1109/bigdatacongress.2017.85
64. Gatteschi, V., Lamberti, F., Demartini, C., Pranteda, C., Santamaria, V.: To blockchain or not to blockchain: that is the question. IT Prof. **20**(2), 62–74 (2018). https://doi.org/10.1109/mitp. 2018.021921652
65. Drug supply smart contract. https://www.biospace.com/article/releases/mediledger-s-blockc hain-pilot-to-assist-drug-supply-chain-stakeholders-in-developing-an-interoperable-track-and-amp-trace-system-for-the-us-dscsa-regulations-has-kicked-off/
66. Katuwal, G.J., Pandey, S., Hennessey, M., Lamichhane, B.: Applications of blockchain in healthcare: current landscape & challenges (2018)
67. Schöner, M.M., Kourouklis, D., Sandner, P., Gonzalez, E., Förster, J.: Blockchain Technology in the Pharmaceutical Industry. FSBC Working Paper, July 2017
68. Siyal, A.A., Junejo, A.Z., Zawish, M., Ahmed, K., Khalil, A., Soursou, G.: Applications of Blockchain Technology in Medicine and Healthcare: Challenges and Future Perspectives (2018)
69. Meng, W., Tischhauser, E.W., Wang, Q., Wang, Y., Han, J.: When Intrusion Detection Meets Blockchain Technology: A Review. In: 2018 IEEE, pp. 2169–3536 (2018)
70. O'Dowd, E.: Utilizing Healthcare Blockchain to Increase Identity Management. HITInfrastructure (2018)
71. Schöner, M.M., Kourouklis, D., Sandner, P., Gonzalez, E., Förster, J.: Blockchain Technology in the Pharmaceutical Industry. FSBC Working Paper (2017)

72. Ahmad, A., Saad, M., Bassiouni, M., Mohaisen, A.: Towards Blockchain-Driven, Secure and Transparent Audit Logs (2018)
73. Tseng, J.H., Liao, Y.C., Chong, B., Liao, S.W.: Governance on the drug supply chain via gcoin blockchain. Int. J. Environ. Res. Public Health **15**(6), 1055 (2018)
74. Gatteschi, V., Lamberti, F., Demartini, C., Pranteda, C., Santamaría, V.: Blockchain and Smart Contracts for Insurance: Is the Technology Mature Enough? MDPI (2017)
75. Tosh, D.K., Shetty, S., Liang, X., Kamhoua, C.A., Kwiat, K.A., Njilla, L.: Security implications of blockchain cloud with analysis of block withholding attack. In: 2017 17th IEEE/ACM International Symposium on Cluster, Cloud and Grid Computing, vols. 978-1-5090-6611-7/17 (2017)
76. Qin, K., Gervais, A.: An overview of blockchain scalability, interoperability and sustainability (2018)
77. Herrera-Joancomartí, J., Pérez-Solà, C.: Privacy in Bitcoin Transactions: New Challenges from Blockchain Scalability Solution. Dept. d'Enginyeria de la Informacio i les Comunicacions. Springer, September 2016. https://doi.org/10.1007/978.3.319.45656.0.3
78. Ademi, E.: A Comprehensive Study on the Scalability Challenges of the Blockchain Technology (2018)
79. Liang, X., Zhao, J., Shetty, S., Liu, J., Li, D.: Integrating Blockchain for Data Sharing and Collaboration in Mobile Healthcare Applications (2017)
80. https://www.greenbiz.com/article/4-ways-counter-blockchains-energy-consumption-pitfall
81. Imbault, F., Swiatek, M., De Beaufort, R., Plana, R.: The green blockchain-managing decentralized energy production and consumption. IEEE, vols. 978-1-5386-3917-7/17 (2017)
82. (2018). https://www.cryptoglobe.com/latest/2018/10/bitcoin-miner-to-build-300mw-solar-farm-for-sustainable-crypto-mining/
83. O'Dowd, E.: (2017). https://hitinfrastructure.com/news/ibm-watson-fda-collaborate-on-healthcare-blockchain-research
84. O'Dowd, E.: (2018). https://hitinfrastructure.com/news/healthcare-blockchain-standards-support-collaborative-development
85. Kakavand, H., Kost De Sevres, N., Chilton, B.: The blockchain revolution: an analysis of regulation and technology related to distributed ledger technologies, 1 January 2017. SSRN. https://ssrn.com/abstract=2849251
86. https://www.congress.gov/bill/116th-congress/house-bill/528/text
87. https://www.congress.gov/bill/115th-congress/house-resolution/1102/text
88. Paech, P.: The Governance of Blockchain Financial Networks. Law society economy working papers (2017)
89. Dagher, G.G., Mohler, J., Milojkovic, M., Marella, P.B.: Ancile: privacy-preserving framework for access control and interoperability of electronic health records using blockchain technology. Sustain. Cities Soc. **39**, 283–297 (2018). ISSN 2210-6707
90. Koens, T., Poll, E.: Assessing interoperability solutions for distributed ledgers. Pervasive Mobile Computing **59**, 101079 (2019)
91. Mosakheil, J.H.: Security Threats Classification in Blockchains (2018). https://repository.stcloudstate.edu/msia_etds
92. Sayeed, S., Marco-Gisbert, H.: Assessing Blockchain Consensus and Security Mechanisms against the 51% Attack. MDPI applied sciences, no. 1788 (2019). https://doi.org/10.3390/app9091788
93. https://ledgerops.com/blog/2019/03/28/top-five-blockchain-security-issues-in-2019
94. Ye, C., Li, G., Cai, H., Gu, Y., Fukuda, A.: Analysis of security in blockchain: case study in 51%-attack detecting. In: 5th International Conference on Dependable Systems and Their Applications (DSA) IEEE, no. 1109/DSA.2018.00015 (2018)
95. Saad, M., Spaulding, J., Njilla, L., Kamhoua, C., Shetty, S., Nyang, D., Mohaisen, A.: Exploring the Attack Surface of Blockchain: A Systematic Overview (2019)

96. Zaninotto, F.: (2016). https://marmelab.com/blog/2016/06/14/blockchain-for-web-develo pers-the-truth.html
97. Atzei, N.: Massimo Bartoletti and Tiziana Cimoli. A survey of attacks on Ethereum smart contracts
98. Konstantopoulos, G.: (2018). https://medium.com/loom-network/how-to-secure-your-smart-contracts-6-solidity-vulnerabilities-and-how-to-avoid-them-part-1-c33048d4d17d
99. Konstantopoulos, G.: How to Secure Your Smart Contracts: 6 Solidity Vulnerabilities and how to avoid them, Medium, January 2018

Short Paper Track

Have I Been Exploited?
A Registry of Vulnerable Ethereum Smart Contracts

Daniel Connelly$^{(\boxtimes)}$ and Wu-chang Feng$^{(\boxtimes)}$

Department of Computer Science, Portland State University, Portland, USA
{danc2,wuchang}@pdx.edu

Abstract. Ethereum Smart Contracts, also known as Decentralized Applications (DApps), are small programs which orchestrate financial transactions. Though beneficial in many cases, such contracts can and have been exploited, leading to a history of financial losses in the millions of dollars for those who have invested in them. It is critical that users be able to trust the contract code they place their money into. One way for verifying a program's integrity is Symbolic Execution. Unfortunately, while the information derived from symbolic execution is beneficial, performing it is often financially and technically infeasible for users to do. To address this problem, this paper describes the design and implementation of a registry of vulnerable Ethereum contracts. The registry compiles the results of exhaustive application of symbolic analysis to deployed contracts and makes it available to users seeking to understand the risks associated with contracts they are intending to utilize.

1 Introduction

Blockchain technologies have reached proportions of popularity similar to other relatively newer fields such as Artificial Intelligence and Machine Learning. LinkedIn, for example, lists blockchain as the most in-demand hard skill in 2020 [1]. Other corroborating data suggests that it would behoove developers, companies, institutions, and governments to adopt blockchain as the technology claims to be a panacea for many problems. However, using blockchain for financial use cases, specifically with Smart Contracts, can be a dangerous gamble. For example, there are many instances where financial losses have been incurred due to insecure programming. These mistakes are often more serious than traditional software system bugs due to the financial consequences (which are uninsured) and the often-permanent bugs on an immutable blockchain.

Fortunately, techniques such as Symbolic Execution, such as the tool *Mythril* [2] that is used in this project, can be used to identify insecure programming. Such techniques can yield comprehensive results for up to 50% of programs and find 78% of the most important bugs [3]. While users would benefit from being able to evaluate the security of smart contracts, without access to significant resources to perform these techniques, they remain out of reach. To address this issue, this paper describes a registry for aggregating and publishing the results of security analyses of smart contracts where users of a blockchain

© Springer Nature Switzerland AG 2020
Z. Chen et al. (Eds.): ICBC 2020, LNCS 12404, pp. 221–228, 2020.
https://doi.org/10.1007/978-3-030-59638-5_15

such as Ethereum can search to see what vulnerabilities a contract they may be wishing to use suffers from before sending it any currency.

2   Symbolic Execution

Symbolic Execution works like algebra for computer programs. The job of any engine is to discover if a particularly vulnerable state may be reached. For example, a state in Ethereum that carries business logic of "send all ETH to the caller of this program" is likely unwanted, but easily discoverable with this method. Fortunately, engines like Mythril work on EVM bytecode to detect this and other disastrous programming logic.

Mythril performs its analysis by taking the bytecode of a contract and decompiling it into EVM opcode instructions where all possible program states are explored over n transactions/calls (two by default). Mythril uses a Symbolic Virtual Machine (SVM) named LASER [4] and a number of analysis modules to determine if any of 16 vulnerabilities, a subset of the Smart Contract Weakness Classification Registry [5], exist. For states where Mythril is not able to traverse due to resource or logic constraints, this shortfall is reflected by the percentage of coverage it returns. In order to prove the vulnerabilities that it finds, it uses the Z3 automated theorem prover, also known as a constraint solver, released by Microsoft Research under the MIT license [6].

3   Methodology

A list of contract addresses was generated by syncing an Ethereum full node, specifically the implementation using the Go programming language, named a Go Ethereum (GETH) node [7]. Once synced, the node was queried for contract addresses. A cluster of machines were deployed using the Google Cloud Platform (GCP) for the purpose of symbolically executing on the addresses obtained from querying the node. Each machine ran a Python program which spawned 10–12 threads. Each thread launched a new bash shell where a Docker container ran an image of Mythril on a single contract address. All output was stored local to the main thread, then written to files/bins depending on the content (exceptions, errors, or output). To alert us when a machine had stopped analysis, an open source messaging system for long running processes was developed through collaboration with another researcher [8]. Figure 1 depicts a high level design of our data collection process.

A hand-coded parser was written to run through the output files, which contained millions of lines of output, to extract contract address, type of vulnerability, severity of that vulnerability, and the coverage that was attained into comma-separated rows. A website was hosted on a Google Compute Engine at the address www.haveibeenexploited.com. The website was written in React and interacts with a Go server that accesses a local MySQL database which holds the obtained results. The website informs its audience of the results of vulnerable countracts as well as miscellaneous details about the project.

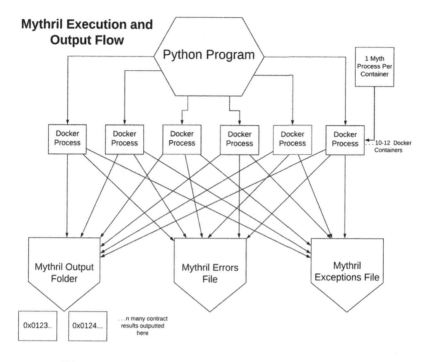

Fig. 1. High-level overview of data collection program [9]

4 Results

After running the GETH node, Mythril was run over the addresses obtained through a portion of addresses (≈1.6 million addresses) in the range 0–≈8.4 millionth block.

4.1 Number of Contract Addresses

The total number of contract addresses created since the beginning of the Ethereum blockchain (up to the 9 millionth block) totaled 3,046,140. The number of live contract addresses (i.e., destroyed contracts have zero length bytecode) on the Ethereum blockchain totaled 2,927,521. Thus, approximately 119,000 addresses have been destroyed over the lifetime of the blockchain. Figure 2 reveals the allocation of live contracts per millionth block range.

4.2 Number of Vulnerable Contracts

The number of contracts indicated by Mythril to contain vulnerabilities in this project, from the partially scanned 0–≈8.4 millionth block, was 797,384 contracts. This means that more than 27% of Ethereum smart contracts have one or more vulnerabilities in them; more for a variety of reasons: we only analyzed

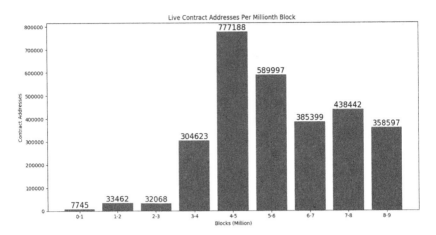

Fig. 2. Live contract addresses in 9 million blocks

a portion of contracts within 0–8.4 million blocks, bugs in Mythril, inability of achieving full code coverage in some cases, etc.

4.3   Number of Vulnerabilities

The number of vulnerabilities discovered during this project totaled 1,224,486. This number does not reflect duplication, for example, when a contract may have repeated vulnerabilities of the same type within a contract. Thus, the number of ways a user may potentially exploit a vulnerable contract is one or more. Figure 3 shows the number of non-repeating vulnerabilities discovered during the analysis, by vulnerability type.

As the figure shows, the most common vulnerabilities are Exception State (ES; 646,957) and State Change After External Call (SCAEC; 327,122). An ES vulnerability has a severity rating of low according to Mythril. A SCAEC vulnerability has a severity rating of low or medium depending on if the external address is a user-supplied address (medium severity) or a hardcoded one by the developer (low severity). The results here indicate that the majority of vulnerabilities present in the contracts are not likely to cause much damage to users as the majority of vulnerabilities are of a mostly low severity rating.

However, even a few contracts with higher severity vulnerabilities could contain a large quantity of ETH and a single potential vulnerability could lead the way to an exploit that could cause damage in the millions of dollars across multiple users of a contract as prior exploits have shown.

Another informative way to examine the data is to analyze what blocks have the most vulnerabilities inside of them. As shown in Fig. 4, among the results obtained, most of the contracts that contain insecure code were created within the 4–5 millionth block. Though these results are partial, vulnerabilities seem to have generally decreased. This could mean that there are factors at work that are

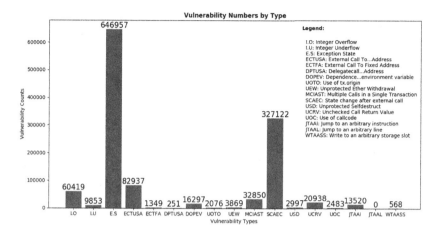

Fig. 3. Number of vulnerabilities by type

making Ethereum contracts more secure over time such as the use of non-Turing complete languages such as Vyper [10].

4.4 Coverage

The coverage that Mythril was able to obtain from each contract was also collected. As the symbolic execution was constrained to 1-h, this was necessary for performance and cost reasons. Overall, the average code coverage achieved for this proof of concept was 76%.

5 Discussion

5.1 Risk Analysis

Perez and Livshits have shown from pooling the results of 5 different academic research articles studying vulnerable smart contracts that "at most 504 out of 21,270 contracts [examined were]...subjected to exploits", representing "only 9,066 ETH (1.8 million USD)...0.29% of the 3 million ETH (600 million USD)" [11]. In the larger context of Ethereum's supply, this amount is small. However, users and the general public do not likely think of amounts in the millinos as small, though other parties may. In fact, if the results from Perez and Livshits are generalized to the larger subset discussed in this research encompassing several orders of magnitude more contracts, if the same percentage of vulnerable contracts were exploited (2%), then approximately 15,948 contracts would be exploitable. If 504 contracts housed 1 million USD then that means, given the same ratio of contracts likely to be exploited (2%), 31 million USD ($\approx$15948/504) may likely be at risk in this dataset. Assuming the same USD:ETH (the value of ETH has risen since Perez and Livshits' research so would in truth be a higher dollar amount) this would mean that, at minimum, 8% of the total Ethereum supply chain is at risk.

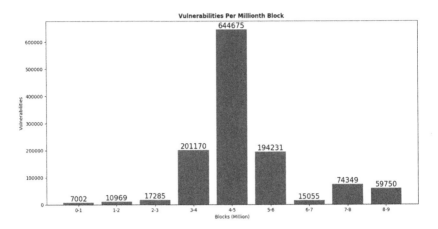

Fig. 4. Exploits per millionth block

5.2 Moral Concerns

Users cannot be alerted directly of vulnerabilities in their contract code. Therefore, a chief ethical concern comes to mind: can this dataset allow malevolent users to exploit vulnerable contracts? Though malevolent parties may use this data as a steppingstone to take advantage of a vulnerability, this project is an attempt at being proactive with exposing and indirectly alerting users of vulnerabilities. Since contract owners and users cannot be alerted directly, at least they can be knowledgeable if they make use of this dataset and, with that knowledge, may attempt to pull money out and/or close a contract(s). For the newest contracts that contain vulnerabilities, if developers and users utilize this service, they will not fill a vulnerable contract full of money and setup a malevolent user for future success.

5.3 Veracity of Results

A small subset of addresses never achieved output or only partial output due to bugs or inefficiencies in Mythril, all of which were documented for reanalysis at a later date. It should be noted, therefore, that contracts deemed to have no vulnerability may very well indeed have one or more uncaught vulnerabilities. Additionally, unless technology improves in some dramatic way, there is no way to deem a contract truly safe and the results in this research conclusively true for all output data. A user should not assume a query to this registry which returns no result is an indication a contract is free of vulnerabilities. Finally, it should be noted that the results here are the opinion of one engine and it is always best practice to get a second opinion before deciding whether to use a contract. Multiple perspectives from engines is a future goal of this project.

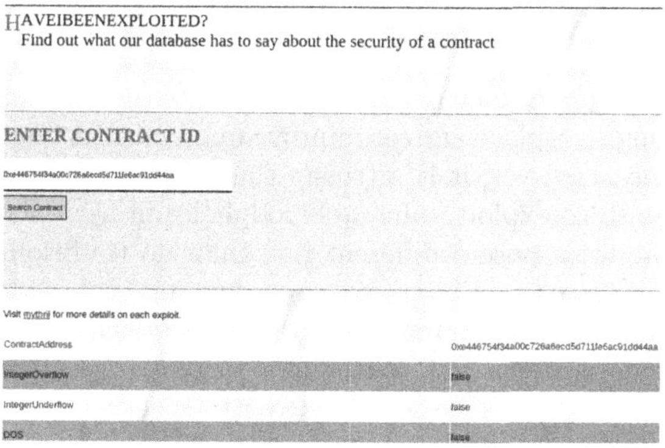

Fig. 5. www.haveibeenexploited.com

6 Registry

www.haveibeenpwned.com is a website that allows users to see if their information has been leaked in a security breach by entering any email address into a simple search bar. Our registry is a similar service, but for Ethereum Smart Contracts, and was named in honor of the inspiration taken. The website, located at the address www.haveibeenexploited.com, acts as a proof-of-concept registry where users can type in a contract's address into a search bar and determine if a contract is safe before use, as shown in Fig. 5. It contains all the results gained from this research.

As it is now, a user may query a contract at the website for vulnerable contracts. This limits the ability for individuals to access the entirety of the database and see all contracts which have vulnerabilities. It was thought that this way honest users who wish to check on the safety of contracts they are concerned with may receive this information. On the other hand, those who wish to obtain a large listing of insecure contract addresses for exploitation purposes may not do so, short of brute-force querying of all of the contract addresses or hacking into the database holding the symbolic execution results.

7 Future Work

Future goals include finishing the Mythril execution and adding new engines to the project to gain multiple opinions on the safety of Smart Contracts [12]. There exist similar work, namely www.contract-library.com, to base off of, but this existing work is limited and mostly involves the use of a single engine. A rating system similar to Consumer Reports [13] and what VirusTotal [14] provides with malware analysis and detection is eagerly planned. Analysis, parsing, and updates to a database may also be automated to provide close to real-time feedback on contracts by a variety of tools. Finally, this type of research idea is not germane to a single blockchain or language and can be used wherever DApps exist.

8   Conclusion

Ethereum is an example of increasing attention to blockchain and decentralized applications seeking to replace and/or improve upon current financial infrastructure. Unfortunately, however, it is a truism that there always exists a group of individuals who wish to exploit vulnerable loopholes in new technologies.

These vulnerabilities pose a different risk than do traditional software systems bugs. Mainly, that these bugs can carry financial consequences and, once deployed to the network, are immutable programs which live on the network, unless the bytecode is destroyed. Without a system to declare contracts reasonably secure, there will always be doubt as to whether a contract or, more generally, the Ethereum blockchain is truly fit for financial use cases.

This research is an attempt to bring attention to the vulnerabilities of this technology and offer such a system – a digital registry of vulnerable contracts – for users, developers, and Ethereum enthusiasts. If users feel that new technology is safe and trustworthy, only then will they give up older technology in favor of the new. By analyzing the state of Ethereum and providing a system that creates transparency in specific contracts which contain vulnerabilities, we hypothesize that the number of users of the network will likely increase and adoption of Ethereum for financial use cases will grow.

References

1. Anderson, B.: The Most In-Demand Hard and Soft Skills of 2020, January 2020. https://business.linkedin.com/talent-solutions/blog/trends-and-research/2020/most-in-demand-hard-and-soft-skills
2. Mueller, B.: Mythril (2017). https://github.com/ConsenSys/mythril
3. Groce, A.: 246 Findings From Our Smart Contract Audits: An Executive Summary, September 2019. https://blog.trailofbits.com/2019/08/08/246-findings-from-our-smart-contract-audits-an-executive-summary/
4. Mueller, B.: Laser-ethereum, October 2017. https://github.com/b-mueller/laser-ethereum
5. SmartContractSecurity: SWCRegistry, January 2020. https://swcregistry.io
6. Microsoft: Z3, September 2012. https://github.com/Z3Prover/z3
7. Ethereum: go-ethereum, December 2013. https://github.com/ethereum/go-ethereum
8. Dulcet, T.: Send-Msg-CLI, December 2019. https://github.com/tdulcet/Send-Msg-CLI
9. LucidChart: High-Level Program Overview, January 2020. https://www.lucidchart.com
10. Vyper Team: Pythonic Smart Contract Language for the EVM (2017). https://github.com/vyperlang/vyper
11. Perez, D., Livshits, B.: Smart contract vulnerabilities: Does anyone care? May 2019. http://arxiv.org/abs/1902.06710
12. TrailOfBits: Manticore, February 2017. https://github.com/trailofbits/manticore
13. Consumer Reports Team: Consumer Reports, February 2020. https://www.consumerreports.org/cro/index.htm
14. Virus Total Team: VirusTotal, February 2020. https://www.virustotal.com//

Author Index

Printed in the United States
By Bookmasters